MESSAGES
AND
MIRACLES

Answers to the 100 most-asked questions
about this most empowering of human experiences

In this moving and compassionate work, one of the pioneers in after-death communication (ADC) research explores the reasons why ADCs occur and how they help the bereaved.

Based on his counseling experience, interviews with numerous people who have had contact with a deceased loved one, and the many questions people have asked him since the the release of his first book, *After Death Communication,* Dr. LaGrand unfolds an untapped source of support for the bereaved and those who comfort them.

Learn whether contact experience is simply the stress of bereavement or an authentic communication, how it can help you establish a new relationship with the deceased, and how to talk to children who report the experience. Read actual accounts of ADCs that have never before appeared in print.

Find answers to these questions, and more…

- Can anyone prove that an ADC is really a hallucination?
- How can an animal play a role in an ADC?
- What does the typical apparition look like as reported by the bereaved?
- How do ADCs change the lives of mourners?
- What types of messages are received?
- How do you know if a dream is an ADC?
- Can the mourner initiate the ADC contact?
- How should I respond to a child who reports an ADC?
- Are there any "negative" ADCs?

"People who have experienced an ADC will by warmly reminded of the beauty of this gift. Bravo to Dr. LaGrand."

— **Geri Colozzi Wiitala**
**author of *Heather's Return:*
*Communication from Beyond the Grave***

"Dr. LaGrand has used his many years of research and knowledge to present an invaluable contribution to the study of ADC in this, his most recent book. Compelling reading."

— **Kathleen G. Moore, Ph.D., LMHC**
Grief therapist in private practice

About the Author

Louis E. LaGrand is Distinguished Service Professor Emeritus at the State University of New York, College at Potsdam, and Adjunct Professor of Health Careers at the Eastern Campus of Suffolk Community College.

A certified grief counselor as well as a trainer for hospice volunteers, he is the author of five books and numerous articles. Two of his earlier books, *Coping With Separation and Loss as a Young Adult* and *Changing Patterns of Human Existence,* are based on his ten-year study of the loss responses of youth. *After Death Communication: Final Farewells* and *Messages and Miracles* are the result of more than eighteen years of interest in the extraordinary experiences of the bereaved.

Dr. LaGrand is a founder and past president of the board of directors of Hospice of St. Lawrence Valley, Inc. and a member formerly on the board of directors of the Association for Death Education and Counseling (ADEC). He is also a member of the Institute of Noetic Sciences, and of the American Society for Psychical Research. He presently is Director of Loss Education Associates and Bereavement Coordinator at our Lady of Lourdes in Venice, Florida.

As a counselor, educator, lecturer, author, and media guest, Louis E. LaGrand brings the fruits of more than thirty-five years of experience, research, and compassion to the lives of those who mourn a loved one. With an open-mindedness often missing in his profession, he encourages clients and counselors alike to accept the healing value of communication with departed loved ones.

Dr. LaGrand and his wife, Barbara, reside in Florida.

To Write to the Author

If you wish to contact the author or would like more information about this book, please write to the author in care of Llewellyn Worldwide, and we will forward your request. Both the author and publisher appreciate hearing from you. Llewellyn Worldwide cannot guarantee that every letter written to the author can be answered, but all will be forwarded. Please write to:

Louis E. LaGrand
℅ Llewellyn Worldwide
P.O. Box 64383, Dept. K406-5
St. Paul, MN 55164-0383, U.S.A.
Please enclose a self-addressed, stamped envelope for reply, or $1.00 to cover costs. If outside the U.S.A., enclose an international postal reply coupon.

MESSAGES

A·N·D

MIRACLES

Extraordinary Experiences
of the Bereaved

LOUIS E. LAGRAND, PH.D.

1999
Llewellyn Publications
St. Paul, Minnesota, U.S.A. 55164-0383

FIRST EDITION
First Printing, 1999

Cover design by Lisa Novak
Cover photo © Eva Rubenstein/Photonica
Book editing and design by Astrid Sandell

Library of Congress Cataloging-in-Publication Data
LaGrand, Louis E.
    Messages and Miracles : extraordinary experiences of the bereaved / Louis E. LaGrand.
        p. cm.
    Includes bibliographical references and index.
    ISBN 1-56718-406-5
    1. Spiritualism Miscellanea. I. Title.
    BF1261.2.L34   1999
    133.9—dc21   99-33212
                                            CIP

Llewellyn Publications
A Division of Llewellyn Worldwide, Ltd.
P.O. Box 64383, Dept. K406-5, St. Paul, MN 55164-0383
www.llewellyn.com

 Printed in the United States of America on recycled paper

Also by Louis E. LaGrand

After Death Communication: Final Farewells

To Jacob
Crews
Alexandra
Olivia
and Chloe

Contents

Part 3: Types of Experiences Reported

Part 4: The Experiencers and the Messages
*Characteristics of Experiencers • Celebrities •
Children and ADCs • Hospice Staff • Atheists and Agnostics •
Types of Messages • Misinterpretation of Messages • Related Questions*

Part 5: Positive Influences
*Changes in Worldview • Dream Interpretations •
Providing Support • Unconscious Effects • Accepting Death •
Unfinished Business • Spiritual Changes • Symbols of Hope •
Therapeutic Benefits • Educational Program • Related Questions*

Part 6: Helping the Person Who Has an ADC

*Expressing Emotion • Establishing Trust • Gifted Intuitives •
Asking About ADCs • Approaches to Helping •
Finding a Counselor • Related Questions*

Acknowledgments

Great people, bold in their outlook on life and strong in their conviction that there is much to learn about the mystery of humanity, have enabled me to forge ahead in my quest to open the importance of the extraordinary experiences of the bereaved to the scrutiny of the general public. Among these are colleagues and friends who have shared their beliefs about the unseen and unexplainable in ways that have been humbling and at the same time motivating. I thank them all for their help in this work and their patience with my questions. This book is a small recompense to all who are courageously open to dealing with a phenomenon we are just beginning to understand.

I also owe a particular debt of gratitude to those who were willing to contact me about their encounters, share them, and allow me to make further inquiries. It is because of your generosity that this book has come into being. I would also be remiss if I did express my deep gratitude to all who read various parts of the manuscript and for their suggestions, especially Shirley Scott, R.N.; Professor Dan Giancola, Department of English, of the Eastern Campus of Suffolk Community College; Professor Emeritus Jan Londraville of the State University of New York, College at Potsdam; and Chris LaGrand, who is a television news writer in San Francisco. Last but not at all least, I am indebted to Astrid Sandell, my editor, whose patience is only exceeded by her ability to superbly edit.

Most of all, I am indebted to my family, who have encouraged me and allowed me to spend so much time on this second project, especially my wife and best friend Barbara.

Introduction

This is a book about one of the most important topics a family member, caregiver, or friend of one who is mourning the death of a loved one should read—especially if she† (or he) has had an extraordinary experience and believes a sign or a contact has been received from a deceased loved one. Researchers call the experience an ADC (after-death communication). Whatever the case, let me begin by assuring you the event is normal, your relative or friend doesn't need counseling, and may, in fact, have received a gift to help deal with the tragic loss.

This is also a book for anyone who is interested in the subject of after-death communication and would like to learn more about it and gain a broad view of related issues and topics. Thus it may used as a tool for personal reflection, a resource for helping the bereaved, and as a handbook for small group discussion. Whether you're a support person and friend, grief counselor, mourner who has had an ADC, or curious inquirer—the questions and answers that follow will provide you with information to stimulate your interest and help you explore the hidden side of human personality, which is all too often relegated to the shelf of fiction and make-believe. Furthermore, the answers will give insight into how millions of people have been able to establish a healthy new relationship with deceased loved ones, finish unfinished business, cope with their massive losses, and let go of regrets and emotions which are stress producing.

Over the years, I have been interviewed on numerous radio programs nationwide, appeared on television talk shows, and given workshops and lectures to both professionals and the general public on the topic of after-death communication. During that time I have been asked a variety of questions about ADC phenomena, some very pointed and demanding. Indeed, I have often had to ask myself many questions as I studied the depth of the experience, pondered the tacky stereotypes associated with the topic, or prepared to interview

† I have chosen to randomly use "he" or "she" throughout the book. Either usage includes both genders and no insensitivity is intended.

xvii

those who have had an ADC. Because the nature of these phenomena are so elusive of scientific explanation and very controversial, I have had to examine my own beliefs before deciding to help others through counseling and teaching.

When grieving the death of a loved one, it is important to habitually ask questions in order to counter the cultural assumptions about grief and move toward reconciling the loss. The very same process has to be followed throughout life if we are to make important choices, reach goals, and develop needed skills. I have attempted in this book to ask questions that will help you grow in your understanding of one aspect of nonphysical reality. The unseen and the unexplainable are rich in substance and therefore could cause you to reassess your value system as well as your worldview. Along the way, this growth will increase your awareness of mystery and provide insight into how we are all connected. Everyone, consciously or unconsciously, searches for meaning. It is the very stuff that fuels our existence. Thus you will benefit most from your reading if you start by asking, "What do I want from this book?" Then turn to the section that will most likely contain your answer.

To facilitate your search, I have organized questions and answers into six categories:

> The Nature of After-Death Communication
> Origins and Causes
> Types of Experiences Reported
> The Experiencers and the Messages
> Positive Influences
> Helping the Person Who Has an ADC

Once you choose the section associated with your specific interest the answer you find may spawn new insights and interests—and ultimately new questions. That's good. Now you can move to another part of the book and add some sense of progression and continuity to your learning. In the meantime, you will be building a deeper awareness of the depth of the subject and how it can be applied to your life.

Should you have no specific questions to launch your journey into ADC simply start at the beginning to get your bearings. Either way, you will gain a new perspective on the mystery of nonphysical reality and its impact on individuals who are coping with loss. On the other hand, your journey—if you are grieving—may even help you accept the death of your loved one and establish a healthy new relationship with him or her. After all, with few exceptions, ADCs are essentially expressions of love because they are all about helping each other. Or if you are providing support, you may be instilled with confidence to help friends or relatives who are mourning the death of a loved one. Your reading may even challenge your beliefs regarding the age-old question of whether or not consciousness survives bodily death.

A question I am often asked which does not fit into any of the categories in the book but deserves an up-front answer is, "What is your background and how did you become interested in the subject of after-death communication?"

Let me begin by saying, when this inquiry is made, I sometimes speculate the person is really asking, "How does anybody become interested in such an unusual topic?" With that in mind, my interest can be traced back to a course I introduced in 1977 at the State University of New York, College at Potsdam. The name of the course was "Dying and Death: Implications for Growth." It was because of this course I began to have students come to me with unresolved losses. Occasionally, the Dean of Students would ask me to see a student mourning the death of a loved one. The upshot of it all was I had to become a counselor-without-portfolio. Eventually, I chose to become a certified grief counselor. But before I did that, I had an unusual visit from an older student (a grandmother) and for the first time was confronted with an astonishing story (documented in *After Death Communication: Final Farewells,* 1997). I was put on the spot when she asked if I thought the ADC she and her grandson experienced could be real. It was a precarious moment in my professional life as I had never had an ADC or knew anyone else who had ever had one.

Her story and those which followed always stirred my view of reality and of how the experiences might have originated. Subsequently, I began to collect stories I would hear or read about. In addition, I began to ask colleagues if they had heard of similar happenings and what they thought of them. The experiences were being reported all right, but the vast majority of counselors dismissed them as irrelevant. They clung to the traditional professional belief the ADC was a simple artifact of grief. Furthermore, they emphasized the experience was due to hallucinations and illusions—or to the disorganized condition of the mourner. Despite this, I continued to collect information from those who had the experience and I continued to believe it could help the mourner. Most importantly, I was still deeply interested in how the phenomena originated. In fact, I began to actively seek out reports of ADC phenomena and request them from audiences whenever I spoke about the subject. This led to the construction of a survey instrument which I gave to those who thought they had experienced an ADC or knew someone who had shared one.

Whenever I am at a hospital or doctor's office, I also routinely ask medical professionals if they ever had a patient who claimed to have heard or seen a deceased loved one. As many times as I have heard them say "no" it is followed with, "But I (or a relative) had this happen to me," and then they relate a beautiful story about an ADC.

Over time, I realized all of these reports might not be simply wishful thinking or ruminations of the imagination. Many were too complex to be simply chance occurrences or coincidence. But most important of all, the experience was helping the mourner, especially when others were supportive and nonjudgmental, and sometimes even when there was little or no support. Consequently, I became convinced of the importance of lending credibility to the experience. This meant informing others the ADC should be normalized and utilized by professionals and nonprofessionals to help the bereaved cope with their losses. I also began to find a few professional counselors who experienced an ADC, who were open to the phenomena, and even routinely asked their clients about it.

Now eighteen years later, the trip has continued to be an exciting one, but not without its share of skeptics and naysayers. The cynics wish I would cease and desist from suggesting the ADC is useful without proof the experience is scientifically verifiable. Of course, that is the big problem, because there is no way, at this point in time, to verify spontaneous phenomena. It is impossible to replicate spontaneity as it is associated with the ADC experience. The scientific method rests on the ability to study and replicate data in order to validate the existence of a phenomena. Research on after-death communication has to hinge on accurate interviewing, which results in descriptive research that often doesn't cut the mustard. In fact, anecdotal data is virtually worthless in the eyes of most scientists. But that is to be expected in a society dominated by the scientific method. In any event, it does not lessen the reality of the experience for anyone who is fortunate enough to be blessed with the ADC. What must balance scientific ideology is the fact that the phenomena occurs to millions of people—helping most cope with the death of their loved ones—even though proof is nonexistent. But as British scientist Denis Burkitt wrote, "Not everything that counts can be counted." Here is an insight worthy of every skeptic's consideration.

One final introductory note. All too frequently the words *after-death communication* somehow connote to many people that we are dealing with gifted intuitives (psychics) or the summoning of spirits as in the Victorian Age. Others have the idea the mourner somehow invokes the deceased person's presence as suggested by some researchers. Nothing could be further from the truth. What we are dealing with here are sudden, unexpected experiences involving our senses, dreams, and symbolic and physical phenomena. These do not have readily explainable reasons for occurring in such a forthright manner. Of course, this is always vexing to the rational mind. In fact, many look at the phenomena as being irrational. Yet, these events occur regularly despite the fact we cannot always understand their origin or place them in a scientific frame of reference.

And now on to the one-hundred most-asked questions about ADC phenomena.

PART

·1·

The Nature of
After-Death Communication

Questions 1 through 11

Definitions • History •
The Near-Death Experience (NDE) and ADC Importance •
Pet Involvement • Related Questions

The probability of life originating from accident
is comparable to the probability of the
unabridged dictionary resulting from an
explosion in a print shop.
—Albert Einstein

1. How do you define after-death communication (ADC)?

Dr. LaGrand, I feel a little confused. Lots of people use the term after-death communication, start talking about it, and I get lost because they're talking about something completely different than what I consider to be ADC phenomena. What is meant by after-death communication? Is there a consensus of opinion about what constitutes the subject matter?

There is an ancient Chinese proverb that says: "The beginning of wisdom is to call things by their right name." Without question, the subject of after-death communication (ADC) is among those controversial issues that have not been adequately studied. Therefore, after-death communication means different things to different people depending on who is doing the talking. Indeed, one of the difficulties of discussing the topic of after-death communication—and finding common ground for agreement—within professional, scientific, and even social circles is the lack of standardized terminology. The same problem exists with many controversial subjects.

Eighteen years ago, when the first person came to me seeking my professional opinion on an ADC she had experienced, I had no idea what to call it. Since that time there have been several names applied to the phenomena such as post-death communication, paranormal experiences, interdimensional communication, extraordinary experiences, afterlife communication, natural experiences, and the ever-popular hallucinatory experiences.

After-death communication is a term of fairly recent origin. It was coined by Bill and Judy Guggenheim who, in 1996, published the first book focusing on the role of ADCs in the lives of the bereaved. It is currently used by researchers and professional counselors. The term is controversial for many people because even though we relate to the dead in a variety of ways, the bias against a deceased person talking to or sending a sign to someone alive is strong. Despite this bias, the phenomena occur regularly. Let me remind you we relate to the dead in a variety of ways: monuments, museums, preserved rooms or homes of historical figures, the celebration of Memorial Day, and the visitation to cemeteries to name a few. Many people, when alone, talk to deceased loved ones either silently or out loud and are even encouraged to do so by therapists as a coping tool. Many more talk to the deceased on a daily basis in their petitions to saints. Of course, we all have a penchant for quoting inspiring sayings from those long deceased. Nonetheless, if you say you have received a sign or message from a deceased loved one, those who hear you make that statement will assume you are a candidate for the nearest psychiatrist.

My own definition of after-death communication is in complete agreement with the Guggenheims, who have interviewed thousands of people reporting the experience. Succinctly stated, after-death communication is spontaneously experiencing contact with a deceased loved one. More specifically, it is the field of study that comprises a variety of experiences in which those mourning the death of a loved one believe they have directly or indirectly received a message or sign or been contacted by the deceased. This is the most commonly accepted definition. Make no mistake: after-death communication is not passive, it's active. It is something you can keep in your memory bank for the rest of your life—draw on it continually for strength, it never decreases in value. It is a piece of personal history giving meaning to existence. It grants the opportunity to strengthen one's inner life and deal with whatever the world has to offer. Used wisely, it is a gift of inestimable value helping people find meaning and personal growth through encounters with death.

However, it is important to understand the experience is not something that is invoked or somehow brought on by the mourner or a third-party, such as a gifted intuitive. There are also some professional counselors who believe they can create the circumstances, through induction techniques in which a mourner can experience ADC phenomena. Although theoretically possible, such experiences are not what after-death communication is about.

Remember: the key word in defining after-death communication is *spontaneous;* it comes unbidden. In addition, the apparent initiation of the event is generated from a source outside of the recipient and is the second defining characteristic. This definition does not preclude the possibility of asking for or praying for a sign a loved one is all right; it will still come spontaneously, if at all. Some mourners also may think they have had contact with deceased loved ones by means of imagery or visualization techniques. I contend that those also are different phenomena, as real as they may seem. To illustrate the ADC experience and its effect on the bereaved, here is an illuminating ADC visitation dream sent to me by a minister from the Northwest.

"It's All Right. He's Still Here."

In 1984, a close friend developed lung cancer, surely fatal within six months. His family consisted of two brothers who disliked him and an alcoholic mother, so I assumed the work of easing his life during his remaining time. When he finally died it was, of course, a relief after his suffering; we moved from praying for a miraculous remission to begging for a quick passage after the cancer had damaged his body so severely that even without the tumor he would have been severely crippled and deformed. After this was over I was simply numb from repressing emotions. Nothing gave me pleasure—or pain, for that matter—as I went about putting my life back in order.

It is necessary for me to have truly intense psychic experiences when dreaming; I was educated as a scientist for three years at Cal Tech. While my parents were confident acceptors of all kinds of psychic experiences, my adolescent skepticism led me to reject their mindset and rebel. My disillusionment with science came rather quickly, but the training in objectivity does not let me relax and receive impressions while awake. But, as you described in your book, the ordinary dream is swept away, shattered—it is like someone ripping the projection screen during a movie and stepping through it.

And that is what happened. Several weeks after his death, my friend simply barged into my dream, scattering the fragments of it like autumn leaves before him. There he was, his old self, healthy, full of fun, not particularly concerned that he had died. He didn't say anything, just eyed me with a typical impish expression as if to say, "Well, you wanted me; here I am."

I said to myself, "It's all right. He's still here." Since I cry easily, I did, shedding torrents of tears of relief. After I woke up—first from the vision and then from the dream—the healing process had begun. It was some months later I boarded a plane and as the plane rose above the polluted city into a fairyland cloudscape of intense beauty, again I began to cry and realized with joy that I could appreciate the beauty for the first time in nearly a year. By the time we landed at the Phoenix airport an hour later, my eyes were red but I was ready to accept and appreciate life and its bounty once more.

The obvious impact of this ADC experience further suggests the path to release and freedom that the mourner is able to find. On the other hand, there are some individuals, including some parapsychologists, who embrace a much larger concept of after-death communication. While the more common version has as its central focus survivors who are mourning the death of a loved one, others include the near-death experience (NDE), premonitions (a forewarning), precognition (the ability to randomly predict the future in a way other than through logical inference), and out-of-body experiences as part of after-death communication. You can begin to appreciate that we have lots of work to do in order to clearly define what we refer to as an ADC and to agree on standard terminology. Again, I would like to emphasize two salient characteristics in defining after-death communication as viewed by those in professional counseling roles and those doing research that focuses on the bereaved: spontaneous occurrence and the apparent origin of the phenomena coming from the outside in.

2. Are ADCs of recent origin or do they have a historical track record?

I feel like after-death communication is something that has been occurring in my family for at least a couple of generations. So I wonder if this is something that has just been discovered or if it has been going on for some time and has been kept hidden for obvious reasons.

What we presently call after-death communication is most likely as old as humanity itself. It can be found in the written word more than two thousand years ago. For example, Cicero (B.C. 106–B.C. 43)—considered to be the greatest Roman orator as well as a famous philosopher, voluminous writer, and master of Latin prose—wrote about a very significant ADC. In an essay entitled *On Divination*, he describes both a dream state and an evidential (when one learns something not previously known) ADC. It involved two friends who were traveling from Arcadia, a mountainous region of ancient Greece, to the town of Megara between the Gulf of Corinth and the Saronic Gulf. One of them decided to stay with friends and the other went to the local inn.

He and his friend finished their evening meal and retired. In his slumber our guest dreamed that his traveling companion appeared to him and said, "The innkeeper has murdered me, flung my body into a cart, and covered it with dung. Please, I beg you, be at the gate early in the morning before the cart can leave the town."

Stirred to the depths of his being by this dream, he confronted at dawn the rustic who was driving the cart out of the gate. The wretch took to his heels in dismay and fright. Our friend then recovered the body and reported the murder to the proper officials. The innkeeper was duly punished.

Can you find the four pieces of information given by one friend to another in the evidential portion of this ADC? Since this event was written—and before—there have been a large number of ADCs experienced in which the recipient has received information not previously known. The information has come from an auditory or visual ADC as well as through an assortment of vivid dreams.

There are many ADC experiences reported in the Bible and elsewhere. ADCs have been standard fare for centuries for many who have been devastated by the death of a beloved family member or friend and who have then received a comforting message from beyond.

Robert Burton (1577–1640), English scholar and clergyman, used the pen name Democritus Junior to publish his famous *The Anatomy of Melancholy*, which appeared in 1621. Focusing on the cause and effects of melancholy, Burton wrote of the ADC experiences of maids, widows, and nuns in rather disparaging terms:

> Some think they see visions, confer with spirits and devils . . . They think they see their dead friends continually in their eyes, observantes imagines . . . [They] are almost distracted, mad or stupid for the time, and by fits.

Although Burton would not recognize the ADC as a normal phenomena, as unexplainable then as it is now, he describes quite clearly the existence of the phenomena.

With the founding of the Society for Psychical Research (SPR) in London in 1882 and its American counterpart, the American Society for Psychical Research, in Boston during the same year, renewed interest in psi phenomena was at a peak. The interest in ADC-type phenomena was also peaking. These societies drew distinguished members from the scientific and educational communities, many of whom were confirmed skeptics of paranormal phenomena. Nonetheless, the SPR launched the first massive study of unexplainable occurrences under the title of the *Census of Hallucinations.* Many of the over 17,000 respondents provided reports of experiences that we now refer to as ADCs.

It wasn't until the 1980s that Edie Devers, a Florida nurse and now psychotherapist as well as author of *Goodbye Again;* Bill and Judy Guggenheim, authors of the first book on the subject of ADCs, entitled *Hello From Heaven;* and I began in our separate ways to develop an interest in exploring the subject from the point of view of the individual who is mourning the death of a loved one. This is a perspective that has been sorely missed by experts in grief theory and not fully utilized by those giving support to mourners. Presently there is great interest in the phenomena as more and more people realize how helpful these experiences can be. Still, I regret to say, the media gives it little coverage because of the taboo against talking to the spirit of someone who has died.

3.   What are the substantial differences between after-death communication (ADC) and the near-death experience (NDE)?

It seems as though the near-death experience has a lot in common with after-death communication because in both instances there appears to be awareness of or contact with those who have predeceased us. Also, it is obvious that both experiences often help people reduce their fear of death. While there are similarities, there must be differences if both phenomena are not considered under the same title. Where do they part company?

First, let's examine the NDE. It is usually defined as an unusual, some say profound, experience that occurs when a person is on the brink of death. Although the NDE has been described for centuries in various writings (e.g., The Tibetan Book of the Dead), the prototypical event currently being studied was first introduced in 1975 by Raymond Moody in his best-selling book *Life After Life*. This book, still available in bookstores, has been translated into a dozen languages and has sold millions of copies. His research suggested a pattern of stages or events, including hearing oneself pronounced dead, having feelings of peace and quiet, experiencing movement out of the body and through a dark tunnel, meeting a being of light and others who had died, making a life review, and finally coming to a border or barrier and then returning. Let me emphasize that there is a long history of NDE-like phenomena that can be traced back in religious literature, Chinese culture, and from many other ethnic traditions.

There are three basic types of NDEs. The one just described is generally called the transcendental experience. A second category involves deathbed visions (DBV), which were extensively studied by Karlis Osis, who was originally responsible for stimulating new interest in near-death phenomena several decades ago. The DBV occurs with a dying person who interacts with others who have predeceased him. The dying person may converse with those he "sees," reach out as though to touch the deceased person, or exhibit nonverbal behavior to indicate peace and happiness at the prospect of his passing to meet relatives and friends. A third type of NDE has been labeled the autoscopic experience and actually involves an out-of-body experience as in the transcendental NDE. However, all of the classic motifs of Moody's NDE are not involved. Often, the person experiencing the autoscopic NDE hovers over his or her body watching whatever action is taking place and eventually comes back into the body and experiences the pain associated with the present conditions.

Here is a typical NDE, experienced by Ray Gorman of Ogden, Utah.

"My Father Came to Me in a Time of Crisis"

I was twenty-nine years old and my wife and I had two children—a boy and a girl. At the time, I worked as a process inspector for a company that made solid fuel for large rocket motors. It was October and I was working with a mixing crew that was mixing a 4,400-pound batch of propellant. There were five of us on the crew and we were preparing to transfer the completed batch of propellant from the mixing bowl to a transportation container when the material ignited and exploded. Two of the crew were killed instantly, and myself and the other two were severely burned. We were immediately taken to one of the local hospitals, where a team of plastic surgeons were waiting. They evacuated the intensive care unit and put us there so they could control our environment to limit the possibility of infection. I only mention this because it is important to understand we were the only ones in this large open room, so everyone could hear what was going on at all times.

The injuries that I suffered were extremely painful, and I was very scared, because I did not believe that I was going to survive. To make matters worse, the doctors had to sew together what was left of my eyelids in order to protect my eyes and ensure that I would continue to have eyelids after the scarring process. They also told me that my eyes would be shut for two months. Needless to say, this made me even more frightened.

After the second day, one of the fellows that was with me expired from his injuries and I could hear them working on him. I heard the nurse call the doctor and advise him of the death. I just knew it was a matter of time until I also expired, and to tell the truth, the pain was so great that I really didn't care. On about the fourth or fifth day, I was in such pain, I was wishing for it to come. All of a sudden, my pain vanished and I could feel myself floating. Although my eyes were sewn shut, I was able to open them, and I immediately looked at my hands, and they were whole again and showed no signs of being burned. I could not see anything else because I was surrounded by a thick gray mist, and I had the sensation of moving, like I was standing on a fast-moving elevator. I could feel the wind in my hair and I could hear the wind on my ears. My first thought was that I had died, and I felt a great sense of relief, because we did survive the death of our physical bodies. I also had the feeling someone was going to meet me, so I was not afraid.

Soon the sense of movement stopped and I was standing, still surrounded by the gray mist. I began to hear footsteps, and they were loud, like someone walking on a boardwalk in a hollow area. As the footsteps came closer, I strained my eyes and saw the figure of a man approaching me. When he got close enough, I saw that it was my dad. He was dressed in white pants, shirt, and shoes, and he was carrying a small suitcase. I said, "Dad, is that you?" and he replied, "Yes Raymond, it's me." I then asked, "Am I dead?" and he said, "No Raymond, you're not dead. I just came to tell you everything will be all right and you should not worry anymore." I then asked him if I could stay here with him and he said, "No, because it's not your time yet." At that time, I began to cry and I said I did not want to go back, that I wanted to stay now that I had come this far. He again told me it was not my time and he turned to walk away. I called to him to ask him to stay because I had so much I wanted to ask him, but he kept walking until he disappeared into the gray mist. When he was gone, I again began to feel myself moving, and soon I was laying down in my hospital bed. The excruciating pain was again racking my body.

I feel I was privileged to have had my experience and I know it was not a hallucination. This experience has truly touched my life and I often reflect on it with a warm feeling. My father came to me in a time of crisis, soothed my pain, and most of all, he gave me some insight into something we all fear: death.

Now for the differences between ADC phenomena and the NDE. As you can observe, the NDE occurs in circumstances where the participant is dying or thinks he is dying, although a number of people have reported out-of-body experiences that have nothing to do with thoughts of dying. This is why the event has euphemistically been called the no-death experience. (A small number of mourners have reported an out-of body experience that preceded the visit of a loved one.) In contrast, the ADC occurs with people who are mourning the death of a loved one and may or may not have unfinished business with the deceased. They have an experience that helps them deal with a specific problem or that gives them encouragement to go on with their lives. So the specific circumstances under which both events occur is obviously different.

Another difference has to do with how both events are initiated. It appears as though the NDE is often a product of an external event. That is, an accident occurs, one's physical condition suddenly deteriorates or one believes they are in imminent danger of dying. Then the series of changes ensues. On the other hand, the ADC most always occurs in a spontaneous, unknown way; a triggering event is absent. The experiencer is not thrown into a set of circumstances, but suddenly comes face-to-face with the deceased or receives a sign when least expected. This is not to deny that a person may have influenced the occurrence of an ADC through prayer or asking the deceased to send a sign.

In actuality, there seems to be more similarities than differences between the two types of phenomena.

4.   How do people who have had an NDE view the ADC?

It is quite clear that millions of people have had either an NDE or an ADC experience, although I understand many more have experienced the latter. While the NDE has received more publicity and more research has been conducted on it, I am wondering if those who have had an NDE have a different take on the ADC experience as opposed to those who have experienced neither phenomena. Put another way, does the person who has had an NDE have a more positive or negative view of ADC phenomena?

There is ample evidence from the research on NDEs to show that those who have the experience undergo a number of changes in the way they look at life and death. The data suggests an increase in belief in an afterlife, greater concern for others, and a return to their spiritual roots. Perhaps most notable is their lack of fear of death and reduced interest in materialism. In fact, many report that death is clearly the gateway to an existence beyond description. In short, there is a world of love and beauty in the next life and to them ADC phenomena is simply another manifestation of contact that is made between this life and the next. They have no problem believing in the ADC as a manifestation of real contact between physical and nonphysical reality.

I once interviewed a woman who had a near-death experience and looked at the ADC as simply another common interface between physical and nonphysical reality. It was no big deal. *Ho hum*—just ordinary. To her, both phenomena were quite normal and often overlooked or purposely ignored because of cultural mores. Let me remind you that building an edifice of belief in the ADC is easily accomplished if you have had a positive experience involving the unseen or other unexplainable phenomena. Despite the fact that scientific reductionist thinking refuses to acknowledge either the ADC or the NDE as bona fide phenomena, they occur continuously throughout the world. My interviewee had a good point in accepting the ADC as a normal part of human existence, because many individuals have extraordinary experiences and dismiss them as anomalies, "my craziness," or misperceptions as science would suggest. In general, those who have had an NDE look most favorably on the ADC as another aspect of total reality that is not accepted by a substantial proportion of the population.

5. Why is it important to become aware of ADC phenomena?

I know much has been written about ADCs and the fact that they result in mourners being able to use them as a tool to cope with their losses. Are there other reasons to suggest and develop that could be used to influence those who may not feel that ADC phenomena is that important?

First, let's begin with the understanding there is substantial evidence that shows that the phenomena does in fact occur in the lives of many millions of individuals. For example, the prestigious Gallup Poll reports one in six adults claim to have had contact with a deceased loved one. The University of Chicago's National Opinion Research Council (NORC), using a national sample of subjects, asked if "you ever felt you were in touch with someone who had died." Forty-two percent of those polled responded in the affirmative. Authors Kalish and Reynolds, in *Death and Ethnicity,* reported in their sample of respondents that fifty percent of the women and thirty percent of men had a contact experience. A recent USA Today/CNN/Gallup Poll, conducted in 1997, found that twenty-eight percent of Americans are convinced that communication can occur between survivors and the deceased. All of these figures do not include children who also experience ADCs. This information alone should spur us to investigate why so many people who are mourning the death of a loved one receive a contact of some sort (apparently from a loved one, or as some believe, from an angel or a Supreme Being) that assists them in coping with their loss. Any phenomena that occurs as frequently as the ADC, and which is not easily explained, should become a prime candidate for research to understand why the experience occurs and where it originates. What is critical to understand and commonly overlooked is these events are not merely immensely helpful to the mourner they also have the potential to influence one's physical well-being and relationships with others. The prevalence of ADC phenomena is in itself a reason we should become more knowledgeable about it.

Second, because the phenomena occurs so frequently and nonphysical reality is often looked down on by the scientific community as a manifestation of wish fulfillment or figments of the imagination, it suggests that we need to maximize the normalcy of this helpful phenomena. For what reason? Not only to assist the mourner who believes he's losing his sanity, but to educate those who provide support. Support persons need to realize such occurrences do not indicate that the mourner is in need of professional counseling. Furthermore, they can have a powerful influence by their response when the ADC is shared. It is critical for support persons to understand the immediate negative response to a shared ADC means they not only increase anxiety in the mourner, but more importantly, they sever the trusting relationship that the mourner needs. (See question 91.)

Third, and most important, the experience is real to the mourner regardless of the interpretation by support persons. Let's examine an ADC that most scientists would dismiss as meaningless based on the lack of hard evidence to support the contentions of John, an eighty-four-year-old widower, whose wife had died six months previously. He had been in a support group I was conducting and called me for an appointment a couple of months later. Here is his account:

"Then I Realized That Was My Sign"

I have prayed for a sign at services, when I make a visit to church, or at night that my wife would be in heaven and is happy. She was a good person and I want to know she is up there and happy. When she was alive, we had jokingly said that if I died first and she had a problem she would ask me about it. If I said "yes" to a particular question I would knock once. If my answer was "no," I would knock twice. I had forgotten about this and was not thinking about it the night I woke up. It was 3:30 A.M. I heard three distinct and forceful knocks. I got up and looked outside; no one was there. I went back to bed and stayed awake, but heard nothing else. I wasn't sure if the knocks woke me up or I was awake and then heard them. Finally, I went back off to sleep. I didn't think anymore about it until the next night and then I realized that was my sign that I had been praying for. I thought about contacting you, but hesitated. Then I received your letter and that made me believe I should call you. {Author note: The letter was a follow-up letter sent to all support group members.}

When he came to discuss the event with me I asked many questions, especially about his feelings and beliefs about what had happened. He responded without hesitation with "I believe" and "I'm reassured." What he was seeking is what any support person can provide: a simple gesture of support for his conclusions—and that's what I provided. I checked with him a year later and he was doing very well.

The fact that the mourner believes that he has had a sign or message regarding the deceased is what must be addressed, not the skeptical inquiry of the support person, regardless of the good intentions. Why must it be addressed and take priority? Simply because the experience has a host of potential therapeutic applications, from affirming the death and going on with life, to establishing a new relationship with the deceased and reordering life goals and objectives. As one woman, whose son was murdered, put it: "ADCs are a helping and healing tool." The event may also reduce fear, initiate value changes, and in some cases prevent suicide.

Fourth, the experience always results in a message for survivors. The message may be symbolic, implied, or explicit. For example, most ADC visitation dreams can be interpreted literally, not symbolically. As a result of the messages conveyed, positive changes in the mourning process may occur that would normally take months or years of therapy depending on the degree of complicated mourning. Sometimes the mourner may need assistance in deciding on how to interpret the experience, or validation for the decision he has reached based on his ADC. There is always a message if one will simply look for it.

Fifth, mourners most often need to share their experience within a non-judgmental framework. In particular, they need someone who is willing to listen and initiate listening with the supposition that what has transpired may be genuine. Nonjudgmental listening provides the initial validation necessary to strengthen the relationship between the mourner and the support person, reduce mourner anxiety, and provide an atmosphere in which emotions can be expressed and life affirmed. Conversely, lack of any validation often adds stress to the mourner when his or her judgment is challenged by a well-meaning friend or family member. In this regard, I remember a young woman at a lecture I was giving who was visibly upset because her mother had shared two tactile ADCs with her. The experiences involved her father, who had recently died. Her mother was convinced of their authenticity and meaning, while the daughter was telling her that no such thing could happen and that she was imagining it all. The conflict was driving a wedge in their relationship and she had come to the lecture to find reinforcement. After normalizing her mother's experiences and hearing others share their ADCs in the group, she was able to see her mother's reactions in a different light. She was unaware that it was possible for her mother to have the experiences, that she was not in need of professional assistance, and that the experiences could be used to help her cope with her loss.

Sixth, for anyone conducting a support group, especially someone who has never had an ADC or heard of the variety of experiences that can occur, awareness of ADC phenomena is a must. It is inevitable that the topic will arise. How it is addressed can have a major impact on how the group responds in future meetings. The same can be said for professional counselors or caregivers providing support for the bereaved. An immediate negative response to the sharing of extraordinary experiences by the bereaved can both add to their anxiety (as they think they are losing their sanity) and destroy the helping relationship. Succinctly put, becoming aware of the whole spectrum of ADC phenomena and its effect on the mourning process is essential knowledge for professionals and nonprofessionals alike who want to be best equipped to assist the bereaved.

- *See also questions 89 and 96*

6. **How can anyone know there is more than one reality, a reality that includes ADCs?**

Although the word reality *is used loosely, I have always interpreted it to mean the way the world is in a physical sense, that it is real—touchable, see-able, and measurable. That IS reality for me. So if there is a nonphysical reality, a spiritual reality, how does one go about proving it exists?*

We all live in a culture that is clearly oriented toward physical reality. In fact, it is accepted by many in the West that the predominant cultural fabric is materialistic in nature. Of course, what plays a major role in this physical orientation is our economy, which is built on ever-increasing the gross national product and highlighting luxury, time-saving devices, vacations, the arts, automobiles and an endless line of toys, gadgets, and objects to satisfy the desires and demands of an affluent society. In annually working toward reaching the goal of topping last year's production totals, new and more glittering forms of advertisement and eye-catching media must be introduced. This focus easily allows us to get caught up in the importance of seeing is believing and the conviction that what is external, or out there, is what brings happiness and is real.

Add to this scenario the fact that the scientific method permeates our cultural ethic and is the backbone of determining what is real—and it is not surprising that nonphysical reality becomes an albatross of the past with little credibility. So how then can we begin to balance such a one-sided view of life with its exclusively physical dimensions? One approach is to look at what experience tells us. Proof lies in human experience.

Subjective experience tells us much about nonphysical reality. Let's begin by looking at the wisdom of the bodymind, which on an unconscious level makes thousands of decisions when a wound has to be healed. We are not consciously aware of the fact that dead cells are removed from the site of the wound and new materials are brought there to begin the job of rebuilding injured tissue. This goes on whether we are asleep or awake. Who or what makes all of those decisions for healing to occur when we experience such a variety of wounds in terms of size and location? The same question may be posed with regard to the immune system that is constantly on guard against bacteria and viruses and a bevy of other invaders trying to do their deadly tasks of destroying the healthy functioning of internal organs. We know that all healing—whether physical or emotional—ultimately comes from a difficult-to-prove and define source, but our culture is reluctant to say that nonphysical reality is somehow involved.

Furthermore, we tend to forget that human life itself is a miracle. What hidden resource could possibly be behind the ability of two tiny cells, an egg and a sperm, to meet and divide and result in the complex of individual cells, organs, and systems we call the body? Sure, we know there is a DNA code that lays it all out for the orderly multiplication of cells, but where do those orders originate and how can they be carried out with such precision? And how can we all have our own unique voice and fingerprints? The complexity is staggering when you think of the billions of people who have lived and died. Looked at another way, where does creativity find its source? If you read some of the biographies of great poets, musicians, and writers—like Puccini, Brahms, Shelley, Goethe, and Keats—it is not unusual to find them saying that their works come from a place or source that they describe as the unconscious, chance, something other than an earthly power, or from some place beyond conscious awareness. Science has yet to agree on the source of such wisdom.

Because the word *spiritual* means many different things to people, let's first clarify how I am using the term. For me, spirituality refers to the world of nonphysical reality, the incorporeal part of our being, our essence—including the heart, soul, character, mystery, courage, and divine spark that permeates humanity. It is the ongoing connection with a Higher Power—a Power that is both within and without. It cannot be measured, weighed, or seen. It is manifested in the altruistic things we do to help our neighbors, the way we serve others who are less fortunate and in need, and the uplifting experiences we have, sometimes mystical, sometimes coming from nature in all its beauty.

The spiritual is a part of humanity, eternal and ongoing long after the body has disintegrated; it transcends the material and sensual, though part of human consciousness. The spiritual unites us all, the common core of humanity. Maya Angelou, one of the best-selling and best-loved authors of our times, puts it another way: "I believe that Spirit is one and is everywhere present." I couldn't agree more. Today, more than ever, physicians, counselors, and mental health specialists are beginning to recognize the need to nourish the spirit and soul as well as the body and are recommending a variety of relaxation techniques and spiritual practices that bring inner peace and tranquillity. In other words, psychiatry is beginning to rediscover that the vast majority of psychological problems are at root an impoverishment in meeting spiritual needs.

Just as some individuals dismiss spirituality and nonphysical reality as wishful thinking, so too do they look at ADC phenomena with the same jaundiced eye. This is to be expected if their beliefs are wedded only to the scientific method, because it is impossible to be open to anything that is not verifiable. That in itself is a self-limiting pattern of thinking. We all suffer from an insufficient understanding of reality because it is easy to become attached to one small aspect of our environment and lose the possibility of awareness of the whole. Such fragmentation is built into contemporary lifestyles as we begin the twenty-first century.

It takes concerted effort in this day and age to look past the immediate trappings of our physical worlds and engage the Greater Reality. However, for those who have an ADC, it is in essence an experience with another reality of a spiritual nature as it puts one in touch with a whole new unexplored universe. Consider the awareness of new realities that opened in the life of Donna Leonard of Burtonsville, Maryland.

"I Am Not Imagining Any of These Things"

My husband passed away on November 25 of this year with a heart attack. This was very sudden and he was in perfect health. Our family was deeply stricken with grief. I have had a very bad time, but the grief counselor I went to see said I was dealing with the grief in the right way. We have a very close family, five children and fourteen grandchildren. My husband and I were together for forty-five years in a great relationship. Everything was done with our children; they were our best friends.

Since my husband's death, three of my children have had dreams where my husband assured them he is all right. I have had no dreams, but I have been fully awake when the following happened to me: I could not sleep at my house after the death of my husband so I stayed at my daughter's house. Laying in bed one night I felt a hand take my hand and I could never describe the warmth that entered my entire body. Several weeks later, I was awakened at 12:30 A.M. by the alarm clock in my daughter's bedroom where I was sleeping. Not familiar with this clock, I grabbed it in the dark trying to shut it off, instead I must have hit the radio button and a message said, "Fear not, you will never be alone."

This morning at 4:00 A.M. I was wide awake just laying on my bed. This was the first time I stayed in my house and my daughter stayed with me in another room. We were having a problem with water coming into our basement and I heard my daughter go downstairs and turn on the wet vac to suck up the water, which was right under my bedroom. I looked at the clock and it was 4:00 A.M. I was thinking my daughter was so great looking out for this for me when out of the blue this came in my head: I saw my husband and my son walk down our driveway. I saw exactly what both had on. I was sitting in our pick-up truck with two of our grandchildren. I saw him open the door and he said the entire family is here except me. Then everything just disappeared.

One other experience. My husband and I always slept with a touch light on the lowest setting because I did not like to sleep in the dark. Since his death, this light has come on by itself on many days, especially when I am having a very bad time. We have had this lamp for sixteen years and it has never come on by itself. I have tried to stamp on the floor near the lamp; I have banged the dresser where it sits and it will not come on unless it is touched. One day, I just could not bring myself to turn it off because I always believe it is my husband turning it on. So I left the light on. That night when I went into my bedroom, the light was on the second level setting. When I left for work it had been on the first level. I am not imagining any of these things, even though my grief is hard to take. All of the above have happened with me being fully awake.

For Donna, there is proof of more than one reality, as she and her daughters have experienced. When the mourner realizes the spiritual dimensions of the deceased loved one, she immediately has another tool to deal with his physical absence. Once you spiritualize the person, you begin the establishment of a new relationship in a meaningful context. In the final analysis, of course, reality has no objective witnesses; the proof you seek is always a function of the perceptions of the observer. But like it or not, subjectivity, faith, and spiritual experience have always been and will continue to be part of the human condition.

- *See also questions 27 and 77*

7. Is the communication that takes place in an ADC experience only one-way—coming from the deceased to the mourner?

Because the phrase after-death communication refers to that which is experienced after a loved one has died, I am wondering if there are any regular two-way conversations that occur. Or is it only an event in which the deceased (or someone) initiates and ends all communication?

Although the vast majority of ADC experiences appear to consist of receiving information from an outside source, there are instances in which conversations and an exchange of sentiments takes place. Many visitation dreams occur in which questions are asked and answers received by the mourner. In some situations, a mourner who is feeling low and hoping for a sign that his loved one is all right receives an answer to a request. This is what happened to seventy-six-year-old Larry who was walking the ocean beaches, asked for a sign, and within seconds had his answer.

"These Five Minutes Will Always Remain Very Precious to Me"

One day during the week of March 10, 1997, I was walking the beach in Venice, Florida, with my wife and thirty-eight-year-old son. From time to time, we would search for shark's teeth (Venice is billed as the shark tooth capital of the world) and shells as waves, which were larger than usual, rolled in. It was a cloudy, gloomy day that reflected my mood as I was mourning the sudden death of my forty-three-year-old daughter, Bev, who had died three months previously.

I paused, scanned the distant gulf horizon, and asked for some kind of message that Bev had found peace. Almost immediately, I looked down at the churning waves battering the shoreline and perceived what I thought to be a very large shark's tooth. I made a dive for it, both with my hand and foot, and missed! But surprisingly it reappeared and I placed my foot on where I thought it was. By this time my son came to my aid and took a position directly in front of me. We were being belted by the high waves and I could feel sand escaping from beneath my foot. We then waited for a more gentle wave, and upon signal, I removed my foot as he picked up a handful of sand beneath. He extracted the treasured tooth from the sand and soon thereafter suggested we mount it in some permanent way along side Beverly's picture. He thought this tribute fitting because Beverly, during her previous winter visits to Venice, had become somewhat addicted to hunting shark's teeth. One day she found 150!

I had not told my wife or son that I had asked for a sign from Bev. From the time I asked for the sign until my son expressed his desire to mount the tooth was only a matter of five minutes. These five minutes will always remain very precious to me.

The shark's tooth that we found measures nearly two inches in length and just over an inch in width. The crown, or blade, of the tooth is serrated on both edges. It is unlike any shark's tooth that I have ever found. It is also the largest.

This type of ADC would be quickly labeled a coincidence by those who are unable or unwilling to see a connection between the great interest Bev had in hunting for shark's teeth, her father's request, and the sudden appearance of an unusually large specimen. But for Bev's father this was an answer to his request from a divine source. What should be noted is even in these situations where a sign is asked for, the experience occurs suddenly and without warning, be it in a dream state, in nature, or in another condition that gives no hint of what is about to unfold.

There is also apparent two-way communication that often occurs with those who are in desperate circumstances and cry out for assistance. I am thinking of those who are deeply depressed or have been without sleep for days and cry out for help in an agonizing plea for their pain to lessen, then suddenly feel comfort or warmth or drift off into a sound sleep. Later they say that their cry for help was heard and the cloak of gloom seemed to immediately lift. Communication took place via a change in their emotional and/or physical condition.

8. Are pets of the deceased ever involved in or affected by ADCs?

Although I have read quite a bit about people who have experienced ADCs, I am wondering if animals are sensitive to unusual phenomena given their extraordinary senses of smell and hearing. Also, it seems to me I have read that owners of deceased pets have reported unusual experiences involving those animals. Is this true?

You are correct. There are a number of pet owners who are convinced they have seen or heard their deceased pets. There are other pet owners who insist that they have sensed the presence of their dogs or cats and still others who believe that their pets have telepathic abilities similar to those described and attributed to humans. (Telepathy is commonly defined as the transmission of information between two people by means other than through normal sensory channels.) Numerous pet owners have said that their pets have an unusual ability to detect when they are returning home, long before they are in range of the house. The animals seem to respond to the action and intent of returning, not to the actual return accompanied by their friendly greetings. There is little, if any, research evidence to support these contentions. However, it is important to keep in mind that some people establish a relationship with a pet that is every bit as strong, if not stronger, than relationships with family members. When the animal dies mourning ensues that is just as real and demanding as when a friend or family member dies.

Those who are mourning a pet need support, comfort, and understanding as though they were morning the death of a beloved person. It can be exceedingly stressful for anyone who is mourning the death of a pet to have their loss minimized. Regrettably this happens all too frequently. This act results in what professional counselors call disenfranchised grief—one not only has to deal with the loss, but with the loss of comfort and support as well. Pet mourners need to review their long relationship with their pet and be allowed to vent their emotions and talk about their feelings. Furthermore, they should not be expected to have resolved their loss in a matter of a few weeks. Accepting the death of a beloved pet can be a long-term problem and can be helped by friends and family who provide open and supportive care for the mourner.

As for whether or not a pet can be involved in an ADC experience, there is no evidence to say it is not in the realm of possibility for a pet owner. The noted expert, Donna L. Reittinger, Professor of Psychology at the College of St. Rose in Albany, New York, says pet owners have reported encounters involving deceased pets. In a personal letter, she stated:

> The bereaved often report they "hear" the pet meowing or barking, "see" the pet in a field, or actually feel it rubbing against their legs. Some will also report that they "felt" the presence of their deceased pet usually at a time of day when they would customarily interact with the pet (i.e., feeding time, bed time, etc.). Apparently, just as we want to hang onto our deceased human loved ones, so do we want to hang onto our deceased pets as well. However, an extensive review of the professional academic literature on pet bereavement revealed no significant dream experience involving deceased pets. I conclude that dreaming of the deceased pet either doesn't seem to be a predominant feature of this bereavement situation or empirical researchers have not investigated this phenomenon.

As to the ability of pets to become aware of an ADC involving a family member or close family friend, there are many ADCs that have brought responses from animals just as though the person or sound that was heard was the person alive and well. I recall a young woman whose father died unexpectedly in an industrial accident and several days later saw an apparition of her father. It took place in the presence of the family dog, who also saw this family member and began to bark in the same manner as when he would normally greet the person. Within seconds, the father was gone and the young woman reported that the dog "went over to the spot where my father had been standing and began to sniff around looking for him." The implications of a pet seeing the same apparition as a family member is indeed an experience that brings up a host of vexing questions: Do dogs hallucinate like humans? Do they have a faculty similar to humans that operates outside of the normal space/time structure we are all accustomed to? Is this faculty innate or a learned response? Can a pet sense the presence of a deceased loved one in a manner similar to the intuitive sense of presence reported by many individuals? Much research is needed to answer these questions.

9. Does the ADC experience ever happen to people who are not mourning?

I am curious about reports of people who are not grieving yet who say they have seen or heard the beloved who died many years ago. Is it possible for someone who is not mourning to receive a sign or message even when there is little or no apparent need for it?

By definition, ADC phenomena refers only to those who are mourning and believe they have had contact, either direct or indirect, with a deceased loved one. However, deciding on when one is no longer mourning is not a simple matter. Some individuals seem to deal with their losses in a matter of weeks or months so they are able to go on with their lives without too much disorganization, depression, and lack of interest in life. Others may take years before they are able to function in a way that suggests they have been able to come to terms with their loss. Grief, therefore, is a highly individual matter that depends on the degree of emotional investment in the person who died, the mourner's belief system, self-concept, previous loss experiences, the nature of the death, whether the death was expected or sudden, and a host of other variables much too long to be included here.

The point is: when someone stops mourning is a topic for endless debate because on the one hand some experts argue grief always revisits and can therefore last for the rest of one's life, while other experts insist normal uncomplicated mourning usually comes to resolution in six to eight months or perhaps a year. Who is right in the debate? Probably both sides since there are clearly mourners who fit both of those models and millions of others who fall in the middle of those two extremes. In actuality, there are probably as many models of grief as there are grievers; grief and mourning are highly individual. No two people experience grief in exactly the same way. Thus, a person can experience an ADC many years after they have officially (or openly) concluded their mourning. They may or may not be in need of the ADC, and it may or may not be reinforcing to the person, though it is almost always a pleasant surprise and welcomed.

There are a number of people who are not mourning, or are not considered to be primary mourners (closest to the deceased), who are involved in an ADC experience that is most meaningful to another person. This is called a third-party ADC. In some third-party experiences, the person does not even know the deceased, but receives a sign or message that is passed on to the primary mourner and has a deep comforting effect on that person. (See question 39 on third- and fourth-party ADCs.)

Now if you are wondering whether people who are not mourning or are not in any way connected with a loss of a loved one have ADC-type experiences, the answer is yes, they do. They see apparitions of deceased individuals, hear their voices, or experience other signs and unexplainable phenomena. I spoke with a physician's assistant who experienced an apparition of her grandmother in her home. She was not mourning but she was expecting the birth of a child. She had no idea why her grandmother appeared to her because she did not feel she was in need of assistance. She was glad the experience took place, but was at a loss to explain why she was given the experience.

Donna, at age eighteen, had the following experience one evening when she was worrying about her grandfather who was ill:

"It Was a Comforting Message to Ease My Anxieties"

My grandfather was sick off and on after Grandma died. I came home one evening early to find Grandpa in bed when normally he would be watching TV or he would have had supper in the oven for me. I went to his room to see if he was okay. He was having a hard time breathing. He told me to go get Aunt Joan. Of course, in a panic, I ran upstairs to tell her. She and my cousin came down and called an ambulance and they took him to the hospital. I was very upset and really thought it was the end. "He's going to die" is all I could think. Grandpa was a tough cookie, but we did get along, and I loved him very much.

The next night, I came home and went to bed as usual. As I lay there, I felt a cool breeze in the room. I was laying on my side and I saw someone standing by the side of my bed with Grandpa's blue plaid bathrobe on. It wasn't like you would see a regular person; it was more like a figure. An arm reached out to touch my arm and the figure said, "Everything will be all right." Now, it was more a thought exchange—the message was clear— Grandpa wasn't going to die. He would be okay. Then it was over. And there I lay just as before.

This wasn't a physical encounter; it was spiritual. It wasn't a dream. It was very real. Needless to say, I was afraid. I thought about it after and thought it might be an angel, but then I thought it was Grandma just letting me know not to be so upset about Grandpa. The blue plaid bathrobe made it so familiar, but I was still afraid and slept with the light on for a while after that. However, I do believe it was a comforting message to ease my anxieties.

There are other instances in which individuals experience deceased strangers and are unable to determine why the experience took place. For example, there are a large number of individuals who have reported roadside sightings of what they thought were individuals needing assistance, or who they thought had collided with their car. Upon stopping their vehicles to investigate, the apparitions suddenly vanish. Much has also been written about incidents that are called the "phantom hitchhiker syndrome" by parapsychologists. A person will pick up a hitchhiker, only to have him or her disappear after a short period of time. Such events may be a real stretch of the imagination for some. Nevertheless, there are hundreds of well-documented cases in the archives of the Society for Psychical Research from highly credible sources. So to answer your question, without a doubt, people who are not mourning do experience ADC-like phenomena.

10. How does after-death communication differ from guided imagery and internal communication?

There are some counselors who use guided imagery and internal communication to help the bereaved deal with the loss of their loved ones. Some profess to be able to bring a survivor in contact with the deceased. How do these differ from the ADC, since some individuals feel they have indeed talked with their departed loved ones?

The use of guided imagery has a long and useful history in professional counseling circles. Of course, autosuggestion (self-suggestion) and visualization, like guided imagery, make use of one of our most important faculties: the imagination. The most sophisticated of modern computers pales in significance and comparison to the power and versatility of the imagination. It is by far one of the most potent problem solvers and, at the same time, potent problem sources, depending on how it is used and under what circumstances. There is even considerable evidence to indicate that when reason and the imagination are in conflict, imagination often wins out.

Generally, the imagination takes a bad rap in our culture, for many of us are brought up on admonitions such as "your imagination is getting the best of you" or "you have a wild imagination." Therefore, we fail to realize how the imagination can be used to help manage pain, organize and manage stressful situations, reduce anxiety and tension, improve health, forgive others, as well as practice and refine coping techniques. And that is only a short list.

We can create images to deal with anything life has to offer, from beautiful scenes that bring peace and relaxation to aggressive scenes for fighting disease or quiet scenes to stimulate the immune system. Guided imagery has one major difference in relation to other image-making-with-a-purpose techniques; it is "guided" by a set of images. We can do this alone or with a therapist, minister, friend, or facilitator who talks us through a particular scenario to evoke a desired response. This guide gives added strength to our imagery and hopefully better results for whatever the therapeutic goal might be. In the question of its use to create a conversation with a departed loved one, it certainly may simulate such a possibility, but it is not the same experience as the ADC. Because guided imagery can be used effectively to forgive someone who is no longer around, and also dissipate anger and guilt, the trained therapist creates an atmosphere that generates emotional exchange and uses the imagination to create a talking relationship with the deceased. This often culminates in a changed image of the self and the deceased as it enhances the reality of communication.

Similar results are achieved with internal communication. In her book, *Your Loved One Lives On Within You,* psychotherapist Alexandra Kennedy suggests that although the physical presence and the old relationship to the deceased loved one has come to an end, the loved one can still live on within the survivor through the development of a new inner relationship. This relationship offers a host of possibilities to develop. According to Kennedy, many people are surprised to discover "the deceased takes for granted that the relationship is ongoing." That is a powerful force in the coping process. The pivotal factor in structuring the ongoing relationship is the imagination. Reaching the presence within demands a commitment to express deep feelings, to listen, be open, and to use dreams as a springboard to inner communication.

Developing the inner relationship is not difficult to manage and often results in the belief that direct contact has been made. While Kennedy emphasizes that there is no proof that actual contact with the deceased occurs, many who have practiced internal communication are convinced their new relationship is both real and comforting; they report having solved many of the problems that were part of the old relationship. At the very least, internal communication "attests to the fact that our loved one lives on within us."

Internal communication and guided imagery are effective tools for coping with the death of a loved one. They have one thing in common with the ADC experience: belief of contact with the deceased. Both of these approaches to dealing with the death of a loved one are induced through the imaginative capabilities of the mourner, and in some cases may have similar therapeutic value comparable to the ADC. Like meditation, prayer, and love, they are capable of stimulating our latent psi ability (also called psychic ability, ESP, clairvoyance, intuitive ability, and paranormal or supersense ability), which is possessed to some degree by everyone. On the other hand, the ADC is not invoked, but is spontaneous in nature.

11. What is considered essential reading for anyone who is interested in learning more about after-death communication?

I understand that it is only recently that books and articles have begun to appear that feature ADC phenomena, particularly from the point of view of someone who is grieving the death of a loved one. Where would you suggest I start in trying to develop greater understanding of ADCs and their effect on the grief process? Is there any material out there that you think everyone should become aware of, or is the available information simply too scattered and sketchy for in-depth study?

From the start, let me emphasize that there are many accounts of ADC phenomena dating back for centuries, but they are mixed with a variety of other unexplainable subjects and one would have to pore over numerous documents before locating the specific material of interest. However, if you have the time, go to your nearest library or the archives of the British and American Societies for Psychical Research and begin the search. For more recent articles, look up words like grief, widows, and hallucinations and you should come across a rather small number of quality articles on the subject. But note the material is not addressed with the title of after-death communication because it is only within the past four or five years this designation has been used to separate the phenomena from all the other types of similar subject matter.

As for books, I would be remiss if I did not begin by recommending *Hello From Heaven* by Bill and Judy Guggenheim, because of the sheer number of accounts of ADCs to be found within its pages. Emphasizing the spiritual nature of the experience, this volume is the first large study of ADC phenomena based on seven years of collecting more than 3,300 first-hand accounts. The authors present a twelve-fold classification of ADC experiences, a vast array of messages received, and great insight into the effects on the mourning behavior of recipients. The authors also use several types of ADC experiences to suggest proof of an afterlife is substantial based on their research. The use of evidential and shared ADCs, in addition to messages from the deceased before the survivor learns of the death, and suicide prevention ADCs, lend support to their contention of life after life. This is a must read for anyone beginning the study of ADC.

A second and equally appealing must-read—especially if you are a professional counselor or caregiver—is *Goodbye Again: Experiences With Deceased Loved Ones,* written by Edie Devers, who teaches at the University of South Florida and is also a practicing psychotherapist. Her rich clinical background offers a plethora of insights into ADC phenomena and the meaning it holds for survivors. It is not only recommended for those who have had an ADC, but also for psychotherapists, those interested in the metaphysical sciences, and anyone interested in the field of psychology. The author does an excellent job of portraying how the ADC can be used in a variety of ways to assist the mourner in the process of adapting to loss and communicates the purpose, power, and healing significance of the experience. The many case studies focus on the use of dream encounters and waking encounters, feelings associated with ADC, and familiar cues provided by the deceased. The final two chapters emphasize the therapeutic nature of ADC and the healing nature of transcendent experiences.

Next, I humbly recommend my own work on ADCs entitled *After Death Communication: Final Farewells,* which is the result of interviewing scores of mourners who have had an ADC, my counseling practice, the study of the existing literature in the field, and discussions with colleagues who also have private practices. At this point, I will defer to Professor David Fontana, President of the British Society for Psychical Research, who wrote a review of the book that appeared in the newsletter of the SPR called *The Paranormal Review.* Here is part of the review.

> *After Death Communication* deals initially with the cause and nature of grief, and with its varying impact upon individuals. Nine chapters then follow, each dealing with one of the forms that contact with the deceased can take. We are then given an interesting chapter on skepticism and its causes, which concludes by drawing attention to the damaging consequences to the bereaved that the trivialization of their experiences by others can have . . . A final chapter provides guidance on how to help a person who experiences a deceased loved one, and there is a helpful glossary and a list of useful addresses.
>
> *After Death Communication* is not concerned with offering conclusive, objective proof of postmortem survival (though it provides some interesting pointers). It stresses instead the sincerity and personal conviction of the people whose case studies are presented, and offers sensitive and

perceptive comments on each of them. It makes clear that the conviction of the individuals is ultimately what counts in this area of such mystery and human suffering. I doubt if there has been a better book on ADCs, or one written with more genuine feeling for the grief—and in many cases subsequent reassurance and rejoicing—of people who have suffered the loss of those they love.

There are two other books I would strongly recommend to anyone interested in ADCs and their effect on those who experience them. One is a volume that only partly deals with ADC from the perspective of the mourner, still its depth in describing pre-death visions and premonitions can provide insight into relationships between visions experienced by those who are dying and those who are living—as in the ADC experience. I am referring to *Parting Visions* by Melvin Morse, a practicing pediatrician in Seattle, Washington. Subtitled *The Uses and Meanings of Pre-Death, Psychic, and Spiritual Experiences*, and with an afterword by Betty J. Eadie, this book not only provides a physician's view of visionary experiences but it highlights the significance of parting visions in everyday life and the undervaluing of the spiritual side of humanity.

Another book that should draw your attention is *Love Beyond Life*, by Joel Martin and Patricia Romanowski. It is based on approximately ninety cases that were drawn from over 3,000 accounts collected over a twenty-five year period. Many of their interviews were with people living in the United States, Canada, and several foreign countries. The authors define after-death communication as "any contact between a living person and the consciousness, spirit, or soul of the so-called dead." Their definition includes NDEs, premonitions, and the use of gifted intuitives or spiritual mediums. This definition of ADC includes any communication, whether invoked or spontaneous, and regardless of whether or not the recipient is mourning the death of a loved one at the time of the experience. Like other authors, they emphasize that love does not die with the death of the beloved and the ADC is a bridge of love between the living and the deceased.

Last but certainly not least is a book by Professor Robert Kastenbaum that I suggest not because it is filled with a variety of examples and issues surrounding ADC phenomena. Rather, it gives a more scholarly and even-handed approach to examining one of the themes found in the literature on ADCs, namely the question of life after death. In *Is There Life After Death?: The Latest Evidence Analysed,* Kastenbaum presents both sides of this controversial issue and backs them up with a number of meaningful resources as well as some very interesting stories—even some ADCs. This book will whet your appetite for the continued study of nonphysical reality and give you much background for engaging in needed discussion about issues receiving very little publicity in the media.

Let me emphasize that I have suggested a variety of readings in order to provide you with different perspectives on the topic. The choice of these books should not be taken to imply that I agree with all that is presented. You must study the material and decide on the validity of claims and the philosophy behind the concepts discussed. For additional readings, see the bibliography at the end of the book.

I also recommend that your learning should not be confined to reading alone. If you are indeed serious about discovering whether or not it is possible for the deceased to stay in touch with the living, I would strongly suggest you make every effort to find people who have had an ADC and talk to them about their life-changing experiences. They will not speculate—they know! Nothing substitutes for talking to someone who has had the experience. This is not as difficult a task as it may first appear. Begin by asking questions in your own family. You may well be surprised at what you hear simply because there are many family members who are fearful of sharing the experience because of the possibility of being labeled in a derogatory fashion. An honest and gentle inquiry may bring out an experience worth hearing. If not, it is possible a family member knows someone who has had an ADC and would be willing to talk to you about it. One caution: Be careful of making decisions about the reality of ADC experiences based on one or two discussions. Give yourself time. Have discussions with as many people as possible including clergy, counselors, as well as those who have had the experience.

You will also receive credible information by talking with those who conduct bereavement support groups at your local hospice, perhaps even the hospital, if you live near a large one that provides support services for the bereaved. Those who provide such service are usually willing to talk about ADC phenomena, will provide many insights, and answer some of your most pressing questions. This will further increase your knowledge of the range of extraordinary phenomena that occurs to those who are mourning the death of a loved one.

PART

ꞏ 2 ꞏ

Origins and Causes

Questions 12 through 35

Intuition • Hallucinations and Illusions •
Angels • Apparitions • Spiritual Experiences •
Unconscious Mind • Related Questions

*Miracles do not happen in contradiction
to nature, but only in contradiction to that which
is known to us of nature.*
—St. Augustine

12. What role does intuition play in experiencing a deceased loved one?

Dr. LaGrand, since everyone possesses intuition, which seems to be a rather mysterious yet powerful faculty finding its way into our daily decision-making, I am wondering if it could be connected to the process involved in having an ADC. In light of the wisdom it appears to command as a part of experiencing the unknown, how do you see intuition being a factor in some ADC experiences?

Consciousness does not allow us to be aware of the sum total of knowledge and wisdom that lies within. In fact, at any given time we are aware of only a tiny fraction of the resources at our disposal. Frequently, unless we are especially diligent to watch the process, we are not at all aware of our thought processing, we just do it. What is of interest in this regard is a part of the intricate mechanism for creating thoughts and arriving at a decision—a mechanism that we all possess—and is a little-known faculty that long ago someone labeled intuition. It could just as well have been labeled inspired wisdom, intuitive inspiration—or a form of ESP. You are right in saying everyone has intuition, but many people do not consider it in a positive light. Its bad reputation seems to hinge on the way it is belittled in Western culture as being a less than reliable source for making decisions. Furthermore, it is often not considered to be a universal faculty possessed by everyone and cannot stand the test of time. All of these are specious assessments.

On closer examination, we find such a reputation to be totally unjustified. More recently it has been shown that intuition is not only involved in most of our important decisions but it can be developed and refined as an integral part of our personality. Many philosophers believe it to be the basis for truth because it is an "instantaneous, direct grasping of reality." Some scientists believe intuition is the manifestation of our deepest instincts. Others are convinced it has genetic and cultural origins leading to the supposition that some people are much more intuitive than others. This may explain why some individuals are referred to as gifted intuitives or mediums. Pitirim A. Sorokin, considered one of the greatest sociologist-philosophers in the West, said in his landmark book, *The Crisis of Our*

Age, that intuition is "especially indispensable in the apprehension of those aspects of the true reality that are inaccessible to the senses and to reason." He and a number of other scholars support the view of intuition as being the basis for truth. This leads to a question without a definitive answer: Is intuition tapping into the unconscious mind or could it be coming from another source of which we are totally unaware?

In any event, it is clear intuition is a natural part of our mental abilities and plays a leading role in discovery, creativity, and problem solving, not to mention its role in suddenly grasping the dimensions of a particular experience and knowing without the facts—the truth of the matter. Of course, that is not very scientific. But just knowing without the facts is exactly what occurs in the lives of many scientists, which leads to break-throughs in all disciplines. Gut feelings and hunches, as well as an ability to read nonverbal signs, have played major roles in the development of theories, drug therapies, and inventions. At the scientific level, good experimentation requires a fine intuitive feel. So, too, in the business world where many decisions—from choosing among several candidates for a key position to acquiring property for expansion—are made in part on incomplete information and more on an inexplicable knowing. Listening for our intuitive promptings by habitually tuning in to inner feelings on a physical and emotional level helps tap out-of-consciousness wisdom and simultaneously enhances its ability to provide useful information. How then does this mysterious faculty affect the ADC experience?

Here we have to introduce another concept regarding the origin of intuition: it is housed in the right hemisphere of the brain, the creative side, and is part of our ability suppressed by the culture in favor of factual and measurable pursuits. Remember, to science, ADCs and NDEs don't exist because they can't be measured. Intuition too, is a slippery unknown to pin down. We certainly do not send our children off to school with the admonition to learn about intuition, the unconscious mind, and nonphysical reality in order to find inner peace and happiness. Nor do our schools make a strong effort to teach about these subjects. Coupled with our inability to find daily peaceful time-outs in our harried modern world, intuition often lies in a poorly developed state. The argument is that if we were more attuned to the existence of nonphysical reality—as a small number of people are—we would use our intuition more and experience many things, not only ADCs, that are a part of our total environment. In short, we would experience more of our spiritual side and reduce the fear that is associated with unexplainable phenomena, because intuition is part of the mystery of humanity.

Some authorities believe intuition is associated with psi ability. Carl Jung was among the first to suggest this concept, although he did not use the term *psi,* but associated intuition with nonsensory perception and as a separate mental function. Since then, others separate intuition from psychic knowing by saying the latter involves a sudden light-bulb-turning-on experience where information appears out of nowhere. I believe this experience is part of what we call intuition; it is possessed by everyone. The reception of extrasensory information is as normal as the regular processing of information through the senses. Culturally, we refuse to recognize its commonness. Obviously (or perhaps not so obviously), we have a faculty that is a gateway to the nonphysical, which gives insight into the entire universe in which we reside, not merely into physical reality.

At the same time, let us not forget, conventional wisdom suggests intuition operates largely on an unconscious level. We don't have full control of when or at what speed it performs its unusual functions. Intuition, more difficult to define than experience, is a factor in sensing the presence of the deceased or other nonphysical forces. Like the ADC, it occurs in spontaneous fashion and often appears to come from an outside source (though few researchers would ever go on record to say that). There are millions of individuals who have had an ADC experience in which, and I will use their words, they "knew he was here" or "I sensed his presence: I had no doubts." These experiences not only draw on our inexplicable intuitive faculty, they bring it to conscious awareness, and open up a whole dimension of existence we tend to normally ignore in favor of what we can see and touch. Here is an example from thirty-five-year-old Beth.

"I Knew My Dad Was Okay"

A friend and I were watching a movie on TV when I sensed my father's presence in a very strong way. The kitchen light started to turn on and off and I got up to check the light. When I sat back on the couch, I could sense my Dad's presence even stronger. All of a sudden my friend jerked his foot

back and said, "Ow, something just hit me on my foot." His foot was
exactly where I felt my Dad was standing.

I knew right away that this was my Dad. I knew my Dad was all right
and was still with me, helping me along. It helped me with my grieving
because it made me see that life does go on even after the death of our bod-
ies. I knew my Dad was okay.

Sometimes the sense of presence is accompanied by lights going on or off or the smell of a particular odor associated with the deceased. These are among some of the most difficult of phenomena to accept for those who disbelieve in nonphysical reality, dismissing them as nonsense and giving physical explanations for the occurrence. Beth made it clear to me in relating this experience that she had checked the light and "there was absolutely nothing wrong with it."

In summary, I am convinced what we call intuition is a faculty we all possess, but it is still not fully understood and may never be fathomed. Its depth and versatility are not recognized by the general public and its nature to direct us to other, lesser known aspects of our existence is ignored by most. It is likely what we refer to as intuition or psychic knowing (whatever you choose) is a lofty faculty that connects us to a higher realm that is always there willing to become a partner in our personal growth.

13. Can anyone prove a hallucination occurred instead of an ADC?

Whenever the topic of extraordinary experiences of mourners surfaces,
specifically ADCs in which the mourner hears or sees the deceased, I con-
stantly hear friends or colleagues say they are normal experiences, but they
are hallucinations, no more or no less. This happens particularly with people
in the field of psychology. What is the basis for deciding when someone hallu-
cinates? Is there incontrovertible proof when it occurs?

In answering these questions it is best I begin by stating that hallucinations and illusions are the two most popular explanations for auditory and visual ADCs given by those who argue against the existence of the phenomena. Some medical researchers also use hallucinations to account for the near-death experience (NDE). Hallucinations, in particular, are a convenient way to explain ADC phenomena because the term has a long history of use in both psychology and the medical profession and can cover a multitude of unexplainable behaviors. Sometimes the explanation includes the added reason that the experience was due to the medication one was taking or to one's disorganized state of mind associated with the loved one's death. Reason suggests that in some instances these explanations may fit. However, when an exchange of information—a conversation—takes place between the mourner and the deceased that results in comfort, acceptance of the death, and a renewed interest in life, then we need to take a second look at the hallucination theory.

A person who hears voices when no one is there or who sees visions is having hallucinations is a common description accompanying the typical definition of hallucinations as "false perceptions of an external object when no such object is present." Another description would be that an hallucination is a sensory perception without the usual external stimulus. There is even a small percentage of the population who reportedly have the capacity to recreate hallucinations.

Hallucinations—auditory and visual—are commonly associated with schizophrenia, a complex psycho-biological mental disorder involving major changes in personality and in the perception of reality. Like many diseases, it commonly begins in early adulthood, and can severely debilitate or mildly affect one's thinking and perceptive skills. Although schizophrenics usually do not think they are ill, outward signs of withdrawal, disorganized thoughts, insensitivity to nonverbal cues, impoverishment in social and work relationships, and delusions are not uncommon. It is estimated that one person in a hundred is likely to be afflicted by the disease some time in life. Significantly, the incidence of hallucinations, especially auditory hallucinations, in schizophrenia is especially high. It is not unusual, therefore, to think of the temporary mental and emotional disorganization associated with the grief process, and then automatically link hearing or seeing the deceased loved one to an hallucinatory experience. Some writers suggest that we all possess a "fantasy-prone mind."

The common circumstances under which ADCs most often occur are contrary to the popular assumption that all mourners who report an auditory or visual ADC are hallucinating. Specifically, most mourners are not in a high state of disorganization as is often believed. Conversely, they are frequently in a relaxed condition (one woman who I interviewed was reading the afternoon newspaper when she glanced up and saw an apparition of her husband) and not thinking about the deceased, or they receive a message that helps them find a lost object. In other instances, they receive information that prevents injury or accident. This is hardly the stuff from which hallucinatory experiences would seem to consistently evolve—especially when the supposed hallucination is witnessed by two or more people. However, there are some parapsychologists who believe apparitions are indeed hallucinations telepathically projected from the mind of the deceased loved one to the mind of the mourner or (and this will strain our rational minds) are residual images from the deceased that have become a part of the surroundings in which the person lived. This latter theory implies that powerful emotions are somehow retained by the places in which traumatic events have occurred to be later played back as apparitions.

How then can one find incontrovertible proof an hallucination has occurred? First, let me say that I have asked many people in the field of psychology whether a hallucination, if and when it occurs, can be proven. In terms of the scientific method there is no way to prove when a mourner is hallucinating or has had an ADC. All that people in the scientific community can do is make an educated guess. More specifically, we have to look at the circumstances surrounding each event. If a person with a schizophrenic personality is mourning the death of a loved one and says he hears the voice of the person who died, we have some extenuating circumstances to consider. If, however, as we have described above, one hears voices that bring a new sense of belonging and comfort, this can indicate something different. Obviously, what the voices say must be considered. Are they suggesting positive or negative or even destructive behavior? We must carefully take into consideration the total situation, including the person's emotional health before the death occurred. If they are withdrawn, if they are delusional, firmly holding on to false beliefs—such as that others can read their minds, or that they are being led and controlled by unspecified outside forces—we obviously have strong reason to not only be cautious but to encourage them to seek professional assistance.

At best, the question of deciding between a hallucination and an ADC can most often be answered by the results of the event and by the person who had the experience. In my experience, time and time again, it appears those who have never had an ADC, or are wedded to science and naturalism, are unable or unwilling (maybe both in some cases) to entertain the remotest possibility a deceased loved one might actually have contacted a surviving friend or relative. So we are faced here with a universal dilemma of life: deciding on whether to be open or rigid in confronting phenomena not culturally accepted as real.

Specifically, let me list four criteria to ponder if you, or someone you know, has an ADC experience and wish to reinforce your beliefs for or against authenticity. Ask these questions: First, was the figure in the apparition someone you knew? Was it your loved one or another figure, perhaps of divine origin? By comparison, there are many people who hallucinate grotesque or nonexistent figures or people they do not know. Also, remember that psychology tells us expectation plus a specific emotional state can result in what is believed to be a ghost. How would you judge your frame of mind at the time of the event?

Second, was information conveyed that you were not previously aware of or that gave you insight into a particular problem you were facing? Usually, hallucinations do not provide material to help one deal with loss or point out coping mechanisms to employ. Nor do they help people find lost items.

Third, can the experience be classified as a collective apparition? That is, did more than one person see the loved one? This, of course, would be a powerful piece of evidence for accepting the experience as an ADC. Collectivity can occur in audio as well as visual ADCs and in most other ADC phenomena, although some people in a group may be able to experience the ADC and others may not. (Sometimes a person in a group who did not know the deceased, for some inexplicable reason, does not hear or see what happened.)

Fourth, were you able to carry on a conversation with the apparition that resulted in your obtaining peace of mind? Hallucinatory experiences often leave a person in an agitated state or spouting information that is not readily understandable.

In making your decision, unless you have had a history of hallucinatory experiences from schizophrenia, alcoholism, or other drugs, consider the results of your experience. If it has helped you deal with your loss, if it is reflective of the love and care you know has been a part of the relationship with the deceased, and if you "know" in your heart the experience was the gift you needed, take it and use it for the purpose for which it was created.

14. Are illusions frequently the cause of some of the ADCs that mourners claim to experience?

You have said that illusions, along with hallucinations, are the most common explanations given for auditory and visual ADCs by those who do not believe in the possibility of contact from those who have died. What kind of illusions could be associated with ADC phenomena and how do they occur?

Illusions are essentially misperceptions of the environment in which we live. Since a perception is usually defined as the personal meaning we give to experience, it is not unusual to find illusions are near the top of the list for explaining certain ADCs. Although we all see with our eyes, we perceive and judge with our brain, which is why we can all see a particular object, person, or scene but give it our own personal spin or meaning. In other words, two people can see the same thing, but draw totally different conclusions about what they saw. So interpretation is a function of needs, emotions, feelings, fears, and a host of other variables from past experience and conditioning. Therefore, what is an acceptable illusion for someone can be easily dismissed as irrelevant, but the same supposed illusion can be extremely important for someone else and may be called an ADC because it fits a need. Only the mourner can decide, which is as it should be.

There is no doubt a number of visual illusions are quite common. For example, the moon in the sky looks much smaller than the same moon when it is viewed as lazily sitting on the horizon. On the horizon, the moon suddenly seems like a gigantic ball perching on the rim of the world. Or if you look at a tree branch or a log that is sticking out of the water, it appears as though the branch or log is bent. On a warm day you can look down a long country road and at a distance it seems as though there is water on the roadway until you close on the distant water illusion and it vanishes.

One of the most dramatic and popular illusions you may want to experience (the Muller-Lyer Illusion) involves drawing two lines three inches long and one inch apart. Then draw arrowheads on both ends of one line and reverse arrowheads on both ends of the other line. The result is that one line looks longer than the other. Why? One explanation is that the reverse arrowheads and the way they appear on the line are interpreted by the brain as being more distant making the line appear longer. It is apparent to science that all of our senses do not deliver a completely accurate picture of reality. Try drawing the illusion for your own experience and to better understand why the illusion explanation is so widely used.

The Muller-Lyer Illusion

There are other optical illusions—the movies are full of them—that create representations of reality that are far from the truth of reality. Can it happen with an ADC experience? Certainly it can. We have all been deceived at one time or another by false and misleading impressions. But once again, when deciding on illusion or ADC, we must fall back on context, meaning and messages, and the resulting behavioral changes in determining authenticity. If one is in a quandary trying to decide on authenticity, it is imperative to share the experience and obtain feedback from others. Again, the perceiver reserves the sole right to making the final decision.

Just how often is illusion mistaken for an ADC experience? No one knows. It would be pure supposition to say the vast majority of ADCs involve illusory experiences, even though it is a handy way to dispose of phenomena so difficult to explain. Certainly shadows in poorly lighted areas, clothing hanging in unusual configurations, or light reflections off shiny surfaces may be deceptively real apparitions for some individuals. So, too, can hearing a familiar voice that had been heard a thousand times before (when the person was alive) be a product of misperception. Anything is possible. In fact, illusions occur in all of our sense modalities and play major roles in the way we perceive. Nevertheless, there are too many positive outcomes from supposed illusions to relegate all of these experiences to the neat package of faulty perception. Clearly, ADCs involving dreams or indirect contacts cannot be summarily dispatched as illusions.

Certainly it was not an illusion for twenty-four-year-old Janet.

"My Aunt Was Fine Wherever She Was"

I was visiting my sister and was sleeping in the same room my aunt had died in a few months previous. I was scared and nervous because I was sleeping in the room, so I was having a hard time falling asleep. As time passed, I glanced up at the door and saw my aunt standing there and she said, "Don't worry or be scared, everything's all right and I'm okay." Then she disappeared. I fell asleep after the incident because I felt relieved. When I awakened, I was confused and questioned whether I had dreamed it or not, but I do believe it happened. I think it was my aunt's way of helping me to feel better about her death. I think it was caused in part by my unease regarding her death. The explicit message I received was that I shouldn't be frightened and my aunt was fine wherever she was. I had been (still am somewhat) questioning what happens after you die. I think this experience made me feel better about her death, because she was in a better place.

It is interesting to note that Janet was relieved and not scared of what took place. Most important was her interpretation of the experience as a message indicating her aunt was well in another place. That is the key consideration.

15. Could angels be the cause of most ADC experiences?

Many people believe everyone has a guardian angel that watches over them and provides protection in times of need. It seems to me the positive nature of the ADC experience could very well be the result of the intervention of angels. Have there been ADCs where the survivor thinks there is an angel behind what occurs? What is your view of angelology and ADCs?

The interest in angels in the United States and perhaps the Western world is unprecedented in modern times. Not only have there been a spate of books on the subject but an entire new industry in angel memorabilia seems to have suddenly appeared, as well as newsletters and magazines featuring stories about angelic messengers. The nationwide Angel Collectors Club has seen a dramatic increase in membership in the past few years. Why the sudden upsurge of interest in angels? It has been suggested angel awareness (or pop spirituality) helps fill the spiritual vacuum that has been created by the increased emphasis on the acquisition of material goods and sensual pleasures and the failure of religious institutions to provide meaningful dialogue to nurture faith.

This is not to imply a strong belief in angels does not exist in various subgroups within the country. It is precisely the strong belief in angels that has helped many Christians strengthen their devotion to God and their interpretation that much of what we label ADCs are in fact the work of angels. For example, about a year ago I interviewed a spiritual medium and described a tactile ADC (where one believes he has been touched, hugged, or kissed on the cheek by a deceased loved one) and asked him his view about their origin. He said: "I believe it's their guardian angel who gives them that sense of comfort. The angel has been with them from the beginning." When I changed the subject and asked him where he obtained the ability to receive information from other than conventional means, he responded with, "Without Christ and the Blessed Mother I have nothing." Obviously, without using the research term ADC, he was convinced that the extraordinary experiences of the bereaved were a product of finite spirits (angels) and a Divine Being. It is noteworthy that his experiences had also increased his spirituality.

One thing is clear: many ADCs can be explained as the work of angels (some would argue all). There are a substantial number of people who have had an ADC and believe it was an angel, not the deceased loved one. In a poll conducted in the early 1990s, nearly seven out of ten Americans said they believed in angels, so it should not be surprising that those who have an ADC might say it was an angel in disguise or in literal form without wings.

History is filled with stories about the work of angels. Throughout the Bible, angels are mentioned more than three hundred times doing all sorts of things from ministering to Christ and appearing to other individuals (according to Genesis 16, Hagar, the slave of childless Sarah, is the first person to be visited by an angel) to freeing Peter from prison. Angels are pure spirits; they have never been humans, nor do humans ever miraculously become angels. The archangel Gabriel revealed to the prophet Mohammed, while he was meditating in a grotto near Mecca, that he had been chosen by Allah. It was an angel in St. Augustine's garden who initiated a turn around from his lustful ways. As for current day angels, stories abound with numerous rescues from comas and accidents, healings, guidance when lost, and comfort when in sorrow. Angel visitations are legion. In their book, *Angels: The Lifting of the Veil*, authors Thomas Keller and Deborah Taylor emphasize how "angels are all around us, willing to be of help." Those in need must ask for help and it will come. Although they provide help, they are God's servants. A number of young children have reported seeing angels.

Traditionally, it has been taught that angels are heavenly messengers who possess powers and intelligence far above those assigned to humanity. Also, each person is said to possess a guardian angel from the moment of conception until death. Not all angels are good, and those who have challenged the will of God are evil spirits or demons. Demons are in the service of the Prince of Darkness, the devil. Interestingly, the importance of angels for moral purposes is the help they can provide in the battle against evil. They also, in the belief systems of many, have the ability to offer comfort, strength, and endurance in coping with the death of a loved one. Just as science can offer a rational answer for any ADC that occurs, I can think of no ADC in which one would be unable to build a case for assistance from an angelic being since they are said to have been given power and abilities far above our comprehension.

For current reading on the subject and the work of angels in the lives of those in need, let me recommend two books. First, *Where Angels Walk Among Us* by Joan Wester Anderson. This book grew out of the author's interest in angels after her son was miraculously rescued when trapped in a car during a blizzard. In her research of the subject, she placed ads in religious publications seeking experiences involving angels, and to her surprise she received a high volume of responses from throughout the country. The illuminating accounts in Anderson's book will stimulate questions and provide a source for formulating answers.

The same applies to the second recommendation, *A Book of Angels* by Sophy Burnham. This book had its beginning in experiences the author and some of her friends had that needed explanations. Worldly logic could no longer explain many of the curious and mysterious events that had occurred. Her research soon led her to include angelic encounters from all over the world as well as some historical background material to explain cultural beliefs. Both books will help the reader understand why many individuals who have ADC encounters believe angels come in spontaneous fashion in moments of stress and bring comfort to the grief-stricken.

16. How are ADCs and the concept of synchronicity connected?

I have heard people say "it was synchronicity" when something good happens to them at the right time. Thus it has occurred to me that ADCs may be synchronicities that happen when people are in special need. Do you see ADCs and synchronicities being the same phenomena?

The concept of synchronicity is one way that those who do not look at ADCs as manifestations of nonphysical reality label the experience. Synchronicity is a term coined by Carl Jung, Swiss psychiatrist and founder of analytical psychology, which is defined as "a meaningful coincidence of two or more events, where something other than the probability of chance is involved." Coincidence, on the other hand, is usually defined as "a striking occurrence of two or more events at one time apparently by mere chance." The major difference between the two is that in one instance chance is the explanation while in the other the relationship between the events cannot be causally determined. So synchronicity is a safe term to be used when a solid scientific explanation cannot be found for an event. Everyone experiences synchronicities that are helpful and life-affirming.

Synchronicities and coincidences happen on a daily basis. Deepak Chopra, M.D., endocrinologist and mind/body guru, believes we can create our own synchronicities if we have the intention and tap into the energy of the spirit. He contends that we are continuous flowing systems of energy and information and can learn to set the stage for bringing about meaningful coincidence. Synchronicities, however, pose a special problem for many because they not only occur spontaneously, as do coincidences, but they are often of such dimensions as to border on the unbelievable.

A few years ago I was leaving a conference in upstate New York to return to my home out on Long Island some three hundred miles away when it began to snow. At the same time, the New York City–Long Island area was experiencing severe rain and high winds, which had closed the Throggs Neck Bridge, my normal route home. When I made my usual approach to the bridge I was detoured to another route and promptly became lost in heavy traffic. I decided to pull over at a gas station for directions, which I received from an attendant. He was overheard by a mechanic, who corrected his co-worker by saying it had just come over the radio that the route he had recommended to me had also been closed. I was sent in another direction that would take me to eastern Long Island. Had he not heard the bulletin and told me about it, I would have lost another hour in traffic before I had discovered the closing.

In the meantime, the storm had turned into a devastating nor'easter, pounding Long Island unmercifully and causing massive flooding. Eventually, many hours after embarking on my journey from Saratoga, I arrived home in one piece. I no sooner walked through the door and the telephone rang. It was my mother-in-law who lived near the water and was fearful of the tides, which were rising dangerously. Frantically, she had been calling me for hours—she was all alone and needed a place to stay and someone to talk to. She was at her wit's end and was immensely relieved to hear my voice. This was synchronicity (or?) at its best. If I had not left the conference early, if I had not taken a route I had never traveled on before, and if I had not been redirected by the helpful mechanic, I would have arrived home hours later or may have had to stay overnight in a motel. My mother-in-law would have been left all alone dealing with her overwhelming fears and the rising tides.

How can this be explained? Meaningful coincidence? Divine intervention? The collective unconscious? Or? The fact remains that these helpful events are a mysterious and continuous part of the human condition and cannot be explained in a conventional manner. I can say the same thing about ADCs: They are prevalent, unexplainable scientifically, and result in meaningful assistance to the beneficiary. You decide! The following story shares two examples occurring on birthdays that were significant to both mother and daughter and helped them cope with their losses. These ADCs took place in Scotia, New York. They were part of a series of ADCs Loretta Frederico experienced after the death of her two grandsons in an automobile accident that claimed the lives of five young men.

"It Helped Both of Us so Much"

I have had several ADC experiences since I lost my two precious grandsons in a terrible car accident. Rocco was nineteen and Tommy was only fifteen years old. Rocco left a little two-year-old daughter at the time who since has seen both of the boys. There were five young men killed in the accident that terrible night. Since then, three more young men from our small community have died and one young girl. The accident that happened on November 23, 1996, left my family grieving and the pain has been unbearable . . . You see, my family lives all around me. Since I had a lot of land, I gave my daughter some of it and she built a home right next door. So my grandsons were always at grandma's and we had a very close relationship. I have found all the things the boys did when they were alive they are doing now, if only to let us know they are around, and to help us with our grieving.

Sometimes, Tommy used to hold the door shut on the other side of my daughter's front door when I was trying to leave. Well, he did this several times even after his death, and as soon as I would say, "Tommy, stop it," the door would suddenly open by itself. On his birthday in May, he would have been sixteen, and he had been looking forward to getting his driver's license. I was over at my daughter's house taking care of her and the baby, both had colds and weren't feeling well. Tommy started a clock that hadn't been wound since the boys died six months earlier. It continued to run for three hours. It helped both of us so much. Then on their stepfather's birthday, a hummingbird flew into my daughter's house and my son-in-law put his finger out—and the hummingbird landed on it long enough for my daughter to take a picture of it. If you are interested, I'll send you a copy.

Obviously, for this grieving grandmother and her daughter these events happening on birthdays had special meaning as part of a pattern of ADCs that Loretta told me have "been a tremendous amount of help." Note also that the apparitions reported by Rocco's young daughter have also strengthened their convictions that the boys are trying to help them. For them these experiences are not synchronicities—they are communications from their boys. It seems as though calling ADCs synchronicities is using one unknown to explain another unknown. Many believe synchronicities are simply a scientific term for divine intervention.

Three features shared by ADCs and synchronicities are their spontaneity, singularity, and consciousness-raising qualities. These are significant connections. (Some would also argue dream ADCs and synchronicities are products of the unconscious mind.) They are not planned events and they are highly individual in nature, effect, and how they are interpreted. Your question remains: Are they the same phenomena? I don't think so. They may well come from the same source, whichever you decide to choose, and their timing is surely unique. Once more, synchronicities occur at a rate far greater than the ADC, but ADCs occur primarily in dealing with the grief process. Their apparitional, auditory, and symbolic features, while timely, seem to me to be a step above most synchronistic events. Perhaps most important is my observation that ADCs often appear to have a more immediate and longer lasting impact on the recipient. They become a part of individual and family history and useful teaching tools within the family. They are not easily dismissed or relegated to luck, chance, or an unknown source. Who knows, some day we may come to recognize synchronicities, ADCs, and NDEs as all facets of the same gem.

17. How can you decide if you have received an authentic sign or if what happened was a coincidence or an illusion?

I have trouble with some people who report having a wide variety of ADCs when a loved one dies. When I hear their accounts, I have my doubts about the authenticity of some of them. Then, too, there are individuals who have a single experience and want to believe they have had the sign they were looking for, but have nagging misgivings about the experience. Is there a rule of thumb for deciding on the truth of the experience? How can one tell the difference?

Deciding on the authenticity of an ADC is a common question spawned by the dominating force of science in our culture. Certainly, it is a critical question to ask because we have all been brought up on the scientific method, which is ingrained deep in the unconscious; it is part of the cultural trance to which we are all subjected. For some people, decision-making is more difficult than for others, depending on how they are influenced by their families or with whomever they chose to share their experiences. The fact remains that we are heavily influenced by those with whom we live and work, as the power of suggestion so readily attests. Therefore, if at all possible, try to share your experience with someone who has had an ADC. Perhaps a better option, if you have one, is to find a counselor who is known to have had an ADC or has worked with others who have had ADCs.

Some ADCs are much easier to authenticate than others. If you have a dream ADC with very specific information and insight given by the dream messenger (deceased loved one), and you awake with a feeling of peace and joy that had been absent since the death, sharing it with a knowledgeable person should erase any misgivings. If, however, you have experienced a situation where on several occasions lights have flickered on and off, pictures have been moved from their original positions, or an object belonging to the deceased has been found in a place where someone had to have placed it, the burden of proof can be formidable. These are the kinds of events that perhaps more than any others are cause for those who have never experienced them to throw up their hands and say, "Wait a minute. Are you trying to say the loved one is behind this stuff?"

Assuredly, these are the kinds of things that have long been associated with fraud in the world of the paranormal and have carried the commercially exploited stamp of the bizarre for decades. They are the trappings for stories around the campfire on a cool summer night and they can cause you to sometimes question your sanity.

Nevertheless, they can be dealt with in a healthy manner. First, make the normal investigations to satisfy your own curiosity: all the light circuits are in excellent working order, no wind, person or other natural phenomena moved the pictures, and no animal or your forgetfulness could have somehow knocked over or replaced the object in question. Having exhausted any and all possible natural explanations, turn to non-physical reality and ask yourself these questions: Is this the kind of thing my loved one would do? What does my heart tell me? Does it fit? Does it fit for me? That is the ultimate question. What does it feel like inside, deep inside, for me? I am reminded of the remarks of William Butler Yeats, the great Irish poet and playwright, who said, "We taste and feel and see the truth. We do not reason ourselves into it." What does it feel like deep in your heart? What does it taste like? Is it truth or self-deception? You will know if it fits your belief system. Each of us has the wisdom within to make the important decisions. Go with your heart and listen carefully; it has the edge on reason.

There is something else you can do. Shop around for several opinions. In doing so, you risk talking to someone who is closed-minded and may verbally or nonverbally—which is sometimes worse—make it clear you are losing it and are in need of medical help. This can be so demeaning at a time when you are already stressed out, and it adds considerably to your feeling of isolation. If it is someone you counted on as an important support person, his or her act will probably sever the support relationship as far as you are concerned. That is the risk of seeking other opinions where you are not sure the listener will be nonjudgmental. Persist! It is worth the effort.

18. What are some examples of experiences mourners have that are not ADCs?

It is obvious that some people have experiences involving deceased loved ones that they realize later were misperceptions or wished-for appearances. I'm wondering if there is a way to help people when they ask about their ADCs, or even before they ask, to tell them about common misperceptions or grief-induced experiences that are normal, but are not ADCs? Of course, the first step is to become aware of the types of experiences that cannot be classified as an ADC. Where do you think we should begin?

Let's begin with letting go of the idea of telling mourners there are common misperceptions when grieving before all of the options for checking out the ADC have been exercised. Above all, don't start talking about misperceptions before the mourner has even decided to share the experience, if he had one. That could be devastating to the helping relationship you are trying to establish. Remember, being an effective support person means allowing the mourner to set the agenda for discussion. Don't be the dominating I-have-my-own-agenda take-charge support person. Gentle nurturing and maintaining an ongoing support relationship is your first responsibility. I would further suggest letting the mourner do most of the talking before launching into what is not an ADC. Your role initially is to be the best listener possible, especially when someone decides to share such a personal experience with you. There may be no need to even bring up the subject of misperceptions, depending on the type of ADC experienced and the confirmed belief of the mourner. Now let's turn to what are not ADCs. Here are four common situations:

1. **The Crowd Phenomena.** Arguably the most common misperception regarding a deceased loved one that has been consistently reported in the literature on grief is what I refer to as the Crowd Phenomena. This phenomena, however, does not always happen within a large crowd. It can happen when you are looking out your window at passersby or walking on a busy street.

   For example, about a year ago I received a call from a grieving widower in a Midwestern state whose wife had died unexpectedly a couple of weeks earlier and he was left with three young children.

On this particular occasion he had gone to a shopping mall and was walking around when he looked some distance ahead of him and, in the crowd, he thought he saw his wife. Actually, he saw the back of the head of a woman whose hairdo and head shape resembled his wife's. He quickly ran to the spot where he thought he would see his wife only to find she wasn't there, although there was a woman who did have some of the physical features of his wife. He was perplexed and was hoping there was some way his wife had been there and that he had somehow missed her in his dash to locate her. The same thing may happen when one is riding in a car or bus and the mourner looks out and sees a person who he thinks is the loved one. He gets off the bus or stops the car and runs after the person, only to discover he has made a mistake.

2. **The Flicker Phenomena.** A second common experience is associated with peripheral vision that we all possess, but in varying degrees. Great athletes are abundantly blessed with this type of vision. Peripheral vision allows us, when facing in one direction, to pick up movement and objects to our side when we have not turned our heads. This means the eye involved quickly registers flicking movement or supposed movement, which is frequently interpreted as a shadow or a blur. Consequently, the person who is alone or thinking of the loved one may think the flicker has something to do with the presence of the deceased. This can be especially misleading if the mourner has been hoping or praying for a sign indicating the loved one exists in a better place. A similar experience may occur involving a venetian blind. If one is again not looking straight at the blinds and a leaf is blown past the window or falls from the roof or nearby tree, it can initiate thoughts of the deceased.

3. **Highly Agitated States.** In some instances when one is in an extremely agitated emotional state, sense perception and its processing phase can be affected. In fact, this is exactly what many believe is behind most ADC experiences—the misinterpretation of sensory input by the brain. It is likely that the degree of agitation causing such faulty processing in a given individual varies significantly with each mourner. But let me stress again the phrase "extremely agitated

emotional state." I can remember seeing my father—three hours after the sudden death of my mother from a massive heart attack—in an emotional state that I find even now as I think about it difficult to describe. In short, I had never seen him in such disarray. I was forty years old at the time, yet I wanted to run away from the scene. When the mind is overwhelmed with the incomprehensible, the unthinkable, when emotions are at fever pitch, certainly one can have difficulty with the normal processing of sensory input and create misperceptions.

4. **The Invoked Sense of Presence.** There are some experts on grief theory who report widows saying they invoke the presence of the deceased at a time when they are having special problems coping with their loss or are in a depressed state. At these times, the procedure of calling out to the deceased apparently was helpful in getting these widows through a stressful period. It is my contention that invoking the sense of presence is not the same as an ADC that occurs spontaneously and without warning. This is not to say that there is anything unusual about calling out to or talking to the deceased at times when one is at their wit's end or feeling isolated and dejected. The mourner may well feel the loved one hears and is present. It obviously helps some individuals whether or not they truly believe they are being heard. For other mourners, the same procedure holds little meaning and gives no comfort.

19. Isn't it possible some demonic force could be the cause of the ADC?

Having talked at length to a lot of people about ADCs, I have come across a number of people who have suggested demonic activity is behind most ADCs. They believe very strongly that the devil plays a primary role in taking advantage of people who are mourning. How would you respond to this charge?

There is a subgroup in the United States who believe very strongly that any communication that may occur between the living and deceased loved ones is the work of the devil. I learned this in dramatic fashion two years ago when I interviewed a young fundamentalist minister in the South. As soon as I asked him if he had ever heard of anyone who had an extraordinary experience while mourning the death of a loved one, he made it clear, in no uncertain terms, that when this type of activity occurs, it is initiated by the devil. On another occasion, I took a call on a radio show from someone with a similar belief who said essentially the same thing. After we exchanged viewpoints, he reminded me that the devil has many disguises and ways to introduce evil and sow confusion. He made it clear that convincing mourners that they have received a sign from a loved one was one of those ways.

In the Christian tradition, the evil spirits who go about doing the bidding of Satan are called demons. Where do these evil spirits come from? Let's clear up one misconception first: evil is not a thing, a commodity, or an object; it is the result of choosing, of intention to go against the order of goodness and stability. Evil lies in the will to choose one path over another, to change the order of goodness. Even the devil was once goodness of a high order, but chose disorder. Evil is a conflict between wills, our will, and the will of the Creator. This is what is believed to have occurred with many angels who had power, wanted more, and opposed the will of God in the grab to take it. Thus, demons are former angels who have the skill and acumen that allow them to be masters of deception, causing conflict and disarray. But they cannot win unless we cooperate and give them an opening.

When I am confronted by those who believe the devil and evil spirits are behind ADC phenomena I always remind them to examine the contents of the experience. Consider the following ADC that occurred to Ann Callahan, who lives in the southern part of Australia:

"This Experience Did Change Me"

The experience I want to tell you about happened in a dream, or in an out-of-body experience, I am not sure which one. I was awakened one night by noises coming from the kitchen. Things were being moved around. I got up to investigate. I remember being naked, but it didn't seem to bother me. I could feel the carpet and vinyl beneath my feet (I never dream with such clarity). As I approached the kitchen I could see my Mum standing in front of the open cupboard. "I'm just rearranging your cupboard," she said smiling. She then came over to me and gave me a cuddle: I felt every part of her body against mine. She then held me in front of her and said something, but unfortunately I couldn't remember exactly what that was, I think because when I woke up the next morning I was in such a state of euphoria and wonderment. I actually felt like I had only seen her last night and it was actually five years after her death.

This experience did change me. Of course, after she passed on I was in a deep, deep state of guilt. I read all I could on life after death, and came to the conclusion that it had to be. But after this "experience" my spiritual beliefs are so much stronger. Yes, I still miss her, but I know she calls in from time to time, and when she's not around my guardian angels are. In honesty, I'm really not sure why it happened when it did. There were plenty of other times and there still are now when I feel I could benefit from a "visit." Maybe we are not meant to know where or when. I don't care. It was just such a wonderful experience, which I guess may or may not happen again. All I know is that I received reassurance of what I believed in and confidence no one else could give.

If we look carefully at the results of this ADC, it is typical of most in the way it helped the mourner reconnect with life by regaining a sense of belonging and put her in touch with her spiritual side. It is critical to understand that the death of a loved one usually causes the mourner to feel isolated because of the loss and the death of part of the self. One feels others cannot possibly understand the pain being experienced. Clearly, ADCs are all about helping relationships. The person who receives such a gift frequently feels peace and warmth, knowing the loved one is happy, whole, and in a better place. Many are confident they will meet again. The contact from the spirit of the deceased is saying "I care." Love is at work.

There is always a double message of healing: I'm okay where I am, and you can be okay where you are too. Would the devil and his brood be into creating this type of assistance to those in need? I doubt it, even though they are deceptive and wily in their approaches. In all the years I have been around people who have had an ADC, I have never heard of a single case in which the ADC resulted in spreading evil and discouragement. Instead, love wins out—there is not a more powerful antidote for grief. A quiet reassurance begins to reign.

20. How do quantum physicists view ADC phenomena?

Quantum physics has brought new questions and not enough answers to our understanding of matter and energy. I understand there is much disagreement within the ranks of physicists over whether or not the innermost workings of the universe can ever be known. Does quantum theory have any implications for understanding the origin of ADC phenomena?

During this century it is quite clear that quantum theory (the study of energy and matter and the motion of material particles) has undergone some astonishing changes. In particular, quantum mechanics (the application of quantum theory) has caused many scientists to think twice about the origins of the universe. Billions of times every day at the quantum level of existence strange things happen, strange to our conventional way of thinking about reality. The residents of the subatomic world—protons, neutrons, and the smallest of the small, the quarks—flash in and out of existence at the drop of a hat. They make bacteria and viruses look like giant buildings by comparison. They are part of a universe completely baffling to science and the microscope as they leave only a faint trace on a photograph, lasting for two or three millionths of a second. (The top quark has never been seen and scientists never expect to see it because it only lasts for a hundred billionth of a trillionth of a second before it falls apart.) Yet, they are the elementary particles, the very basic building blocks of the physical world.

The big stumper persistently remains: what is the ultimate origin of matter and energy? Or, to put it in quantum terms, where does the quark—considered to be the last of the fundamental particles of matter—come from? No one has the answer, not even the most sophisticated modern computers. Where matter and energy come from and how they behave begins to raise more questions than can be answered. The great physicist Richard Feynman, who shared the 1965 Nobel Prize in Physics, once said: "I think I can safely say no one understands quantum mechanics." Why such a statement from a man who also was part of the duo who first hypothesized the existence of the unseen quark, a most fundamental type of elementary particle? Well, when we descend into the realm of the subatomic world, we are not merely struck by the randomness found there, but by the contradictions.

For example, two photons having once met and now separated by great distances (even a continent away) and long periods of time, still know what the other is doing. Having once met, they seem to be a team for all time, no matter where they are. Thus what affects one affects the other—spontaneously and faster than ever thought possible. (The information passed between the two occurs faster than the speed of light, which goes against Einstein's special theory of relativity.) We can only speculate that there must be a memory network so complex and mysterious that acts as a constant transmitter and receiver of messages in the subatomic world. The idea of information existing everywhere and at the same time (it is not transmitted, it is everywhere) is referred to as being *nonlocal* by physicists. Some think the notion of nonlocality is applicable to all facets of nature and the universe, even to the mind. Back in 1900, author Camille Flammarion wrote *The Unknown:* "It is certain that one soul can influence another soul at a distance, and without the aid of the senses." If nonlocality turns out to be a universal principle, it opens up an exceptional new way to perceive the world and ADC phenomena. This would imply our minds are linked to whatever they contact, past or present. It would also mean, as nonlocality suggests, mind and consciousness do not recognize cumbersome space/time boundaries. Thus, at some level we do not understand, the mind and consciousness is everywhere, eternal, and everlasting. If this is true, it does not signify that we can send messages whenever desired, but maybe someone with greater intelligence and purpose can.

Perhaps most mind-boggling of all—and this occurs within the body—is that something material comes from nothing. Just as a quark or a photon comes into and out of existence from nowhere, a single thought can produce a neuropeptide (a chemical informational substance) that sends messages to every cell in the body to physiologically express that thought. How can a thought produce a material, in this case a physical substance? Practically speaking, how can the immune system be stimulated into action by a molecule that wasn't there less than a second ago? In other words, for every thought or emotion there is a corresponding physical manifestation of that thought or emotion. We can truly talk to our bodies and they will listen.

If something comes from nothing, if information can be everywhere at once, if something can simultaneously exist and not exist, then it certainly is conceivable that signs, apparitions, and visitation dreams can occur that help the bereaved. Can we find a quantum physicist to say this? Perhaps if we looked hard enough, though at this time I know of no pronouncements on the subject. What we need to focus on is that mystery has always been, and will continue to be, an integral part of existence for energy and matter, and for communication between physical and nonphysical reality. If all of this is too much of a stretch for your openness and imagination try reading *Cosmos, Bios, Theos,* coedited by Yale physicist Henry Margenau, who is convinced only an omnipotent, all-knowing Intelligence could be behind the intricate laws that govern the universe and, as some believe, allow ADCs to occur. Follow up with physicist Nick Herbert's *Quantum Reality* and *Elemental Mind.* He believes that all of reality is nonlocal. Finally, try some of the writings of British physicist David Bohm who has done much to bring science and the spirit to a meaningful dialogue.

In the meantime, remember that we can learn from history. If history tells us anything, it clearly sends out a clarion call that points to the fact that our understanding and learning about the mystery of humanity and the universe is still unfolding. It may be more accurate to say our understanding and learning is just beginning when it comes to recognizing that there may be a hidden order to everything that we think is coincidence, chance, or synchronistic. Rest assured that we are far from knowing everything about the laws of nature.

• *See also question 44*

21. Do some ADCs originate from Christ encounters?

It has been said many people who have what you call ADCs are in reality having encounters with Christ, who hears the cry of those in deep anguish and comes to give comfort and reassurance. In your research, have you come across any experiences that suggest Christ or a Supreme Being—and not the deceased—is present?

Christ encounters have received very little media coverage, and the phenomena is hardly known outside of some religious circles and an occasional article appearing in church or diocesan newspapers. Even in Christian congregations and in the leadership of these churches, the topic of contemporary encounters with Christ is not a popular topic because the personal encounter is considered rare as well as a challenge to established orthodox teachings about past encounters. These spiritual encounters also remain hidden because of their personal nature and fear of the recipient that others would not be open to hearing about such a momentous encounter. On the other hand, a number of near-death experiences have included Christ encounters and provided a powerful experience that changed the direction of the life of one who has had an NDE, as well as his belief system. However, one book, *I Am With You Always,* by G. Scott Sparrow, makes it clear there have been many Christ encounters in modern times, some of which could easily be classified as ADCs. Like ADC events, they occur to people from all walks of life, such as Bill Wilson, the founder of Alcoholic's Anonymous, and Edgar Cayce, known widely for his clairvoyant abilities, and often to those who feel unworthy and unsuspecting.

How is Christ encountered in the ADC? Typically the experiences are similar to those in which the bereaved become aware of the deceased loved one. Therefore, dreams, which have historically been a consistent access to communication with God, become the framework through which comfort and love emerges. Jim, who has strong faith in God, had the following Christ encounter in a dream after the death of his infant daughter.

"Maria Was Alive"

One night, shortly after her death, I dreamed of the Resurrection of Christ from the dead. As Jesus rose from the dead, there too was my daughter rising anew. It was vivid and clear. Maria was alive and well, safe with the Lord.

This dream was very comforting for Jim and was instrumental in helping him accept the death of his daughter. He also shared the dream with his wife, an important action to take, which was reassuring to her although she was not as comforted by the event as Jim was. It is important to share the ADC with others in order to reaffirm its meaning and impress its detail on both the conscious and unconscious minds.

The ADC as a Christ encounter also occurs as an apparition and in auditory form. Sometimes the encounter does not involve a personalized Christ figure, but the recipient encounters a dazzling bright light that immediately brings a sense of love and warmth. Some may interpret the light as an angelic being instead of Christ. There are also a host of symbolic and natural phenomena involving unusual behavior by birds and animals, which are believed to spring from the hands of Christ. This is based on the conviction that a Supreme Being can use natural things for spiritual purposes because He is the Lord of natural processes. In any event, when these encounters occur, the bereaved display a newfound sense of peace.

That the Christ encounter occurs and can be classified as an ADC is obvious. Whatever terminology is used, the fact remains that the bereaved are assisted in their grief work by the experience. Some people believe these encounters would be much more frequent if the bereaved would reach out more and ask for assistance through their religious beliefs. Great resilience often emerges from the ADC, especially when it is perceived as a spiritual experience. When it comes to deciding on whether or not a Christ encounter is valid, Sparrow suggests using the biblical evaluation yardstick. He quotes Jeremiah in the Old Testament, who says, "When the word of the prophet comes to pass, then shall the prophet be known, that the Lord has truly sent him." In other words, if what the Christ encounter says or implies comes to pass, count on it as authentic.

22. What are some of the reasons given for why apparitions occur to survivors and people who are dying?

I wonder if there are reasons, other than giving support to the bereaved, for why a deceased loved one would come back. The apparition seems to have been around for a long time as a topic for debate and I'm wondering if, in theory, other reasons have been put forth to suggest these "visits." Is there any reading that gives additional viewpoints?

The realization that apparitions of the deceased—or ghosts, if you pre-fer—have been consistently interacting with the living is one of the little-publicized hallmarks of human history. However, the experience is not new to the bereaved, nor is it rare for a selected number of people who are not mourning the death of a loved one. Your question also reminds me of the interesting question of why the bereaved do not experience more apparitions instead of the less dramatic signs that are more frequently received. But let's start with what is arguably the most commonly suggested reason for why bereaved people experience visions and apparitions: they need help at a critical time.

1. **To provide comfort and reassurance.** When we examine the variety of messages resulting from ADCs, and in this case messages that derive from an apparition or vision, it is clear the content at root is to give comfort and establish the fact that love still prevails, even though the loved one is no longer physically present. Here is a visual example from Carol whose daughter died at a very early age.

"This Experience Helped Me in My Grieving"

I was in my home several months after Breanna's death. It was in the morning when suddenly I saw a vision of her trying to walk down the hallway. I could smell her presence. She was there because I had a tremendous longing of wanting her again—one way, anyway, some way! You know, you always hope for that spiritual connection after your loved one dies. This experience helped me in my grieving. It was a driving force to help me go on day to day.

This ADC, involving the sense of smell as well as sight, exemplifies the comfort and support to deal with the pain of loss that is a common result of the experience. Also, the interpretation of the vision as having a spiritual origin brings a special meaning of an ongoing and everlasting connection that helps the mourner deal with separation. Consolation in time of sadness and remorse appears to be the most logical reason for the ADC experience.

2. **To assist the transition at death.** There are many people who insist it is rather common for deceased loved ones to return to help those who are dying. The appearance of deceased friends and

relatives may well be what produces a sense of joy and acceptance of dying that is often reported by the dying person just before he dies. Death bed visions are a major type of near-death experience that have been reported by many medical and hospice personnel and NDE investigators. The presence of deceased loved ones appears to reduce the fear of death for the dying person. The presence can affect the mourning process of survivors in a positive way. There have also been a number of reports of appearances of deceased relatives to those who have been seriously ill but are not expected to die. Not infrequently, the result of the "visit" hastens recovery.

3. **To finish unfinished business.** When there has been no time for goodbyes because of sudden accidents resulting in death, or when other matters have been left undone, the appearance of a deceased loved one may bring closure to a problem that has been a nagging hurt and an energy drain for the mourner. What other types of unfinished business brings emotional turmoil that an apparition may heal? Guilt over not being present at the moment of death is a common occurrence for many mourners. Another is the feeling that one had not done enough for the deceased during the illness. On other occasions, the deceased may assist the mourner in locating important papers, money, or objects that the survivor is unable to find. In these and other circumstances, the deceased is thought to return to help the living in their readjustment and to reinvest in life.

4. **To suggest ways to solve problems.** A number of individuals have had apparitional appearances from loved ones or angelic beings when they were wrestling with difficult problems. I have come across instances where mourners have received specific information for solving a problem. One situation I am thinking of occurred with a young widowed mother who received a "visit" from her grandfather. She had been having great difficulty dealing with the behavior of her young children, and the grandfather made it very clear she was to take a stronger stance in her child rearing. In other instances, one may be encouraged by the deceased to take the first step in patching up relationships within the family or to reach out to others. This advice invariably results in the mourner being able to

cope with and eventually master the problem. In a similar vein, sometimes information is supplied that results in the prevention of problems.

5. **To emphasize love is eternal.** One of the most frequent interpretations of all ADCs is the belief the deceased loved one is showing that love doesn't die and he or she is still concerned about the mourner. Sometimes you will hear the bereaved express these sentiments with remarks such as "Her spirit will always be with me" or "He is still watching over me." Sometimes the deceased will say "I love you all" or "I know you can do it." The expression of belief in a reunion also suggests that love is strong and death has not broken the tie.

6. **To protect.** There are numerous ADCs that seem to have as their sole purpose the physical welfare of the mourner. In this vein, a message is received to help the mourner out of a potentially harmful situation before it occurs. In other situations, if the person is in the midst of a harrowing scene, he is given information that neutralizes the potential harm. I have heard of situations where the deceased loved one was heard giving a message to exit from a roadway. In following the advice, the mourner was spared a dreadful chain-reaction accident. Others have reported sensing the deceased's presence (or perhaps an angel) in situations where they felt they might be harmed by another individual. Reminders and warnings may also fall into this category.

For additional reading, I would recommend Andrew Mackenzie's *Hauntings and Apparitions* and Eleanor Sidgwick's *Phantasms of the Living*. Although both of these books are old and sometimes difficult to find, they still are among the best in providing information on apparitions. Most books on parapsychology will have a chapter on apparitions, if you are unable to locate the above suggestions in your local library or through interlibrary loan.

There are other reasons, in addition to the above mentioned, for apparitional appearances. They are not included here as they are not directly related to the ADC topic. You should also know, contrary to popular opinion, that apparitions seldom, if ever, scare the bereaved. On the contrary, they bring a feeling of warmth and goodness to the mourner. I also recommend at the appropriate time to allow your conversation with friends and acquaintances to turn to the question of apparitions and nonordinary experiences, and you will be surprised at the information that surfaces that will help you in your understanding of the intentions of apparitional figures.

23. What is meant by "believing is seeing" as an explanation for why ADCs occur?

When I first read the phrase "believing is seeing" I had to think twice about its specific meaning. Then I realized it could have more than one meaning. You have indicated that some people may use it to suggest an explanation for ADCs. How do you see it being used?

For comparison purposes, let's begin with the commonly heard phrase "seeing is believing." This has been tossed around for centuries with very clear intent. I can remember my mother and other family members saying "I'll believe it when I see it" or "If you see it then you can believe it," which are simply other ways of expressing "seeing is believing." Of course, that phrase is no longer as true as it used to be. There are lots of things that we see and that literally are not true and shouldn't be believed—as the movies, magicians, and other masters of deception have shown. Or as some medical researchers have put it, "Sensory experience is not the true test of reality." This statement is also applicable to some natural phenomena as well (see question 14).

In contrast, the concept "believing is seeing" is used to express the role of belief, hope, and faith in life. Enthusiastic belief in any endeavor you undertake has long been considered a proactive effort for a successful final outcome. Hope and faith provide a huge untapped source of energy to deal with the problems of life; they effectively limit the propensity to think the worst in any given situation. The fundamental meaning of "believing is seeing" is a spiritual message, a mindset quite different from what contemporary society endorses: believe and look beyond what your senses tell you is true. There is more than what meets the eye. There are some things you only know through faith.

Faith is the port of entry to the unexplainable and the unseen. The more we widen our conscious awareness of nonphysical reality, the more we find increasing options to deal with loss, change, and the unexpected. The vast majority of people who are fortunate to have an ADC always look on them as positive spiritual experiences. As Blaise Pascal, a French mathematician and philosopher, suggested—and recent studies of the impact of spiritual beliefs on health and longevity confirm—belief in something outside of and greater than the self is a deep need of every individual. The first step in adopting the "believing is seeing" approach is extricating ourselves from the bondage of physical reality and being open to spiritual reality in all of its manifestations. Faith in the unseen brings miracles, nurtures unconditional love, and a consciousness in which we become aware of one unified reality encompassing all.

Here is an example of "believing is seeing" as told in this symbolic ADC as experienced by Gina Cox of Hillsborough, North Carolina.

"There Was No Doubt in My Mind"

I have had an incident for sure that I know was a contact from my deceased mother. It took place about two weeks after my mother died of cancer. She fought a long, drawn-out battle and suffered a lot, so her death was expected and a blessing and relief for her and all of our family. I am a very spiritual person who definitely believes in a life after death and I felt certain my mother was in a wonderful place beginning a new life—but that tiniest bit of doubt and wonder kept me praying for some kind of a sign she was okay.

Anyway, my mother grew beautiful African violets and was always trying to give them away to family and friends. I had taken many plants, but never could keep them alive or didn't have the kind of light so they would bloom. I went to see my mother in July, after she found out she only had around six months to live. Because I live far away from her, I really thought it would be the last time I would see her alive. As I was telling her goodbye, she again gave me an African violet to take home, and because I knew this would be the last flower I would ever receive from her, it was important that I keep this one alive. She told me when to water it (Monday and

Thursday), and exactly what kind of violet food to use. Over the next seven months, I took great care of it, trying different windows for different lighting. The plant was full of blooms when I brought it home but, as in the past, they died and it stayed pretty and green, but it never bloomed again.

In February, we got the call the end was near and we quickly went to be with her. She died on February 16. We returned to our home and the pretty green plant she had given me. I continued to water it as she told me, wanting more than ever to keep it alive. If you know anything about violets, you know the blooms are tight little balls on the end of stems that take a while to grow away from the leaves before they open. But my plant just continued to be leaves. However, one day, about two weeks after her death, I went to water it as usual and to my surprise it was absolutely full of opened, beautiful flowers. I was so shocked and surprised and yelled out to my kids, "Oh my God, Mom made my flower bloom." There was no doubt in my mind, and there still isn't any, that she (or God or my Guardian Angel, maybe) made this violet bloom to let me know she was okay. It was just what I needed and I said many prayers of thanks. Shortly after that, the flowers died and then the plant died. But I wasn't at all upset because it had fulfilled its purpose, as far as I was concerned.

That is "believing is seeing." And it happens frequently.

With regard to ADC phenomena, "believing is seeing" may be used by critics as well as those who endorse the phenomena. Critics suggest that those who have the propensity to believe in ADC-type experiences will look for them more and interpret any unusual or coincidental happenings as a contact. It is charged that such choices are made without careful thought, inquiry, and reasoning. Believers in the ADC experience counter with this thought: If you don't believe in or are not at least open to the possibility of the experience, you will dismiss whatever happens with the usual coincidence, chance occurrence, hallucination, or illusion explanation. Reality has no objective witnesses.

Although there are a number of people who are not believers before they have an experience—and then switch sides in the debate after having an ADC—I believe it is more likely that one will experience an ADC, and many more uplifting adventures in life, if one has a belief system that allows for phenomena that cannot be verified by science. I am well aware of how the acceptance of all unverified phenomena can be troublesome in the long run, even set a dangerous precedent, but there are just too many positive results of faith leading to greater happiness, seeing signs and wonders, and providing the ability to cope with massive change, to suggest otherwise. There are certain age-old immutable truths that we seem to keep rediscovering; *believing is seeing* is one of them. It is easy to forget the truism that when you believe, you see more. Faith often results in seeing more than meaningful coincidences and using them in dealing with life. Its regrettable that we have a penchant at times to look for signs and wonders in order to bolster faith.

24. What are the strongest arguments against the reality of the ADC?

I'm convinced that no matter how much "proof" is uncovered for or against the reality of the ADC, there will always be a war of words about the meaning and validity of the experience. You have probably come across many arguments from the scientific community that refute the possibility of the ADC as a real event with a purpose. Are there any arguments that have caused you to review your beliefs or have at least caused some doubt?

At one time I came up with approximately fifteen different explanations for ADC experiences, most of them critical of the phenomena. Generally, these explanations range from judging the experience as a normal but insignificant part of grieving, to many natural or physiological origins, and finally suggesting a spiritual connection. I have already indicated elsewhere (see questions 13 and 14) that hallucinations and illusions are often the first explanations given by those who doubt the validity of the experience. That may satisfy some when it comes to explaining events in which the deceased is seen or heard, but it has no application to ADCs that are symbolic, derived from the dream state, or result from natural circumstances (a flower blooming at an unusual time). While I personally feel the hallucination/illusion answer is oversold and overdone, and that many of the accounts of seeing or hearing the deceased are credible, I am sometimes stretched in considering physical phenomena without apparent cause or explanation.

I am thinking here of many situations I have come across where the sense of the deceased's presence is preceded or accompanied by the lights in a room flicking on or off, a picture on a nightstand changing position from one day to another, or a mechanical toy or clock starting or stopping in an unusual manner. Is it possible for the deceased to influence these things in such a manner? Can they affect electromagnetic fields? How is it done and why isn't something more realistic used to send a message? (To some mourners these are realistic ways to make contact.) Is there an angel behind the switch or a Supreme Being? I usually make every attempt to rule out electrical or battery problems, consider whether it has happened before, and then see if and how this phenomena fits into the belief system of the person who had the experience. The symbolic significance to the bereaved—since they alone know the degree of emotional investment they had in the deceased and how he might respond—is an important insight to understand and develop.

Notwithstanding all possible natural explanations, science tells us how we humans are notorious for the way we think when unusual events occur that do not have a ready explanation. And in many ways they are correct. If an event occurs seldom in one's life, from an objective point of view, it should not be of particular significance. It is when unusual events occur with predictable regularity that we should sit up and take special notice. In other words, because there is so much randomness and unpredictability in the universe, there is a tendency to ascribe to the seldom occurring event a highly unusual cause.

With this in mind, there are two major arguments that are consistently made as reasons why so many ADCs are nothing more than products of our inability to discern the facts of the case and maintain objectivity. The first is centuries old. In brief, it states that if a particular event or belief provides comfort there is a tendency to disregard reasonable explanations to the contrary and embrace the comforting thought or event. This has been used to explain away dogmatic theological precepts and certain religious beliefs as well as the surging interest in the rash of religious figure sightings throughout the world. From the scientific worldview it sounds convincing. If something provides comfort from the harsh realities of the world, it seems logical to cling to that which eases stress and discomfort. Here is an example as experienced by Doris Stewart of Dix Hills, New York.

"I Believe it Was My Grandfather"

My grandfather passed away in November, 1995. One night in December, 1995, I was trying to put my four-month-old son to sleep. I was nursing him at the time, so I brought him into my bedroom, laid down on the bed, and started to nurse him. The room was dark at the time and my son was still not happy. I began to feel a sense of frustration. Suddenly, I was calmed by music. My son's crib was at the foot of my bed and the mobile started to play by itself. I sensed a feeling of calmness and my son instantly fell asleep.

Then I was startled when I thought about how the mobile started, although I was not frightened. Not only did it start by itself, but it played for several minutes longer than when it was wound up. I called my husband on the intercom and told him what happened and I put the phone up so that he could hear the music. My husband said a spring must have broken in the unit. I believed otherwise. My grandfather loved children very much and children loved him. I believe it was my grandfather who made the mobile play; it was his nature to ease a situation. To this day, August 19, 1997, the mobile has never done that again. (Nor before!)

Was this experience so comforting for Doris she simply threw all reason to the wind? Could there be another reason why the mobile played and never has since, or could this be something more than a synchronicity? This is a good example of contrast: the scientific paradigm held by the husband and the spiritual paradigm lived by the wife.

A second major explanation that occurs in the writings of debunkers of the unseen is faulty reasoning and judgment, often referred to as probability misjudgment theory. Succinctly stated, the implication is that one will ascribe the miraculous or the paranormal to any unusual event if one is inclined to believe in the unseen. In this vein, one may allow expectations to rule. Thus, it is said that there is a tendency to remember details of an experience that fit expectations (sometimes referred to as selective memory) and conveniently forget those that might disprove what actually occurred. Looked at in the probability misjudgment perspective, beliefs have a major influence on how one decides to examine and interpret the experience. If you have faulty beliefs they result in faulty perceptions of events (this is analogous to the "garbage in, garbage out" computer terminology). Furthermore, personal bias is indeed supported by a commonly accepted observation: We are not necessarily astute observers of our environment or nonverbal behavior unless we have been specially trained. Recently, in speaking to one of the producers of the television program *Unsolved Mysteries,* she made it clear—and I would agree with her observation—that people she has interviewed for possible inclusion on the show often do not tell their stories in exactly the same way over time. Slight differences crop up from one telling to the next.

Lawyers know full well how most of us have the tendency to forget details as time goes by or embellish our stories, albeit unknowingly, and sometimes knowingly. This brings up the possibility of purposely fabricating stories. First, let me say that faulty reporting of an experience has always been a concern of mine when I am talking to someone about his ADC. But more than that, when one relates an exceptional experience, I often later ask myself whether this person might not be telling the truth. Not infrequently, people may wish to tell a good story like fishermen like to tell good fish stories and hope to find someone, anyone, to listen. I had this happen once when a well-respected professional (I won't tell you what profession) told me of an apparition she experienced, and when I tried to find corroboration, it was clear one of the main characters in the account could not back up the story.

You are right in contending there will always be strong arguments in both camps. Therefore, in evaluating the evidence for or against the reality of the ADC, one must take into careful account the emotional disposition of the person before and after the event, the nature of the experience, the details given or changed, and the personal meaning it has for the experiencer.

25. Does each of us have a faculty that operates outside of the conventional space/time framework?

It seems literally impossible for some ADCs to take place if we look at our sense organs because they simply do not operate in the fashion in which some information is apparently transmitted. I'm thinking in terms of receiving messages when the deceased loved one does not speak in a conventional manner. Would you say there has to be something else we have within ourselves that is yet unrecognized by science?

Yes! I believe we all possess an unrecognized faculty, nonlocal in nature, which is able to pick up information originating in a place unknown to us. How such information is transmitted and received has yet to be fully recognized and determined by science. This opinion is based solely on my analysis of ADCs in which there is little other explanation to be found for how someone knew about a particular event before they were actually informed. I'm not talking about intuition and that feeling some people get about an event prior to it happening. So let's look at an example.

In *Phantasms of the Living,* authors Gurney, Myers, and Podmore present a number of cases in which they examine the development of telepathic hallucinations. The one we will start with concerns a nineteen-year-old woman who was rekindling the fire in a kitchen fireplace when suddenly she began to hear beautiful music. As she looked up she was astonished to see thousands of angels in close proximity to each other seeming to rise above her for a great distance. At the same time, her best friend appeared in front of the angels. Almost as quickly as they had assembled the angels began to fade away and the music began to grow faint. Although she was only able to see the head and shoulders of the angels, once they vanished like smoke she was convinced of what she had seen and immediately went to tell an older woman what she had experienced. This woman remarked that she (the nineteen-year-old) could be sure her friend was in heaven. Subsequently, the young woman learned her friend had died that day.

How did this young woman receive the information indicating her friend had died before she actually was informed of her death? The hallucination/illusion explanation does not fit here. Her vision was impressive enough for her to immediately inquire about the health of her friend and learn of her death. Let me assure you this experience is not one-of-a-kind or an anomaly. Through the years a number of similar cases, well documented, have been reported. Those who believe in the reality of the event assume telepathy is involved. Telepathy, originally called thought transference, is defined as the transmission of information between two people by means other than normal sensory perception—in short, mind to mind contact. There is quality research to back up the assertion that mind to mind communication is a reality. Those who dismiss the possibility of mind to mind contact would say the young woman hallucinated, it was a chance occurrence, or pure coincidence her friend died on the same day she had a vision. Let's consider one more extraordinary "crisis situation" that is the most commonly documented telepathic experience.

Terri Stanton was recovering from knee surgery and was rehabilitating her knee at a fitness center where she met Don Jackson. Weeks later . . . but let Terri tell us:

"I Felt Him Say Thank You"

And then, Don asked me out. The date began with a quick workout on a Friday afternoon, followed by dinner and drinks, and a romantic dance under the moonlight on Palm Beach. For just a few moments, Don made me feel like a princess. He was strong and handsome and someone who I was extremely proud to be seen with. Although it would be our first and only date, Don wrapped his arms around me and treated me as though I was his very own.

Over dinner that night, Don—who along with his Greek-like beauty had a colorful past—discussed how his faith had deepened recently, how his father's death six months earlier had affected him, and how much he admired his mother's victory against breast cancer, which he said was largely waged with prayer. It was an incredible conversation for a man who I knew had lived daringly and paid the price. I was touched deeply by his honesty and earnestness, and a little surprised such a tough guy would reveal such deep emotions to someone he barely knew.

Yet, Don would disappoint me. Despite our romantic evening, and tentative plans to meet the next day, I would never hear from Don in the physical world again. A week later, on March 24, two days after my birthday, Don was killed suddenly and instantly when his Ford Explorer slammed head-on into a UPS truck on his way home from a very successful golf game. The accident was so traumatic traffic was shut down for hours, and the jaws of life was used to literally cut away the entire passenger side of Don's Explorer to pull his 210-pound body from the wreckage.

However, despite the news coverage the accident received, I was not aware of Don's death for a few days. I was still angry at him for not calling me after our date.

That Monday, the day of Don's death, I went to the gym as I normally did. However, on this occasion, instead of chatting with my buddies, I moved rapidly through my workout hardly pausing to take a drink of water. As I was leaving the gym at about 7:10 P.M., I was overwhelmed with sadness. I looked around the gym for a moment, and thought, "It's as though Don has died."

I drove home immediately, changed out of my gym clothes and into shorts and a t-shirt, and felt compelled to lay down. It was as though a weight pushed on my body and made my eyelids heavy. I laid on the left side of the bed, not the side I normally do, but the side where I had slept when Don spent the night.

And then, I felt him. Without any doubt, I could feel Don's muscles, the weight of his chest and the strength of his arms around me. For a few moments, I laid in the state of consciousness between awakeness and sleep. I could feel his golden warmth, yet I did not and could not open my eyes. Although I had thought of him often in days previous, this was not a fantasy. I could feel Don all around me. When I awoke from my half-conscious state, tears were flowing down my cheeks. I got up instantly, feeling almost dizzy, and tried to wipe away my tears. Again, I was struck with sadness. But because I was feeling rejected by Don as logic suggests, at the time, I did not understand my feelings. When my roommate asked what was wrong, I told her I was crying over Don Jackson.

Later that night, as we were watching the evening news, videotape appeared of a tragic car accident that had stopped traffic in West Palm Beach. A dark Ford Explorer sat cut open with boxes of toys and clothing poking out from behind the back seat. My roommate turned to me, and said, "Isn't that Don?" But because of the appearance of clothing and toys and a baby car seat, it seemed unlikely to me this could be Don's vehicle.

A couple of days, later my roommate phoned me at my office. She asked if I was sitting down, and I said, "Yes, why? Has someone died?" My roommate gasped and then said, "There's a reason Don hasn't called you." Then, she paused. "Don's funeral is tomorrow," she said. I was shocked, but somehow I wasn't surprised. I knew that Don, for all his beauty and lust for life, had not yet learned not to take risks. But at the same time I was *terribly sad, having met someone who I had thought might be a special person in my life. Little did I understand just how special he was.*

Although I did not attend the funeral, it was a celebration of Don's life. Two days later, I picked up two bouquets of red roses and approached Don's mother's home. I had called ahead, and although she and her family had never met me, they told me to come over right away. When Mrs. Jackson came to the door, I held out the two dozen roses for her. She said, "Oh, Don always brought me roses. This is what he would have brought me." Inside sat Don's sister, his niece, and his cousin. Mrs. Jackson went into the kitchen to put the roses in water, and I cautiously entered the living room where the other women sat. They welcomed me and asked me to join them.

I then explained how I had met Don, how he had raised my self-esteem simply by paying attention to me, and how though I knew him very briefly, he had affected me and made me feel attractive again. They shared pictures with me of Don, snapshots of him riding dirt bikes, and told me stories of living with him on an island in St. Tropez, of Don's lust for life, and of his loving effect on each of them.

I told them briefly of my encounter with Don, the feeling of his presence and the sadness I had felt at 7:10 P.M. on March 24, 1977. Then, they told me Don had died nearly at that very moment, and that each of them— either driving home in their cars from work or preparing to go to a church meeting—had felt his presence. "I think Don was going around checking on each one of us," said his sister. They told me the toys and clothing I had seen on the news had been intended as donations for his local church. But Don was never able to make the delivery himself.

Then I turned to Don's mother, and told her how he told me so much about her over dinner on that single date, how he had loved his father, and respected his mother—that they had both been his heroes. Whether or not Don had ever told his parents that, I knew I had to repeat his love to her. Although I felt a little uncomfortable, the Jackson family was kind and endearing and thanked me for visiting them. I have not seen them since, but when I moved to California, I dropped a note to Mrs. Jackson, telling her again how her son's love for life had encouraged me to pursue my own dreams.

Later that afternoon, after I left the Jackson home, I was standing in the tack shed where my roommate and I kept feed and saddles and bridles for our horses. As I bent over to pick up a bucket of grain, I felt Don's arms around me again, as though he was standing behind me and encircling my waist. I felt him say "Thank you" and again I could not help but cry.

What is most unusual about this crisis ADC is how more than one person was involved in sensing the presence of the deceased before any of them had been notified of the death. This is a rare occurrence when four people sense the presence of the deceased near the time of death. How can we account for all of them having the experience particularly when each were in different locations? They somehow exercised a faculty to perceive beyond the five senses. Perhaps this is a good example of telepathic communication that would make most skeptics wince. But don't forget: we still do not understand how hypnosis or the power of suggestion work either.

26. Is there any one consistent positive link that you have found between all ADCs?

Assuming ADCs have a pattern or standard source from which they evolve, what could be the common threads that run through most, if not all, of these experiences? History is certainly on the side of the consistency of the experience, but I am looking for other links that may forge a mutual bond among all who have had an ADC.

Having talked to and collected data from hundreds of people about ADC experiences, as well as having spoken to colleagues and other professionals about the subject, I am struck with at least two consistently clear links between all ADC phenomena. First, there is absolutely no doubt that these experiences assist mourners in adjusting to the loss of their loved ones. Over and over again, in some form, I hear the refrain "the experience was comforting." I am assuming, of course, the ADC has been accepted by the recipient or validated by a friend or counselor because there are some experiences that cause mourners to question their own judgment. They need input from someone they trust. That aside, one repeatedly finds mourners emerging from their experiences with a sense of encouragement that life is meaningful. Something is learned from each event that awakens a spark to continue the long endurance race of having to start life over again without loved ones.

ADCs do not magically eliminate the grief process. They make grieving more bearable because the often arduous task of reordering priorities, learning new skills, and forming new relationships—the core of grief work—remains. Still, the ADC becomes a versatile coping mechanism used in times of distress strengthening one's resolve to assume new responsibilities and reinvest in life. The highly individual nature of the ADC has varying degrees of impact on the experiencer. It may be a problem solver for one and a confirming set of beliefs for another, a source of insight on the one hand or the initiator of a whole new paradigm on the other. For the child, it can instill a sense of wholeness in a few moments that would perhaps take half a lifetime to learn. Let's look at an example that, though easily overlooked in importance due to its brevity and seeming insignificance, was an immediate source of peace and joy when most needed by Jean Pantaleo of Riverhead, New York.

"I Knew I Was Not Alone"

It was Christmas Eve day and it was snowing. I was twenty-four years old, the mother of three little girls, and had just put them to bed for an afternoon nap. It was quiet and depressing in the house. I'd been waiting for company, but because of the snow, they hadn't come. My husband was at work and I was at a really low ebb. I sat by the window and my thoughts went back in time to my youth and how Christmas used to be. I became even more depressed and started to cry.

I turned away from the window, and when I did, I smelled an odd, different kind of smell. It was vaguely familiar to me, but I couldn't put my finger on what it was! I began to walk around, trying to find the source of it, but was unsuccessful. What was it and where was it coming from? In a few more minutes I'd been all over the house and looked in every cabinet and drawer, every nook and cranny. It was coming from nowhere and coming from everywhere. What was that smell?

I think it took me about a half-hour to finally put a name to the over-whelming, yet pleasant, smell. It was wintergreen—oil of wintergreen—and I definitely didn't have any in my house! So why was I smelling it? And where was it coming from? My grandmother had used wintergreen, right up until she died, to ease her arthritis, and as soon as I remembered this, I felt a rush of peace and joy flood my senses. I simply knew my dear grand-mother was there with me, beside me, all around me. My sadness disap-peared, and I knew I was not alone.

"Merry Christmas, Grandma," I said.

The smell remained in the house for the entire afternoon, until the chil-dren awakened, and then it was gone. Yes, they smelled it too.

This brings us to the second consistent theme of the ADC: LOVE. The word connotes a number of meanings. In the ADC, it most often comes through for the recipient as meeting one of the most important of all human needs: I am special, I am important. We all need to feel we are still unique and special when a part of us dies. Once lost, it is not easy to regain. It can take a long time to reestablish self-esteem when we are con-vinced the world is going on its merry way and is oblivious to the fact someone we love has died. Anger, guilt, and depression drag us down, but the ADC reverses the downward spiral to make us feel whole again. There is always a sense of reconnection when you feel loved. The specter of isola-tion, even when surrounded by friends and family, is breached when the sense of love is felt in the ADC experience. Because the ADC breaks the perception of isolation (a major stressor and risk factor for poor health), it anchors the belief most hold deep within—their love for the deceased will never die—and, in fact, the departed is loving them back through symbol, sign, or apparition. Peace ensues. Love is eternal and seems to shine through the anguish of loss, but so too does the awareness that the bond of love is still reciprocal.

27. Is there any proof, beyond a shadow of a doubt, that the ADC is a spiritual experience?

My idea of a spiritual experience would involve things like the soul, spirit, or incorporeal being as distinguished from physical reality. Many ADCs obviously include this type of spiritual meaning. It is easy for me to conclude most ADCs have a spiritual basis. Is there any proof for my conclusion?

As with most questions pertaining to nonphysical reality, it all depends on whom you talk to. I would suggest that there is too much precision in the universe, too much mystery and complexity in humanity, too much intricate balance in our ecological systems (despite the way they are being plundered) to have all come into being by accident. Clearly it is not trendy to use words like *spiritual,* or worse, *supernatural,* as explanations for ADCs or any unexplainable phenomena for that matter. In fact, for many, such references suggest archaic or oversimplified thinking. Nonetheless, the scholarly approach to the search for truth must be open to all paths and possibilities.

Science has extreme difficulty in proving metaphysical phenomena exists because it simply doesn't have the tools; it wasn't designed for the search. A couple of lines from William Saroyan's *The Human Comedy* are appropriate here. Although he was directing his remarks to physicians, it applies to scientists as well: "[Scientists] don't know everything really. They understand matter not spirit. And you and I live in the spirit." This statement has profound implications in that energy and matter applications cannot begin to provide insights into spiritual experiences; it is an oil and water mix. Yet, we can still use our reasoning abilities, tainted as they are by strict naturalism and scientism, to examine experiential evidence and the behavioral results of these encounters. People do change as a result of their ADC experiences. Thus, there is nothing wrong with looking at positive results as a starting point—and investigating back to the origin for these changes. There are all too many positive responses to relegate the phenomena to chance or evolution, or solely to the wisdom of humanity. Science has an impressive history of acting on results long before it understands causation. Here is a typical ADC most scientists would dismiss as pure chance, but it was a spiritual experience for Peaches Haas, whose husband was killed in a motorcycle accident.

"I Know Rick Is Nearby"

Five days after Rick died, and on the day we had his memorial mass, I was playing golf. I am NOT a golfer, playing only twice in 1966. I played with a very old friend who had come for the services for Rick. The game was a chance to get away from the phones and all of the company that was around me. I felt wonderful and relaxed. For some strange reason on the last green I silently spoke to Rick. "If you are okay," I said, "let me sink this putt." The strange part was that the ball was at least fifteen feet from the cup and I'm really lousy at putting. I took aim and that ball shot off my club and made a direct line for the cup and went in. I truly felt contact with him.

The way I look at it, Rick wanted me to know he was okay and that he was spiritually nearby. The response to my request was so swift and direct it left no doubt in my mind. Repeated experiences have helped me with my grief. I know Rick is nearby and comes through in definite but different ways. Even my housemate has experienced his presence and she is basically a nonbeliever in these matters. Rick's sister called me one morning and told me she had a "visitor" in her car that morning on her way to work. She wanted to know if I thought she was crazy. Rick is getting around. She lives in Cincinnati.

Was this a spiritual experience? It was for Peaches and untold others like her.

It should also be pointed out that many people who have an ADC become convinced that there is a spiritual dimension to existence. Others actually become more spiritual in their orientation to life, return to their spiritual roots, strengthen their faith in a Supreme Being, or move from atheist or agnostic to believer. More than that, most people who have an ADC are either reminded of their beliefs in an afterlife, and embrace them more readily, or change their view of death to become less fearful and more accepting.

No doubt, in this day and age, all of the above is looked upon by many as pure chance occurrences that bereaved people grasp for and embellish in order to deal with their pain. Such an observation should be expected in an atmosphere in which psychology rules and has much to say about the nature of grief. But let me remind you it is likely much of psychology—particularly in helping people heal from trauma of various origins—is about spirituality in disguise. In the spiritual realm, so intimate and personal, great transformation and changes in behavior has its roots, though psychology steps forward to take credit. The ADC as a spiritual experience distinguishes itself as a contrasting agent between physical and nonphysical reality, supporting the premise that there is an ultimate authority, bringing the latter into focus as a part of life, and as a source for adjusting to the changes imposed by loss. A cursory analysis of responses by those who have experienced ADC phenomena points out the existence of a spiritual framework in which they find meaning in life and death. By its very nature the experience taps into the depths of the spirit of humanity. Just as serving others puts us in touch with our spiritual connectedness, the ADC resonates with that same spiritual reality.

In summary, many individuals come to believe ADCs have spiritual origins. This conclusion is reached in the following ways:

1. They experience the ADC and its spiritual base;

2. They study the evidence and witness the spiritual changes in those who have had an ADC;

3. They develop their intuitive gifts and see the ADC as simply another manifestation of spiritual reality; and

4. They have other spiritual experiences of unexplainable origin (such as NDEs) and believe the ADC is similar.

Keep in mind that the ADC is only a tiny slice of a huge unexplainable universe. As for scientific proof of ADCs being spiritual experiences I am afraid it will be a long time coming. Your "proof" will only come from the subjective experiences of the bereaved.

• *See also questions 6, 60, and 77*

28. Isn't it quite plausible most ADC experiences are simply the work of the unconscious mind?

Many people suggest that much of what is passed off as an extraordinary experience when mourning is actually the work of the unconscious mind. It seems plausible that visions, voices, and especially dream ADCs could come from the unconscious. It is said to store everything experienced and is also connected to an exceptional network of information. What is your response to this claim?

Ever since Carl Jung suggested the unconscious mind is far more than a mere repository for instincts and fears, there has been endless debate about the power and abilities it possesses. Currently, there is much to indicate that Jung's conception of the unconscious as a treasure trove of wisdom and influence in our lives is accurate in many ways. For example, it can readily be observed that the way we are programmed at an unconscious level early in life can have a major effect on how we feel about ourselves, the quality of our relationships, and the nature of our perceptions. A feature of the unconscious mind—which causes unnecessary confusion—is our unfamiliarity with the way it works and with its contents. In particular, it is hard for most of us to understand how we value, choose, and believe on an unconscious level. There is more: these unconscious values, choices and beliefs end up playing major roles in our conscious behavior.

How does the unconscious make itself known or how does it express itself? The answer to this question will give us insight into why many ADCs are thought by some observers to be the unconscious at work. We can begin with a few historical facts: many of the greatest scientific discoveries were the products of visions, dreams, intuition, and instant light-bulb flashes of wisdom and knowledge. Elias Howe's lockstitch sewing machine, August Kekule's contribution to understanding the structure of benzene, and Otto Lowe's discovery of nerve impulses possessing electrical as well as chemical components (which won him the Nobel Prize in Physiology and Medicine), all came from sources hardly considered scientific then or now. Hypnosis, as used in medicine to aid burn victims or for other health reasons, is predicated on the belief that suggestions to the unconscious have a direct effect on physiology and the healing process. Perhaps one of the least known pieces of information—one of those best kept secrets that has great implications for human health and happiness—is the greater proportion of mental activity takes place at the unconscious level and has direct relationship to how we view the world around us. No wonder some individuals believe ADCs are the result of the wisdom of the unconscious mind, since creativity is the overriding characteristic that is consistently manifested.

But don't tell that to forty-eight-year-old Phyllis Wynn of Colorado Springs, Colorado. The healing she experienced in her dream after the death of her father was more than a product of her unconscious. You decide.

"The Grief Had Finally Lifted"

When my father passed away suddenly from a massive heart attack, I could not believe it. I was totally inconsolable, and I took it extremely hard because we had a nasty argument a few days before, and I didn't get the chance to apologize.

I cried nonstop, couldn't eat or sleep. I took time off from work because I was so upset that I couldn't concentrate on my duties. I was unable to help in the funeral arrangements. I cried when I saw the coffin the family chose and had to leave the room. I was such a mess, I refused to go see where we were going to have him buried. I could not even handle that part. The very idea of my dad inside that box, getting placed into the ground, forever, overwhelmed me. I believed in God and heaven with all my heart, but when a loved one dies you take it very personally.

We buried him in a very beautiful ceremony. The church was filled to capacity with friends, coworkers, and family. That night, I finally fell asleep and began to dream. In the dream, the city had an unusually severe rain storm. The rains devastated the cemetery grounds and washed my father's coffin down the hill on to the road below. The funeral director couldn't reach the head of the family by phone so he called me down to see the disaster.

I was met by my smiling father who said, "I'm glad you came. I want to apologize for our argument." I also apologized and said, "I'm sorry you passed away." He told me he was okay now, very happy in heaven, and he will always love us and be with us always. I said, "I love you and will miss you and now I think I can go on with my life." He laughed and said, "In heaven is where life is really at. Now, please, rebury me and be happy." I reburied him all by myself and I immediately felt better. The grief had finally lifted and I was my old self again.

The transformation in Phyllis' life, the turning point in her grief, was the visitation dream in which unfinished business was taken care of and the love between father and daughter was expressed. She also expressed the hope to me that her story could help others in similar situations and closed with: "The deceased can visit you in dream form and when they do, healing occurs. I thought I might have to see a professional because of my grief and the lack of sleep, which I so desperately needed, but my healing came in a dream."

If we go one step further into the collective unconscious, where Jung suggested we are all connected, then we have to entertain the belief there are nonlocal characteristics as well. Or as Jungians are wont to say, "in the collective unconscious there is no space or time." If there is no space or time, then whatever occurs in it can occur everywhere and at the same time. Therefore, given the creativity of the unconscious, the ADC, it can be argued, could easily be a device in which the unconscious helps the conscious mind to accept the loss and begin to deal with life again. This is most clearly suggested in the dream ADC. However, I would counter that given the common understanding that the unconscious speaks in symbolic language in dreams, it is clear that the dream ADC is literally interpreted. There is little need for symbolic interpretation because the messages between the deceased loved one and the mourner are unusually logical and clear, either verbally or visually (consider the exchange in Phyllis' dream). Sometimes the exchange between the loved one and the mourner is so rich in meaning and clarity as to cause the mourner to later describe the event as real as life itself. "I know it was him because I asked him to show me this was not just a dream, and he did." Sometimes the proof comes in terms of a hug or a kiss. Note that there are other dreams, not ADCs, which do require symbolic interpretation. Not all dreams of the deceased are visitation or ADC dreams.

As for other ADCs that involve signs or symbolic messages (involving birds, animals, or other natural phenomena), I find it difficult to stretch the abilities of the unconscious mind to be able to control these kinds of events. This is especially so with those who are convinced that physical signs, such as the movement of pictures or objects, or lights going on or off, are from the deceased loved one. Those who believe in the unconscious mind would put these occurrences in the category of synchronistic events.

Given the unusual capabilities of the unconscious mind, with its exceptional creativity and flair for retrieving memories that have been held within for decades, it is also argued by many people that the unconscious is the Spirit of God working within. This is the message in 1 Corinthians: "Or do you know that your body is a temple of the Holy spirit within you, which you have from God, and that you are not your own. For you were bought with a price." Every case made for the work of the unconscious can also be applied to support the contention of unusual abilities being manifestations of the conviction that "we are made in the image and likeness of God." If the unconscious can operate outside of a conventional space/time structure, so too can a Supreme Being.

In summary, my response to the claim that all ADCs are a product of the unconscious mind is to question the assumption that the unconscious (in Jungian terms) has the kind of power necessary to consistently abrogate the laws of nature and the universe. This is not to negate the assumption that the unconscious contains so much more information than can ever be held in the conscious mind or its ability to generate solutions to problems. The variety of ADCs, the highly individual nature of the experience (I doubt if any ADC is identical or interpreted the same way by recipients, even though there are similarities), and the spectacular timing with which some take place lead me to conclude that individuals—even on an unconscious level—do not possess the kind of wisdom and power to initiate these events. As I have suggested before, the ADC comes from the outside. With deep respect for Jung, remember, the unconscious mind is still a theory.

- *See also question 76*

29. Is the ADC a clear indication that there is an afterlife or a heaven?

Because so many people, and some authors, claim that the ADC is a spiritual experience, I wonder if a case has ever been made for using the experience as a means of proving there is an afterlife. You obviously have talked to many individuals who are convinced they will see their deceased loved ones again. What is the evidence that supports their beliefs?

You are asking a question that is on everyone's mind at some time in life and is a perennial subject of debate for millions. For those who have had an ADC, one of the most consistent messages received, either explicitly or implicitly, is that the deceased person is alive and well in another environment. This idea is reinforced again and again when the deceased loved one says "I'm all right" or "Don't worry about me" or "I'm in a great place." The belief that a contact has occurred automatically implies that there is another existence where the soul or spirit of the deceased is alive and well. This is enough for the recipient to have his or her beliefs reinforced with regard to another life beyond the present one; but it is not enough for the general public or for those who have not had an ADC. Therefore, we need to look closely at the nature of some ADCs to determine if they warrant inclusion in the body of information suggesting consciousness survives bodily death.

Not surprisingly, there are experiences reported by mourners that are difficult not to consider as proof for another existence. I am thinking, for example, of crisis ADCs when the mourner learns about the death of the loved one from the deceased (or?) before being informed by authorities or another family member. (Disbelievers argue it could be a telepathic message from a living person or pure coincidence.) There have been a number of these highly unusual occurrences involving children as well as adults. One of the most intriguing cases comes from Eleanor Sidgwick's abridged edition of *Phantasms of the Living*. It concerns a three-and-a-half-year-old boy who knew his father had died before the family was notified. He had been resting on the bed with his mother right after lunch when he suddenly sat up and said, "Daddy is dead." His mother responded to the contrary but, because the little boy persisted and appeared distressed, she thought it best not to pursue the matter. Soon his mother received word of her husband, a captain, having been killed in the war a couple of days before her son had made his startling pronouncement. The Society for Psychical Research (SPR) has a number of these cases in its archives. How do these events happen? Where does this information come from and how is it received? The reception can occur in a visual form, an apparition, by way of the sense of presence (intuitive ADC), a dream, or through an auditory ADC. What is perfectly clear is that information is conveyed regarding the death before official notification takes place. It seems unlikely the message would come from the unconscious.

Other ADCs suggesting the existence of an afterlife are in the form of protective messages. They result in preventing injury or death, come at the most opportune moment, and clearly help mourners deal with another stressful event that could add immeasurably to their woes. Depending on the circumstances, sometimes these protective ADCs may even prevent a distraught mourner from taking his own life. In these situations the deceased (or?) reminds the mourner that his demanding predicament will change for the better and taking one's life is not a solution to the problem. It is not unusual for common ADCs to result in a change in the deep depression that often leads to thoughts of suicide. I remember an older gentleman who approached me after my presentation to a group of parents of murdered children, and in the conversation about his visitation dream he said, "That's the only reason I'm alive today. It's the only thing keeping me going. If it hadn't been for my dream and knowing my son is okay, I wouldn't be able to go on." His only son had been murdered and this father was convinced his son was in an afterlife. The ADC had made inroads on his depression and his pervasive feeling of helplessness.

Not to be overlooked in the consideration of the continued existence of consciousness are those incidents where a message is received by someone who is a friend of the mourner, but was not necessarily close to the deceased loved one. In some instances, the person does not know the deceased or the mourner. Such messages have significant impact on the mourner; however, the question of origin is important to our discussion. When a third- or fourth-party is involved and the message received is to be relayed to the mourner, the indirect contact is generally a complete puzzle to the person who has the initial experience. "How was I chosen and why am I the messenger," are not uncommon thoughts. The messenger usually concludes the sender is in another realm. The third party often has no idea why he was chosen for this particular function involving this particular mourner, but believes the contact was authentic and the person who died is in another existence. The fundamental fact is that the experience is indeed transforming for the mourner and causes him to believe the deceased loved one lives on.

We should also note ADCs that occur and are witnessed by more than one person. Shared ADCs may be of particular significance because they tend to rule out explanations such as hallucinations. Would three or four people who see an apparition or hear the deceased all hallucinate the same images and sounds and at the same time? What about those who together sense the presence of the deceased in their midst? These are among the most interesting ADCs and beg for research and understanding. Invariably, when more than one person is involved in witnessing one or a series of ADCs, as sometimes happens in families, there is common agreement that the deceased is in an afterlife or a better existence. ADCs have much to say about the further existence of consciousness after death and descriptions of peace and happiness in another realm. But let me hasten to say, according to the scientific method, they are not proof positive. However, if you have the ADC experience, it doesn't matter what science thinks because there is more than one way to obtain information about reality, especially spiritual reality. Perhaps the key question you have to ask yourself is, "Does mind exist independently of the body?" If you believe it does, then you are well on your way to believing that the ADC is a spiritual experience.

Finally, there are many people—and some researchers—who believe we are wired to connect with a Higher Power. Specifically, it is believed the temporal lobe of the brain contains what has been called a God module. This dimension of the human brain may also house the faculty that facilitates much ADC phenomena. Perhaps everyone has the hardware but not everyone is open to using it.

30. Why is it that some people have several ADCs and others only have one or none?

I realize millions of people have experienced ADC phenomena; however, even if more than sixty million have had an ADC, that still leaves a couple of hundred million who have not. If the experience is so common and helpful, why isn't it even more common? I know lots of people who have mourned the death of a loved one and have not had the experience. Why?

At the outset it is important to recognize that deciding who receives an ADC and why that person receives it, and someone else does not, is akin to asking who made the world and for what purpose. There will be lots of speculation mixed with common sense and some bias. Assuming such an admixture, let me begin with perhaps the most obvious reason of all.

Some mourners do not need an ADC. Recently, after I gave a lecture, a young woman approached me red-eyed and obviously very distraught. She proceeded to inform me of her sister's death several months previous. At the same time, she was taking a college course in which the instructor was extremely demanding in terms of the work required. She had linked the excessive demands of the course with her sister's death and now—having to take the same instructor in another course—was reliving her grief and stress a second time. She also had some unresolved guilt associated with the death. I suggested it was important to talk about it when she was ready and especially to talk about it with the deceased, which she agreed to do. Then I suggested that there was nothing wrong with her looking for or praying for a sign that her sister was okay. She quickly responded, "Oh, I know she's okay." There was no need for her to obtain reassurance. In her belief system her sister was happy in her new existence. Such beliefs, held by many individuals who are convinced of the existence of their loved ones in a happy setting, require no verification.

Too personal to disclose. For some individuals, the nature of the ADC is so intimate and intensely personal that they are unwilling to share it with others. Sometimes the unwillingness to share is

linked to protecting another family member. I have heard of two
instances in which children, now adults, did not share their ADCs
because they did not feel the adults were ready to listen because of
their own problems in dealing with the death. One child interpreted
the behavior of the surviving parent as being so emotionally overcome she did not feel the parent could endure hearing of the ADC
experience. Some individuals may also interpret the ADC as being
an intimate bond with the deceased and not made to be shared.
There may be a large number of ADCs that simply are not shared
due to the beliefs of the experiencer.

Fear of the unknown. Some individuals who have an extraordinary
experience are fearful of it. This may be due to early childhood
training or the influence of television or the movies. Religious
training could also be involved if one believes that the ADC has its
origin in demons and their devious work. The result of intense fear
may lead to complete repression of the experience. That is, the ADC
could be pushed deep into the unconscious, buried to prevent the
pain of dealing with the fear associated with the experience. On
the other hand, there may be people who choose to suppress the
experience. In this instance, the individual freely chooses to push the
experience out of conscious awareness and not process it. Whenever
it surfaces in memory, it is dispatched and replaced by other
thoughts or activities. In any event, there are a number of people
who have an ADC and are afraid to tell others about it. What I am
implying is that there are probably many more ADCs experienced
than we realize because people refuse to talk freely about them.

Inability to receive a contact. It has been suggested that some
individuals may not be able to receive a contact from a deceased
loved one. One reason given is the refusal to believe in the possibility
of the experience. When something extraordinary occurs involving
the deceased, some people dismiss it as the craziness associated with
grieving. They could not possibly believe an ADC would take place
involving their deceased loved one. Another reason given is the
possibility that many people do not have the innate ability to receive

or discern a contact. St. Paul, in his first letter to the Corinthians said, "The particular way the Spirit is given to each person is for a good purpose. One may have the gift of preaching . . . another prophecy, another the gift of recognizing spirits."

Emotional blocks. It can be argued that some people may not be able to receive an ADC because of the intensity of emotion they are dealing with at the time. Intense anger, for example, limits awareness and the possibility of being open to the experience. The anger may be directed at the deceased or other family members. It may constantly occupy the thoughts and affect the health of the person. The same could be said of the overwhelming guilt some mourners take upon themselves. They are in no condition to understand the commonness of neurotic guilt and how it is almost to be expected after the death of a loved one. Who can live with and love another and when that person dies not find something in the past he could have done better—when using hindsight. Preoccupation with these emotions or intense suffering may limit one's ability to notice signs or symbols, or even affect the nature of one's dreams. In a similar vein, some individuals are much more aware of subtle reactions in their bodies that act as cues to become more alert to outside phenomena.

Other possibilities. I have heard several other reasons given that, like the above, are merely speculative. It is possible that some people do not receive an ADC because of the nature of the relationship with the deceased. An ambivalent relationship may preclude the possibility of the ADC. If there was not a deep emotional investment in the deceased, it is likely an ADC is not hoped for or needed. For others, they may think they need an ADC, but in reality can cope without the experience. And, of course, there are some individuals who have the experience, but are afraid to tell anyone for fear they will be told to seek professional assistance, or will become the brunt of stories or jokes. The possibility one might rely too much on the ADC and not fend for themselves has also been offered as a reason why some individuals have never experienced the phenomena.

With regard to your question of why some mourners receive more than one ADC while others do not have the experience, I am frankly at a loss in finding an answer. It is possible that some mourners need more than one to deal with the aftermath of their loss; they are, perhaps, more aware of their surroundings and open to the phenomena than are relatives and friends. At the same time, some who claim to have had several experiences may not have had as many as they claim. On occasion, when talking to or interviewing someone who claims to have had several encounters, I am skeptical about the nature of some of the contacts, which could be readily explained as a result of a natural cause. One might even suggest, as is true in most subject areas there are, for want of a better term, "ADC junkies." It seems like everything they see or touch is a sign and has some connection to a deceased loved one. While possible, it does not always seem probable. Then, too, there appears to be no good reason why one member of a family may have three apparently authentic experiences and no other family member reports a contact. Yet one member of the family may need an ADC more than another to cope with the massive internal turmoil taking place as an aftermath of the death. Why one mourner receives the gift of an ADC and another does not is essentially a mystery that may never be fully understood.

31. After all of the time and energy you have spent over the years in the study of ADC phenomena, what do you think is the origin or reason behind why it occurs?

You must have had enough contact with people who have had ADCs, as well as with other researchers, in order to draw some personal conclusions about the origin and meaning of the ADC. Are you willing to give us your personal thoughts about the experience or will that put you in a precarious position with colleagues who still believe the ADC is nothing but an internal device used by the mourner to keep from having to let go of the deceased?

Yes, this question puts me on the spot, to be sure. However, I have no qualms about stating my personal beliefs about the phenomena. In retrospect, let me begin by saying that I have been influenced by how ADCs affect the lives of mourners. When I talk to people who have the experience, or who write to me about their ADCs, and they tell me how an ADC has saved them so much pain, eliminated feelings of abandonment, or finally brought them peace and meaning in life, I am inspired, and in some instances awed, by what I hear. One of my fantasies is that some day we will be able to demystify the ADC so that it is looked at by all as a normal part of human wholeness and not an aberration to be endlessly debated. Like, "Hey, its normal; let's get on with it." It's a shame as we head into the twenty-first century we still have people who have an ADC and they have to be very careful about sharing it with others. Why? Because of fear of being ridiculed. That's only the half of it: others who share their experience, feel the stabbing nonverbal responses of rejection—sometimes even from counselors. So they learn not to talk openly about it. We all lose much valuable data when this happens. This data could add to the body of knowledge to help others when mourning, give researchers a better understanding of the grief process, and offer humanity new insights into the world in which we live.

So, where do I think the ADC comes from? In my judgment, it is an experience that occurs as the result of a Loving Intelligence who has forever permitted the interface of physical and nonphysical reality just as this Intelligence has permitted us to use our reasoning abilities unencumbered. ADCs are simply one of a number of little understood phenomena that have always accompanied human development. The Love associated with these events has been referred to as a Supreme Being, the Universe, Allah, God, the Absolute, Infinite Wisdom, and other names. These are all metaphors for what we do not have the ability to properly describe, because we have no vocabulary to give voice to the richness and wisdom behind what happens. To my scientific colleagues this view may appear rather simplistic. Nevertheless, I have no doubt our world is only the tip of the iceberg, that we are here to learn how to practice loving, use our talents in the service of others, and discover how love transforms everything in the most unimaginable ways. Whenever I am asked about origins, I can't help remembering Albert Einstein's insightful remark, which is the opening quote for the first section of this book.

Of equal significance to our discussion is a quote by Sir James Jeans, an English physicist and mathematician: "The universe begins to look more like a great thought than a great machine." I wouldn't take these remarks lightly, for like Einstein, this great scientist has looked at the physical laws of our universe and concluded that there is order and design on a grand scale, far from some chance occurrence, with all due respect to the Big Bang theory. What we in our inadequate vocabularies label as NDEs, ADCs, and OOBEs (out of body experiences), are events that have been occurring in every form imaginable from time immemorial. History, in all countries worldwide, has examples of what many classify as extraordinary phenomena. Yet, if we pause and look at it from a purely historical perspective, it is not extraordinary at all. In fact, it is quite ordinary. Once more, if the Copernican revolution (the cultural shift from religious to scientific authority coupled with the recognition that the earth was not the center of the universe) had not been carried so far to the extreme, so-called extraordinary phenomena would be much more commonly accepted and used as a normal part of life. Perhaps Lois Miller's ADC, in which she saw her mother who had died after a long illness, would be considered nothing other than a beautiful gift, not something unusual to be questioned.

"The Message I Received Was One of Inner Peace"

I awoke one evening to go to the bathroom. When I came back and went to lay down in bed, I flipped my feather pillow and was about to stretch out when I saw my mother. There she was at the foot of my bed with white light all around her. She was facing toward my father's bedroom and she was motioning to him to come with her. My mother loved my father for taking care of her when she was bedridden for seven-and-a-half years. The message I received was one of inner peace—that the end here is a new beginning there.

Two days later while I was cooking dinner, my father came in from working in the garage. He said, "I'm going to take a nap. Wake me when dinner is ready." He sat down in the recliner, put his feet up, and went to sleep. One hour later I was going to wake him but my three-year-old said, "I'll wake grandpa." He came back a few seconds later and said, "Grandpa won't wake up and he's real cold." I rushed in and found my father had died.

The ADC is love in action! The timeless wisdom of the ADC is expressed in giving and receiving love. For the mourner—the sign, symbol, dream, or apparition is saying we are still connected—love is the bridge. The deceased (or whomever) is the giver and is saying, "You are loved." The mourner, as the receiver, has her sense of love and attachment renewed, often when most needed. What is continually overlooked in this transaction is how the ADC encourages the mourner to reach out again to love and end the self-imposed isolation. The expression of love drawn from the ADC by the mourner often manifests in three forms: a needed source of renewed energy, a bridge for transformation from the old to the new, and motivation to take action to adapt.

Furthermore, there appears to be a global double message: we can both make it, although separated; I from where I am, you from where you are. Most mourners may have to be reminded of this subtle message, but once reminded, they embrace it with meaning and joy.

In short, I see the ADC as love coming from Love for the purpose of learning and enjoying life to the fullest. ADCs are self-evident and brimming with truth, once you get past the cultural shield. This, of course, is not part of established wisdom. Perhaps, over time, German philosopher Arthur Schopenhauer's observation will hold true for ADC phenomena: "Every truth," he said, "passes through three stages before it is recognized. In the first, it is ridiculed. In the second, it is opposed. In the third, it is regarded as self-evident." Soon ADCs will become self-evident for their place in the lessons of life we all must learn and they will be recognized as another road to higher consciousness.

32. Is the ADC becoming a topic that is openly discussed?

There are many topics in the paranormal arena that seem to be getting lots of press these days. You turn on the television and most evenings you can find something about the unseen and the mysterious that grabs your attention. Surprisingly, in all of this media blitz I don't see much at all about mourners who have ADCs. What's the problem here? Are we becoming more open as a society to discussing the paranormal in general but not ADCs?

Yes and no. Yes, there is much more coverage than ever before on paranormal phenomena of various types, and considerably more discussion ensues. No, we are not seeing much coverage of ADCs in the lives of the bereaved. While many of the topics on television and radio are presented with the goal of promoting a specific view, too many appear with a heavy commercial overtone. What I am inferring is that most networks dramatize materials in order to get good ratings and in the process tend to be inaccurate in content. Then there are some programs promoting call-ins from viewers for the sole purpose of making money. These ventures result in adding to the abuse of the entire subject of the paranormal as they stoke the fires of memory of many viewers about past fraud and deceit.

With the topic of ADCs there is a slightly different problem. Not only is there an issue about confusing terminology (see question 1) affecting credibility, but although ADCs have been occurring regularly for centuries, as a special research focus the subject is a newborn. Very little has been done in an area teeming with research questions on how, when, and why ADCs occur and with such spectacular timing. I have no doubts whatsoever that the general public and many professional counselors are hardly aware of the breadth and depth of the phenomena. What is worse is the mainstream media, with the exception of the sensationalized shows previously mentioned, will have little to do with ADCs because of the strong taboo against reflective discussions about signs or messages from the dead. On rare occasions, when ADCs are the main focus of a program, many good experiences (from the point of view of the mourner) are not used because a producer decides there is not enough corroboration to make it appear "legitimate." Consider this auditory/olfactory ADC that helped Letha move on with her life.

"I Needed To Move On. I Wanted To Move On."

I was bent over with my head in the refrigerator getting food out for dinner when I smelled something familiar. I inhaled the fragrance for a moment and stood upright as I recognized it as the favorite cologne of my fiancé who had died seven years prior. I whirled around as I heard him speak to me from the corner behind me.

"Umm, so you want to get married again, huh?" I was struck by the fact that everything about the tone of his voice and his distinct personality was exactly as I had known them to be. I was somewhat alarmed by what was happening and also resolute about my own loneliness and desire for companionship. So in a very firm voice I said, "Yes, I do" and ran out of the

room. In my heart I was still bound to him emotionally. I had begun to feel extreme loneliness, however, and spent a great deal of time crying and praying for a companion and friend to come into my life. I think the experience happened in order to release and empower me to move on.

Although the message was explicit, there was history of relationship woven into the experience. Reg had asked me once while he was dying if I would ever get married. Getting married or having a future apart from Reg was something I never thought about, but I told him that perhaps in five or ten years I would. He told me he could never imagine me "marrying some other guy." Smelling the cologne during the ADC brought all the memories associated with Reg flooding back. The words he spoke invoked in me a resolute decision that, yes, I did want to move on now and marry.

As I stated above, I was so struck by how unchanged he was. His personality, voice, and intonation were exactly the same. Reflecting on this caused me to question my religious background and its paradigm that said we are not acceptable to God as we are. Perhaps God, whom I believe had a great deal to do with our creation, really could accept us just as we are, rough edges, imperfections and all without having to change anything about us. I was also intrigued by the fact that Reg knew what was going on in my life. He must have been able to hear my mournful, gut-wrenching sobs and cries to God about my loneliness and my desire for someone to fill the empty place in my life.

Yes, it helped me in my grieving as I was able to see that I had been living my life as if I was still involved with a dead man. I needed to move on. I wanted to move on. I must admit, however, it honestly took me twenty years to totally release Reg to whatever he was doing and wherever he was.

This ADC, and most others where the recipient is alone when the experience occurs, cannot be corroborated and do not make good copy or viewing because there is little concrete evidence to convince audiences. Such an observation reflects both the producer's bias and his fear that potential viewers will not see the show as credible. Then ratings will go down. I see this as a sad situation because there are millions of people who have the ADC experience without corroboration from others. They need the openness of family and friends to be able to talk about their experiences and use them to cope with their losses.

It is particularly disconcerting to see major newspapers and magazines give ADC phenomena little coverage when such notice could give it the legitimate recognition it deserves—and in the bargain help so many of their readers. The one light at the end of the tunnel I occasionally see is the positive coverage that occurs when someone on the staff of the newspaper has had an ADC or knows a family member who has had one. The same is true with radio or television coverage. Otherwise, when you use the words *after-death communication,* the immediate negative response comes through nonverbally, as the phrase is all too often associated with the occult or the use of mediums. Perhaps over time the ADC will reach the status that the near-death experience now enjoys, with fewer detractors and more acceptance of the possibility of the occurrence being normal and a welcome event to experience. As for now, ADC phenomena needs to be given more exposure to the general public so questions can be asked, information obtained, and the process of normalization begun.

33. How do you respond to someone who says, "If a person dies and goes to heaven or hell, how can the person come back and 'visit' the survivor at the same time?"

I have noticed a conflict in the belief that when a person dies he goes to heaven or hell and you say he frequently visits the mourner. How can you reconcile the seemingly opposing viewpoints? Are you saying it is possible for the person, as a spirit, to be in two places at the same time?

Steve Allen once asked me a question like this. Here is how he put it, which I thought at the time was quite unique and yet very practical. He had called to wish the talk show host, Paul Gonzalez, a happy birthday. Then he went on to say: "If I may just drop one question on the table and then I'll get out of the way and Dr. LaGrand can comment on it. My own mind is open on all unresolved questions, which I think is a rational position. But on the other hand, I am frankly skeptical of reports of ghosts and that general sort of phenomena. I don't think they can possibly have any relation to reality. Again, I am skeptical. But the question has nothing to do with that, but more with traditional theology of the Christian sort. We have been told for centuries, though there is great debate on the issue, that when we die there are four possibilities. One is the ever popular heaven, although there is some unclarity as to exactly who is entitled to go right there and who isn't. Another possibility is the world-famous hell, consisting of actual fire—not in the poetic, mythical or loose sense—but very specifically fire. And then there is a third state, called purgatory—where to approach a more rational position, perhaps just about everybody would go at the moment of death—because it's for the special temporary incarceration of those who are good now and then, but not good enough to be rushed into God's presence. And the fourth state was called limbo, and as I recall from my early training, it applied only to those infants who died before baptism. So if we assume all that is reliable, which I am sure hundreds of millions do, then how do we account for people who imagine that they see Uncle Bob eight weeks later in a motel in Cleveland or wherever they may encounter him in their home. The location really doesn't matter; I'll leave that for Dr. LaGrand to explain."

We really are faced here with essentially a theological premise as a basis for asking a very rational question, so I will begin my reply with a theological answer. Most people who believe in a Supreme Being also believe this Being is all-powerful and omnipotent, that He can be anywhere or everywhere, and that He can use things from a natural setting for a spiritual purpose. That is, being the Lord of natural processes, He can use natural things for spiritual purposes. Or, as many people believe, in the midst of coincidence or natural psychological phenomena, there can always be a moment of grace in which illumination occurs. Theologically speaking, an all-powerful God could certainly allow the soul or spirit of the deceased loved one to return to fulfill whatever purposes deemed necessary. (Some people believe a spirit can simply think about a place or a person and be there at that place or with that person.) A God of love would, it appears, help mourners deal with their catastrophic losses in a variety of ways, and an ADC may simply be one of those supportive ways. And why not allow signs and symbols to occur as manifestations of love?

I do not, however, always believe it is the soul or spirit of the deceased who contacts the mourner. It could be any number of angelic beings, as many people report. It is also quite possible that God sends the loved one back as a messenger, just as angels have been His messengers through the ages. In some instances, it is believed the mourner has actually experienced

God. Call it a mystical experience in the classical tradition. Some may also find an explanation in the words of an anonymous writer: "Those who die go no further than God, and God is very near."

Now for the last part of the question. To our human way of thinking, it is impossible to be in two places at the same time. On the other hand, as previously stated, on a spiritual level to think about a place or a person is to be at the place or with the person. Who knows? Perhaps this can occur and is one of the gifts of recognition given to some for reasons only known to a Supreme Being. As irrational as it may seem to our finite minds, it could be a simple truism on the spiritual level. With faith anything is possible. Lest we forget, Judeo-Christian religion is filled with paradox. For example, in Ezekial, in the Old Testament, the Lord talks about taking a shoot or branch from the top of a cedar tree to plant on the mountainside. Such an action, as every horticulturist knows, goes against natural law: you can't stick a branch from a tree in the ground and expect it to grow. The point is: the natural order of things is often reversed by God. What is irrational to our minds is not so in the spiritual realm, as many of the parables in the Bible indicate. Simone Weil, the French mystic, puts it this way: "God only does the impossible. The possible is left for you and I to do." There will forever be a need to value the irrational and subjective aspects of life or risk losing the delicate inner balance that we are wired to maintain.

34. What are some of the other common explanations for ADCs, other than illusions and hallucinations?

Depending on one's belief system, there must be many possible explanations you have heard for why so many people experience ADC phenomena. Having said that the most common explanations you hear are hallucinations and illusions, especially from the scientific community, what other ways are ADCs explained away?

There is much that is exotic and challenging about trying to explain ADC phenomena. When all the possible explanations are studied they seem to fall into three general categories: not real, real, and the fence sitters who say "well, they are real for the mourner, but . . ." I have already written about hallucinations (question 13) and illusions (question 14). Other possible interpretations are believing is seeing (question 23), coincidence (question 17), the unconscious mind (question 28), angelic beings (question 15), demonic forces (question 19), the ADC as a spiritual experience (question 27), and Jung's concept of synchronicity (question 16). Let's examine three other possibilities keeping in mind, with the exception of the spiritual explanation and divine intervention, no single explanation can account for all types of ADC experiences.

1. **Normal Yearning and Searching.** An early psychological rendering of ADC experiences is said to be the result of the yearning and searching phase of the grief process. Many years ago, British psychiatrist John Bowlby introduced a four-phase model of the grief process subsequently adopted by a large number of counselors and medical personnel in their attempts to understand a universal yet complex phenomena. After the initial stage of shock and numbing, he suggested the mourner goes through a very normal phase of searching for the deceased loved one as a function of being unable to accept the death and absence. This search is accompanied by a deep yearning for the return and recovery of the loved one. The mourner is looking everywhere for signs of return and continuance of routine patterns.

   Consequently, sensing the presence of the deceased, dreams, "hearing" familiar sounds associated with the deceased, and occasionally "catching glimpses" of the deceased in crowds, the fulfillment of the hoped for return is carried out. All of this is considered rather normal behavior under the circumstances, but the experiences themselves are not valid or real, only a symptom of grieving that will eventually fade into the background. The following is a typical sensing the presence or intuitive ADC coupled with an olfactory experience that would be considered simply as a manifestation of searching behavior. This was reported to me by a middle-aged woman whose mother died of cancer.

"We Have Both Felt Her with Us"

The day after the funeral, my sister and I were sitting on my mother's bed talking when we suddenly smelled cigarette smoke and felt her presence. Both of us were comforted as we, especially myself, were so deeply close. To this day I still miss her. Since that time we have both "felt" her with us on numerous occasions. Other things that happen frequently, usually when I'm feeling low, is that my angel ornaments will move. They only move one at a time, so it can't be vibration turning them around. This also can't be anyone else touching them as it occurs when I'm alone in the house.

The yearning and searching theory to explain ADC phenomena does not account for third- and fourth-party ADCs, the many signs through nature or symbol, and other indirect means, all bringing comfort to the mourner. Also, let us remember there is no more proof to back this theory than I can muster to convince anyone of the authenticity of the ADC. It is a nice, rational explanation many caregivers and counselors have bought into in order to explain otherwise unexplainable behavior.

2 . **The Communion of Saints.** The ancient Christian doctrine of the communion of saints states that the living and the souls of the deceased are connected through all eternity. Some Anglican communities, and all Roman Catholic and Eastern Orthodox communities, believe a spiritual union exists in which intercessory prayer can take place. Thus the living can pray to their deceased loved ones (who are saints if they are in heaven) to intercede to God for them. Some ADCs, therefore, can be assumed to be a form of assistance from the deceased or from their intercessory powers. Mitch Finley's Whispers of Love: Encounters with Deceased Relatives and Friends, is an account of many ADCs that fit into the doctrine of the communion of saints. Does this theory imply all apparitions and hauntings are a part of the communion of saints? Not at all. As best-selling author and Presbyterian minister, Frederick Buechner, who himself experienced a most dramatic ADC (see *Spiritual Quests: The Art and Craft of Religious Writing* by William Zinsser), says:

Who knows what the communion of saints means, but surely it means more than just that we are all of us haunted by ghosts, because they are not just echoes of voices that have years since ceased to speak, but saints in the sense that through them something of the power and richness of life itself not only touched us once long ago, but continues to touch us.

And is this not similar to the beliefs permeating the New Testament and reflecting the awareness that there is much more to reality than the space/time box that we are taught about in this day and age? The power and richness that Buechner contends still touches us today may well occur through the communion of saints despite the fact that most religious communities are very careful in dealing with the issue of ADCs and are noticeably absent in promoting the essence of the doctrine, with the exception of one annual celebration on November 1, All Saints Day.

3. **Latent Human Nature.** Another approach to explaining ADC phenomena is to declare that the ability to receive impressions and information from another realm is a natural process. Everyone has the latent ability, but it lies dormant because it is not recognized, and therefore not developed. The zenith of this latent ability is found in those who have become highly gifted intuitives (or mediums or psychics, depending on your choice of terms) and claim to be able to receive messages and signs from another dimension. In this regard, there have always been individuals purported to have this ability. They were called seers or oracles. In the Judeo-Christian tradition, they were referred to as prophets and received information directly from God The Holy Spirit. The question remains: Are there a select few who possess the ability to receive information by unconventional means, or is this an inherent part of human nature hardly recognized because of the technological orientation of society?

As an end note, I should mention one explanation researchers do not like to hear more than any other (with the chance exception that the phenomena is drug induced) is the possibility of many ADC experiences being products of conscious fabrication. Everybody, it has been said, likes a good story—as many fishermen know. Perhaps, as the reasoning goes, there are many gullible researchers who fall hook, line, and sinker for a good ADC story.

35. What should you do if you have an ADC experience?

You have written a great deal about ADC experiences, but I would like to have you explain what one should do, if and when, he or she has the experience and wonders how to deal with it. Are there any specific procedures you would recommend in order to utilize the experience and gain the most from it?

The first step to take if you are fortunate to have an ADC is to get paper and pencil and write it down as soon as possible—in detail. It is part of your personal history and it is an event to be cherished. Because you will be able to use your ADC in a variety of ways to help cope with your loss, make every attempt to capture the rich detail of the experience, so as time goes on you can indelibly imprint it on your memory. You may want to place it on audio tape first, if you have one easily accessible, and then later transcribe it. In addition ask yourself a number of questions:

1. How do I interpret what happened? What caused the experience?

2. Was it a spontaneous experience?

3. What message, explicit or symbolic, did I receive?

4. How will I use the experience to cope with my loss?

5. Is this experience something I would expect from my loved one or from God?

After you have written or taped your ADC, decide whom you should share the experience with. Obviously, it should be someone you have the utmost confidence in, who will listen intently and give whatever encouragement and support is necessary. Your choice should be carefully made after reviewing those closest to you and considering their possible responses given your understanding of their beliefs about phenomena that can be controversial or a possible source of fear for them. Their fear could take the form of concern for your mental health or actual fear of the experience itself and that it is originating from a negative source. If, after careful thought, you do not feel you have someone to share the experience with, then consider seeing a counselor.

Let me emphasize that it is important to make a special effort to find someone to share your gift with, even though you risk being labeled sick or crazy. If you look hard enough, you can find someone who will help you by listening with an open heart and who will allow you to express what the experience means. This connection can especially help you normalize what has taken place and decide on authenticity, if you have any doubts. It is a piece of personal history you can use for the rest of your life. If you feel the event was real, but too personal to share with others, please consider how sharing your experience could help others who are dealing with the loss as they try to find meaning in the death of the loved one.

* *See also question 95*

PART

ᐧ 3 ᐧ

Types of Experiences Reported

Questions 36 through 52

Multisensory ADCs • Bird and Animal ADCs •
Auditory ADCs • Third- and Fourth-Party ADCs •
Visual ADCs • Olfactory ADCs • Symbolic ADCs •
Tactile ADCs • Out-of-Body • Dream State ADCs •
Evidential ADCs • Crisis ADCs • Protective ADCs •
Sense of Presence (Intuitive) ADCs • "Negative" ADCs •
Related Questions

The mark of wisdom is to read aright
the present and to march with the occasion.
—Homer

36. Are there any multisensory ADCs reported?

Dr. LaGrand, I am wondering if the ADC experience only involves one sense modality when it occurs, or can it include many of our senses as we use them in our everyday life. I am under the impression that many ADCs are single sense experiences. Am I right or wrong?

I would say there are nearly as many multisensory ADC experiences as there are single sense experiences where one hears a sound associated with the deceased or sees a vision or an apparition. There are also a significant number of ADCs involving a combination of the senses such as hearing and seeing the deceased, or first smelling a particular scent associated with the deceased and then experiencing the sense of touch. So the experience may come in a wide variety of ways and involve any or all of the senses with the exception of the sense of taste. Here are two examples.

A young woman I first met at a local community college had an experience where she was sound asleep, only to be awakened by the familiar touch (tactile ADC) of her mother's hand—in the exact same manner she used to be awakened by her mother as a child. Her mother then proceeded to engage her daughter in conversation (auditory ADC) involving an exchange of questions and answers. At the same time, she was able to see (visual ADC) her mother during the time of this conversation, which lasted for several minutes. Incidentally, when touch is experienced it is a very significant healing event for many; there is no more powerful form of communication. Touch expresses great love—and this should be emphasized to the mourner.

On a recent trip to El Paso, Texas, I spoke with a middle-aged woman whose husband died unexpectedly when they were on a trip. Several months later, as she was about to fall asleep, she was suddenly jolted upright by her husband sitting at the foot of her bed (visual ADC). He told her (auditory ADC) he was all right and gave her some rather startling information with his final comments. He said their daughter was expecting, which the widow knew nothing about and was sure she would have been told if it was in fact true. Furthermore, he told her the baby would be born on the following June 10. The next morning, the daughter came to visit and announced she was not feeling well. Checking with her physician, the daughter discovered she was pregnant and ended up delivering the child on the exact date, June 10. What makes this evidential ADC even more interesting is that neither the husband nor his wife believed in an afterlife. Needless to say, the widow is now a believer. In both of these multisensory experiences, the mourners were able to relate to the deceased in a manner similar to when they were alive.

Multisensory experiences also occur when mourners are visited in their dreams by a deceased loved one. Again, one may feel the hug or kiss, smell an odor associated with the deceased, or hear and see him. Following is a dream in which Maria was visited by her deceased aunt and one of her cousins who, along with another cousin, had been killed by a drunk driver as they waited on the divider to cross the street to get to their car.

"She Just Hugged Me and I Felt Safe"

I was back in my uncle John's old house (after the accident he sold the house). I was alone and suddenly felt a presence. So I went upstairs and went into my aunt and uncle's room. I heard someone calling my name, turned around, and in floats my aunt Cathy. She looked vibrant and pretty but, most importantly, peaceful. She reached out for me, but I was extremely scared and backed away. I told her what I had told her before in other dreams, to leave me alone. She told me not to be afraid of her and that she watches over me and will always love me. Then she said Malissa (one of my cousins who had died) wanted to see me.

I walked into the hallway and saw Malissa, and for some reason I wasn't scared of her. I just cried and told her I loved her. She then hugged me and I felt safe. After the hug she said she had a place to show me. Before I knew it, I started floating up with her. At first, I was scared, but when I got there I felt comfortable. It was the most beautiful sight I have ever seen. There were big puffy clouds below my feet and there were birds everywhere. The entire sky was a rainbow: that was the most amazing part of the place. The sky was every color you could think of. I didn't want to look away. At that moment I felt like I had no problems or worries. I then asked her why she took me here. She said she wanted me to see where they stay and that they were in no harm and were very happy. Suddenly, I started to descend and I got upset and didn't want to leave. She told me I had to. She said I'd be here one day, she just wanted me to see it. I kept begging her to stay and she said it wasn't my time yet. Then it got black and I woke up very dazed and I couldn't speak. I just went to the breakfast table with the family and told them my dream.

In this dream we see Maria has experienced the sense of touch as well as having heard and seen both her deceased aunt and cousin. The vast majority of ADC dreams are multisensory in nature.

37. Can you give an example of how a bird or an animal can play a role in an ADC?

I have heard some people say they have received a sign that they are convinced came from their deceased loved one through a bird or an animal. They are not saying they heard the deceased speak through the bird or animal, yet some of their interpretations really would stretch your imagination for credibility. What are some of the more meaningful signs that people receive and believe are somehow associated with their beloved?

Keep in mind, any person who experiences phenomena that he thinks is a sign from the deceased, whether a bird, animal, or whatever, is in a much better position to make a judgment regarding authenticity, regardless of the fact that he is mourning. I make that statement because so many signs are highly individualized and have personal meaning only to the individual who receives it. Often the sign would be most meaningful only to the mourner and the deceased when alive. There are also some situations more easily accepted by friends and family as well as the bereaved, but not by outsiders.

One of the most dramatic examples of an ADC involving a bird happened to the award-winning author David Morrell, who introduced the character Rambo to the general public in his book *First Blood*. The real life event, however, concerned the death of his seventeen-year-old son Matthew who was battling cancer, but died of septic shock. Morrell and a dozen other mourners were in the mausoleum at the cemetery where Matthew's ashes were to be interred. The door to the mausoleum was open and in flew a mourning dove. At first, in startled fashion, it flitted and zoomed among the ceiling rafters and then suddenly came down and gently landed right next to the podium, where the urn containing the ashes lay. Morrell quietly rose from his seat, went to the podium, and picked up the dove. He walked to the entrance of the mausoleum to release it. He opened his hands—but the bird would not budge. It stood perched and looking him in the eye—for nearly fifteen seconds. Then, as suddenly as it had entered, it flew off.

As you may well imagine, the mourning dove is a flighty bird not prone to allowing a person to pick it up, and especially not willing to stay in the palms of the hands. Was there a message in this unexpected experience? Certainly, one could say many things about the meaning of this ADC, but for the twelve who witnessed the scene, especially a distraught father, the message was clear—Matthew was at peace and was whole again. Later, one of Morrell's friends remarked, "It's getting harder to be an agnostic." This was one of three ADCs that Morrell experienced after the death of his son, about which he writes beautifully in his book *Fireflies.* If you have suffered the death of a child, this is a book you should read.

Ed Jones had the following experience when he was unable to find his mother's grave after going to the cemetery to make a visit.

"My Mother Did Communicate to Me"

For about twenty minutes, I could not find my mother's grave site. The name on the stone was blocked by some plastic flowers that someone had placed there. I silently asked my mom to guide me to the grave site, when I had been actually standing about ten feet away from it. Suddenly a bird flew on to the stone or next to it showing me the grave I couldn't find.

My immediate reaction was to thank my mother for hearing me and communicating to me. My mother did communicate to me through her spirit. I can't explain exactly how. Was it her spirit at the grave site? Or was she able to communicate to the bird? The explanation doesn't matter to me. What happened helped me in my grief. I felt my mom's connection and was in awe of the experience. Talking to loved ones about it helped me grieve.

Interestingly, Ed also sensed the presence of his mother (an intuitive ADC) in addition to his experience with the bird. These two aspects of the experience and his willingness to share what happened with others was important in the course of his grief work.

Another ADC, this one involving a dog, was brought to my attention by Richard Morsilli, whose thirteen-year-old son was killed by a drunk driver. Subsequently, he and his wife experienced an ADC that was written up in *Reader's Digest* and, having been read by millions of people, brought a deluge of telephone calls and letters. It was one of those contacts that left an indelible mark on his memory as it also involved a young boy who died at a very early age. In this account, the youngster loved collies, but was unable to have one due to restrictions in the apartment complex where he lived. However, after his death, at the graveside committal service, there appeared the most beautiful collie you could imagine. No one knew who owned it and it left as mysteriously as it had appeared. The impact on the family, of course, was a positive one.

Kevin and Teresa received what they knew was a convincing sign from their deceased sons.

"Kevin Said He Knew it Was His Birthday Present from the Boys"

It was May 29, 1997, my husband Kevin's birthday. I had the front door open as usual. Kevin and I were just sitting and talking. Any birthday or important event is always hard after you lose your children. Getting through the day was difficult.

My husband has always had a fascination with hummingbirds. He said he wished he could see one up close. They never stop long enough to really see them; yet the hummingbird is a messenger.

All of a sudden this beautiful hummingbird flew right through the front door. I started to flip out: how are we going to get this bird out of the house? My husband went into the living room and put his hand up to the bird. I said, "Yeah, right Kevin, hummingbirds are afraid of everything. They fly away whenever you get near them." In less than thirty seconds that bird was on my husband's finger, just sitting there perfectly content. He walked around with it for awhile and then let it go out the door. I even took a picture of it sitting on his finger.

*We stood there for awhile in shock, not believing what had just hap-
pened. Chills were running through us, yet we had a wonderful feeling, one
you just can't explain. Kevin said he knew it was his birthday present from
the boys. We will never forget it and we will always treasure the memory.*

For additional examples of ADCs involving birds and animals see chapter 7 in my book *After Death Communication*.

38. What types of auditory experiences are commonly reported?

*There is often a question about the authenticity of auditory experiences due
to the prevailing belief in the scientific community that auditory ADCs are
always hallucinations. Could you describe the characteristics of the auditory
ADC and the circumstances under which it occurs?*

Auditory ADCs are rather common and occur in a variety of circumstances, including those experienced by more than one person. The voice
location varies. Some people describe the voice as coming from outside, as
in talking directly to another person. This is referred to by some authorities as an auricular locution. Others report they heard a voice within, an
imaginative locution. Not infrequently, a message such as "I'm okay" or
"Everything is all right" is heard. Still others experience receiving a message and believe it is telepathic, not accompanied by a voice, or are unsure
of its origin (an intellectual locution). By far the most common is the
voice sounding as if a normal conversation is about to take place as illus-
trated in the following auditory ADC, which occurred to thirteen-year-old
Anthony just before Christmas. His grandfather had died on December 5.

"I'm Not Afraid to Die Anymore"

*We received a package in the mail from my mother's niece. I opened it up
and took out three wrapped gifts; one each for me, my sister, and my
brother. There were small pieces of Styrofoam shipping material inside and
it was filled pretty high. After we opened the gifts, my mother instructed me
to throw the box outside at the curb. Just as I picked it up and walked out of
the room to discard it I heard my grandpa (Pop Pop) tell me as clear as*

day, "Look under the flap, Dumbo, look under the flap." My Pop Pop
always called me Dumbo when I was about to make a silly mistake. It was
our private little joke. I was a little frightened and ran to my mother with
the box. We pulled up the flaps and there was an envelope with a card in it
containing $300. Each of us kids was to be given $100.

This experience showed me that my Pop had not gone away leaving me
without a grandpa, but that he was still very much beside me looking out
for me and still helping me avoid mistakes. He still loved me. It made me
feel much better because I knew that my Pop was happy where he was
because he could still joke with me. It makes me less sad to know he's okay
and still visiting me and my family. My mom also has had visits from him.
I am not so afraid to die anymore because I know now only our bodies die.
Pop proved that to me.

Although Anthony heard his grandfather just once as he was disposing
of the box, Barbara R. was driving home from her sister's house when she
repeatedly heard her brother-in-law, sensed his presence, and then briefly
saw him.

"I Know He Was with Me"

Shortly after George's death, I was driving home from Nancy's on I-95 cry-
ing, with a thousand thoughts running through my head all at once, think-
ing about George and his last hours. I can't tell you all the things I was
thinking, because my mind was racing so fast. But all of a sudden, I could
hear George saying to me, "But Bobbi, I'm fine, I'm okay." And with each
of my thoughts countering what he was saying, George kept telling me he
was fine. I could also feel him sitting in the front seat of the car. I looked
over at him and it was George, sitting the way George sat with his head
kind of forward, so that you wanted to take your index finger and poke him
in the back of the neck to get his head up straight.

I can't tell you exactly what he had on, other than a flannel shirt and
dark jeans, and when I reached over to take his hand, he disappeared—as
if I was reaching into another dimension. But I know he was with me. For
awhile I didn't tell anyone about this because I was afraid it would be

attributed to the couple glasses of wine I had had at Nancy's. But perhaps the wine made me more receptive to George coming to me, because their weren't any "barriers." I don't know. But I know he was with me for that brief time, telling me he was okay.

In both of these accounts the recipients received a clear message. They did not believe the events were auditory hallucinations and, of course, in Anthony's experience, he has the money to prove it.

Sometimes auditory contacts are heard by more than one person. Parapsychologists refer to this as collectivity. Similarly, a domestic animal together with a mourner may hear an auditory contact and react accordingly. These events may occur in virtually any setting, either in the familiar confines of the home or outside in a natural environment. How the mourner(s) interprets the experience often results in his being reassured the loved one is near and concerned for his welfare.

- *See also question 49 (read the second ADC)*

39. What are third- and fourth-party ADCs?

The terms third- and fourth-party ADCs are new to the literature on extraordinary phenomena. What do they imply, and can you give me some examples of these kinds of ADCs?

There are several indirect ways in which mourners may receive a contact or sign indicating a deceased loved one is all right. Once experienced, the indirect ADC can be used to help them accept the death and go on with life. Two of these indirect contacts involve other people who often are not primary mourners (intimately and directly connected with the deceased). That is, they are individuals who may or may not know the deceased or may or may not be deeply emotionally invested in the person who died. So the message comes through a third person, hence the designation "third party." Or the message may come through two other people, one a gifted intuitive, before it reaches the mourner, hence the designation "fourth party."

Sometimes the ADC seems destined only for the third party, yet it helps the primary mourner. Here is an example: A third-party ADC recently brought to my attention occurred to Meg, the primary mourner, who lives in the northeastern part of the country. Her husband died very suddenly when he was only forty-eight years old. Of course, at the time of his death she was totally shocked, for even though her husband had been battling his disease for seventeen years he was not expected to die. His death was the most painful event she had ever experienced, even considering the loss of her father when she was only ten years old. The third person in this instance was her sister. As Meg tells it:

"He Thanked Her for Helping His Family"

The week after his death, my sister left my house and was thinking, "Why did this have to happen to you (meaning me)?" when she saw him sitting next to her in the car. He talked to her, which she heard in the center of her chest (her heart—her spiritual center). He said he was okay and he thanked her for helping his family. She saw him again, less intently, in her car during a snowstorm when she was frightened about the drive. He was saying that she'd be fine.

In this instance, even though the contact was apparently meant for her sister, Meg was encouraged by what had transpired. On some occasions the third-party recipient may only hear the voice of the deceased give encouragement or ask the person to deliver a message to the primary mourner. Or the contact may come through a dream.

Some time ago I was on a radio show when a woman called in from Louisiana with a third-party dream ADC. She had been invited to visit a friend whose fifteen-year-old daughter had died from a crippling disease some months before. She accepted the invitation and was asked if she had any reservations about sleeping in the daughter's room. She did not and turned in at a normal hour. During the night she had a dream in which her friend's daughter came to her and asked her to tell her mother, "Please stop grieving for me." Upon awakening, she was faced with the dilemma of whether she should tell her host about the dream. She decided it was best to tell her and she called in to the show to ask whether she had done the right thing. I agreed that as difficult as it must have been, she had made the right choice. Sharing these kinds of experiences in a gentle loving way allows the mourner to obtain information that can assist in taking action to change the course of one's grief work.

One of the most unusual, and what I believe to be among the rarest of ADCs, is what I have come to label the fourth-party experience. I first learned of this occurrence when I was attending a conference on complicated mourning for clinicians in Rhode Island. During one of the breaks a counselor came up to me and said she thought I would be interested in the following account from her practice.

This clinician worked with people who had ALS, or what is sometimes referred to as Lou Gehrig's disease. She had been helping one young man who was in his forties when he died, leaving his wife and older daughter. Many months after the death of her client, she decided to have a birthday party and invited old friends and neighbors. One of the invitees to the party was a friend who was a highly gifted intuitive whom she had not seen for eight months. This friend knew nothing about her client (whom we shall call Mr. M) who had died.

Upon her arrival, she asked the host if they could go somewhere in the house away from the other guests because—to use her exact words— "Someone is knocking on my head." In short, she was getting a message she had not been expecting. As she began to talk, the host grabbed a pencil and some paper and began to write down what her friend Claudia was receiving. Within a few minutes she realized her gifted friend was talking about Mr. M, who had died several months previously. She ended up with two pages of notes.

The next day she was faced with the decision of what to do with the information she had in her hands. "Can you imagine me calling the family and saying I have some information from your deceased loved one? I was perplexed," she said. She held on to the information for two weeks. Finally, she decided she had to call Mr. M's daughter, Ann, and ask if she would like to get together for lunch. Somehow she knew she had to tell Ann what had happened the night of her birthday party.

The eventful day arrived and she tactfully broke the news of what she thought could have been an ADC from the young woman's father. Lo and behold, the daughter was overwhelmed and believed it was an authentic contact from her father because of one piece of information: her father, through the gifted intuitive, said he approved of the man her daughter was going to marry—but Ann had told no one of their wedding plans. She immediately asked the counselor to set up a meeting with the intuitive and proceeded to share all of the information with her mother. They both believed Mr. M had sent information through a fourth-party. The information had come spontaneously in a roundabout way from the father, through the intuitive, to the counselor, who finally relayed it to the family. Remember, the intuitive was not seeking to make contact with Mr. M., nor had she known anything about his death or the fact he had been a patient of her counselor friend.

End of story? No. I couldn't let it rest there. Although the experience took place some three hundred miles from where I lived, it just so happened I was to give a speech in a nearby city two months later. So I called the counselor and asked if she would set up interview appointments for me with her gifted friend and the mother and daughter. I left a day early and interviewed all three on the same day. But the mother and daughter did not know I was interviewing the intuitive, nor did the intuitive know I was interviewing the mother and daughter. Both interviews went exceedingly well and all parties willingly cooperated, thanks to the counselor who graciously assisted.

On my drive home two days later I had lots of time to consider the results of my investigation. To begin with, let me emphasize that I have always suspected some sort of misrepresentation from those who claim to have the ability to communicate with those who have died. However, in this instance I was convinced Claudia was sincere and her abilities genuine. Furthermore, it was abundantly clear that both mother and daughter were convinced of the authenticity of the contact. Most importantly, Ann was relieved of a great deal of guilt she had been carrying since her father's death. In fact, during the interview she told me, "I was able to talk to my father tonight on the way over here." This was in reference to a very normal practice many survivors engage in, talking to the deceased loved one, even though it is a monologue. This is not abnormal and is often an excellent way to reduce anxiety and stress while expressing feelings and emotions. It is encouraged by many counselors. For Ann it was a big step forward. Again, this fourth-party ADC occurred spontaneously and it came from the outside in, the two chief defining characteristics of after-death communication.

40. Isn't it commonly believed by professional caregivers and counselors that hearing voices is a bad omen?

For years I have been under the impression that if someone hears voices they are automatically a candidate for the psychiatrist's couch. At least that's what I remember hearing when I was around adults as a child. To hear voices when nobody was around was a sign of mental disorder. How does this view square with professionals today and with the authenticity of the auditory ADC?

Certainly any professional counselor is going to explore all of the possibilities for people who say they are hearing voices. It has always been and I suspect will always be a symptom that can have serious implications for a mourner. As I indicated in question 13, audio hallucinations are commonly associated with schizophrenia. Not only is hearing voices a bad omen among many caregivers and counselors, but the general public has been enculturated to believe the same. In fact hearing voices is often thought to be a sign of instability, even though throughout history people have heard voices when no one was present in the flesh, which resulted in good things happening.

Socrates is said to have stood for hours, apparently in an altered state of consciousness, and regularly conversed with a voice he believed came from a Deity. He even gave it a name: it was his *diamon*. At the time, this word was used interchangeably with God or Theos. Joan of Arc, French saint and national heroine, was burned at the stake in part for her insistence that she conversed with voices. It all began at a young age when she believed she heard the voices of St. Michael, St. Catherine, and St. Margaret. At age sixteen, her voices told her to give assistance to the dauphin (French title of the eldest son of the king). This all led to victory in battle and her eventual death for heresy for her refusal to accept the church hierarchy.

Even Carl Jung, Swiss psychiatrist and founder of analytical psychology, reported how he conversed with a figure he called Philemon when he was in special need. I am reminded here of a statement he made in *Memories, Dreams, Reflections* in which he said that in his psyche there are some things "I do not produce but that produce themselves and have their own life." And of course many voices have been heard by religious figures over the ages. St. Francis of Assisi heard a voice that told him to rebuild St.

Damian's chapel while Jacob, Moses, and the Virgin Mary all heard voices from heaven. And there are many poets who have reported hearing voices from the Muse!

The point has to be emphasized: voices heard are often meaningful and do help the person who hears them. There are a number of ADCs in which a person hears a voice that provides guidance and protection. This occurred to Priscilla in a northern state when she was driving her car on an icy road and went into a skid. She heard her deceased husband's voice say, "Turn the wheel to the right." She reacted immediately and pulled out of the skid. Such protective ADCs are part of the historical record of hearing voices. While hearing voices is thought to be a sign of the need for professional assistance in this day and age—and it peaks the interest of professional counselors when it is reported by a client—like so much other human behavior it has to be carefully examined for alternative meanings and for the context in which it occurs. If you are providing support for someone who reports hearing the deceased, seek additional information and find out how the mourner interprets the experience before making any type of judgment. The experience may or may not be useful in coping with the loss.

With auditory experiences there is always the possibility of misinterpreting a voice for one's hopes and wishes. Regardless of where the voice comes from, the test is *does the message have personal meaning? And if so, what do I need to bring into my circle of awareness, examine carefully, and take action on if needed?* These are questions a caring support person can assist the mourner in analyzing and using when appropriate.

To conclude, let me suggest that we have to use common sense in making decisions regarding hearing voices or deciding on the validity of other spontaneous contacts. Common sense is every bit as credible as science in obtaining knowledge upon which to base sound judgment; it is an integral part of everyday living. (I emphasize this point well aware that science tells us, according to experimental evidence, everyday judgment cannot be completely trusted. Once more, we are generally poor observers of our natural environment, and underestimate probabilities.) Nevertheless, if you were walking down a street in an exclusive section of Southampton that included mansions with high shrubs and walls, and heard someone on the other side, whose voice you recognize, call out your name, would you immediately dismiss it and say, "I was just hearing things." No, you would check it out. And that's exactly what we have to do anytime we are helping someone who is grieving and has a similar experience, or if we have the experience. Let's not jump to conclusions, based on early childhood influences, that voices are surely trouble for the person who hears them and we should dismiss them as meaningless or as sure signs of mental illness.

41. What is the most common ADC reported?

Of the millions of ADCs that have been reported, is there any indication some ADCs are more common than others? If there are ADCs that occur more frequently than others, what do you think can explain the difference?

Because the systematic collection of data on ADC phenomena is in its infancy, one can only provide an educated guess on what is the most commonly reported ADC. What is currently reported to researchers may actually be different than what occurs in the lives of many mourners because there is much data out there that goes unreported due to fear of the consequences. With that in mind, let me speculate as to the most common ADCs based on my research. It is my belief that the sense of presence or intuitive ADC, symbolic ADCs, and the dream state ADC are probably the most common types of ADCs experienced.

Patricia Garfield, author of *The Dream Messenger,* has spent her life working with dreams and their implications. After studying nearly fourteen hundred dreams of the dead for her latest book, she is convinced that there is a vast volume of dreams about the dead that take place in a pattern that she has dubbed the "universal dream about the dead." The pattern includes nine major symbols she has uncovered in dreams about the dead. If you are interested in dreams of the dead as one of the most common ADCs, Garfield's book is must reading. Obviously, all dreams about the dead are not visitation or ADC dreams with dramatic messages. This is not to imply that many symbolic dreams about the dead cannot be helpful in coping with the death of a loved one. Many, many more dreams than we realize—both symbolic and those which can be literally interpreted—do occur and bring peace and strength to continue on.

There are also numerous symbolic ADCs that include natural phenomena like flowers, rainbows, and butterflies. Here is a beautiful account from Irene. The experience took place shortly after the death of her close friend and brought a special appreciation.

"Every Time I See Sunflowers I Think of Her"

I had a very interesting experience. A very dear friend of mine passed away. She was very fond of sunflowers. Some time before, when she visited me, she always brought me sunflowers. And when she was very ill, I brought her sunflowers. A few months after she passed away, there was a weed in my flower bed (I thought it was a weed anyway), and I was going to pull it up. But I was too lazy to walk over and pull it out. About a week later it turned out to be a sunflower. And I said to my husband, "I know that's Betty. She's coming to say hello and all is well."

I've been in my house for forty years. I have never planted sunflowers. It never came back again. It came that one time and I know it was her. I've had a brother that passed away. Of course, my parents are gone, and many other people, and I've never had anything like that. But this was such a wonderful, wonderful feeling and every time I see sunflowers I think of her.

The symbolism of the sunflower in this experience was not only comforting to Irene, it was also the basis for establishing a new and healthy relationship with her friend. It is just such sustaining experiences that make most ADCs sources for renewal as they provide a sense of connection even though there is physical separation. Relationships are eternal and can be maintained through dreams and memories associated with ADC phenomena.

In trying to determine why some ADCs occur more frequently than others, one can only speculate given the nature of the phenomena. It is possible that the dream state may be most conducive to receiving messages; it has a long and colorful history of doing just that sort of thing (as well as posing questions and highlighting issues). The intuitive sense of presence may be a common ADC because of the heightened intuitive ability of some people and it is an easy route of access to the mourner by the loved one. Symbolic ADCs may be the most natural and meaningful way to impress some mourners (perhaps because of their creativity) and fill them with insight and meaning.

42. What are the most hard-to-believe ADCs you have come across?

There are skeptics and then there are still more skeptics who believe in nothing of a nonphysical nature. I have a feeling that most believers in nonphysical reality and the unseen must, at times, have their doubts about some aspects of ADC phenomena. How about you? Are there some things you have come upon that make you think twice about authenticity?

Oh, yes. Over the years I have heard lots of accounts of experiences, some of which were very moving and inspiring, and others that caused me to say to myself, "You've got to be kidding." At the top of my list are experiences that involve lights blinking on and off. The usual interpretation of this event is that it is a sign from the deceased loved one. Now, when lights blink on and off and then the mourner senses the presence of the deceased loved one, that is a different story. I am more easily convinced that it is part of the entire ADC experience with which the mourner has been blessed. Lights blinking without additional phenomena causes me to especially question the source and the person, although many believe the spirit of the deceased can affect electrical energy.

I am also much more open to situations in which lights come on for no apparent reason and stay on until someone in the house turns them off. I recall this happening to a middle-aged woman whose husband had died. On two occasions she awoke to find the light on under his picture in the hallway—and she lived alone and had turned off all lights before retiring for the night. The first time it happened, she called her son at 2 A.M. and asked him to come over because she thought someone might have broken into her home. He checked out the house and then thoroughly checked the electrical system. All was in perfect order and there was no indication of any type of a power outage or surge during the night. The next time the light came on under her husband's picture, she believed it to be a sign from him. It may well have been.

When lights blink on or off on one occasion and someone says it was a sign I usually cannot agree—unless there are other predisposing factors to consider. Here is an example from Edna Foster who lives on Long Island and whose husband had died several months previously.

"It Was His Way of Reassuring Me"

I was reciting the rosary (Catholic prayers to the Virgin Mary) just before leaving for work one morning. I was reciting the Sorrowful Mysteries. As I read "Ask Him to be with you at the hour of your death," I said, "God please be with me and let my husband be there to help me make my transition. Let him be there waiting for me." As I said this, the lights in the kitchen (which were on) went off and on a couple of times and finally stayed on. This startled me and I looked up and said, "Hon, is that you? Are you letting me know that you're here with me? Thank you." I decided to check the microwave because had it been a power surge the light on the microwave would have gone off. It hadn't; it read 7:53 A.M.

I interpret this experience as my husband communicating with me. It was his way of reassuring me that he would be there waiting for me. I believe I was and am very receptive to any means of communication. I truly believe that since I was very calm saying the rosary, he saw this as an opportunity to communicate with me in a way I would understand. The message I received was also one of divine intervention. Without God's permission my husband would not have been able to communicate with me as he did. He allowed my husband to let me know that he will be there waiting for me.

This experience certainly helped me with my grief. It allows me to continue believing that someday my husband and I will be together again. We were inseparable and we always believed we were soul mates. Knowing that I'll see him again makes life a little easier for me now.

When someone experiences the off-and-on light phenomena, preceded by a request, as Edna had, it is more logical for me to assume that indeed a message was delivered. Of course, I know some of my colleagues would quickly step forward to explain the lights blinking at the moment Edna asked her question as merely coincidental timing. But who really can tell? Perhaps only Edna knows.

43. Have there been any ADCs that have saved a person from a dangerous situation?

Much has been said about ADC experiences that provide support and reassurance to mourners as a rather common occurrence. Have there been any recorded instances where a mourner has been saved from physical harm or kept from doing physical harm to others or themselves?

I have heard of a number of protective ADCs that were literally life savers or prevented added emotional or physical distress for the mourner. There have been some protective ADCs reported involving the prevention of automobile accidents. In these situations, survivors usually hear a voice directing them to take a particular turn to avoid a disaster that has occurred (a bridge was washed out), a chain-reaction collision that is taking place around the bend in the road, or to avoid a one-car accident as discussed in question 40. I also recall a young woman who said when she has been in situations where she feared for her safety, she commonly sensed the presence of her deceased father, which helped her deal with her fear. In one instance, she was convinced her father's presence was the reason a potential mugger who approached her in a secluded area did not take action.

It is noteworthy that Bill and Judy Guggenheim, in *Hello From Heaven*, have a chapter titled, "Saving Grace: ADCs for Suicide Intervention." Several accounts are provided showing intervention when survivors were considering taking their own lives. An impressive account in this chapter concerns a thirteen-year-old girl who became deeply depressed and was contemplating suicide some three years after the death of her beloved grandmother. She cried out in her pain for her grandmother to help her when suddenly, there at the foot of her bed, she appeared. She reassured the young girl that all would be well, told her to say a prayer, and sent her love. The impact on the thirteen-year-old and her self-concept was strong and immediate. Her suicide thoughts abated. In another account, thirteen years after the death of her father, a thirty-four-year-old bookkeeper decided to end her life only to be confronted by her father who convinced her to change the way she was thinking and move on with her life. I suspect there are many more instances like the above that go unreported for obvious reasons.

44. When talking about ADCs involving birds and animals, are there any indications we, they, and the universe are all somehow connected?

With so many ADCs occurring that involve natural phenomena as well as birds and animals it seems to follow that we should look for a link of some type between all living things. I know there are no scientific proofs for ADCs involving birds, animals, and nature. But are there any theories on the possibility we are all connected in ways yet to be proven?

What you mean by "connected" is our first issue. There is absolutely no doubt we are all connected on an ecological level, including everything in nature. All you have to do is look around at how humanity has affected the environment and the connection is obvious, from the ozone layer to our drinking water. Whether you live in a rural area or a big city, good quality drinking water is hard to find even though most communities have water systems monitored by professionals. Yet, according to the Centers for Disease Control, hundreds of thousands of people become sick each year because of contaminated water improperly or insufficiently treated, or polluted by industry. And that's only the beginning of the environmental story. Back in the 1940s, the bald eagle was disappearing as a species because it was eating contaminated fish from streams that were once pristine.

If you are talking about something other than an ecological connection, as important as it is, then, as you can guess, we are into a more controversial subject. To begin with, we have to deal with the pervasive cultural belief in separateness backed up by the dominating specter of science that is rooted deeply in the same belief. All this despite the fact that connectedness and order are continually being uncovered by members of the scientific community. Jung's idea of synchronicity is based on a belief that there is a meaningful connection between humanity and the universe, just as he believed that we and all who have gone before us are joined in the collective unconscious. It can reasonably be argued that synchronicity is a link between the physical world and the unseen world of the mind and soul. Of course, there are millions of people who believe we are all spiritually connected. The ancient belief system of Shamanism has long held that the universe is interconnected. Spirituality, by its very nature, is about the unity of all things, and most ADC experiencers are convinced the ADC is a spiritual experience.

Quantum physics suggests a unity beyond our wildest dreams. At the subatomic level the connections are obvious, but stubbornly unexplainable. For instance, there is experimental evidence to show that everything in the world in which we live is essentially connected. It is known as Bell's Theorem and supports the concept of nonlocality. That is, all events and objects respond to each other's changes of state. It implies that information that exists in one place can exist everywhere at the same time. More specifically, if two particles have been closely associated with each other and are then separated—regardless of the distance—what affects one instantaneously affects the other. And this transfer of information occurs faster than the speed of light, which is impossible, according to Einstein's theories. How can the information be conveyed instantly from one particle to another ten light-years away? It all seems irrational to our current way of thinking about reality. But the mathematically proven theorem on which it rests puts a lasting dent in the idea that a specific phenomena can only be explained in terms of the immediate space/time framework in which it exists.

What other explanation can be given for how two objects not connected, yet separated by space, can still intimately affect each other's actions? There is none. Perhaps this is why British astronomer and physicist, Sir Arthur Eddington, said, "When the electron vibrates, the universe shakes." So, in terms of nonlocality, we are all very intimately, even mysteriously, connected. Many individuals, including some physicists, believe the principle of nonlocality applies to everything in the universe. Physicist David Bohm's holographic theory of the universe suggests it is one gigantic hologram in which everything in the universe contains a copy of the whole. The world and everything in it is intricately connected in a limitless expanse of energy; everything is an extension of everything else. Most interesting of all is his suggestion that the fundamental and primary reality, what he calls the implicate order, is invisible. Certainly, it can be argued that psi phenomena, especially telepathy, is another demonstration that we are connected to each other in ways not fully explainable. You might want to explore the phenomena of remote viewing, the ability to describe structures and experience activities at distant places. It is considered by some researchers as strong proof of mind-to-mind and mind-to-universe connectedness. It is my contention that if we were not trained in the opposite assumption—of being separate individual islands of matter and energy—we would be aware of experiencing much more undivided wholeness.

Many years ago Fyodor Dostoyevsky wrote, "My brother used to ask the birds to forgive him; that sounds senseless but it is right; for all is like the ocean, all things flow and touch each other; a disturbance in this place is felt at the other end of the world." Perhaps we all need to contemplate the wisdom of his message. The unity of matter and spirit, body and soul has always existed. Hopefully, we are beginning to rediscover this profound truth, for there is virtually no evidence to support the dominant fragmented scientific worldview. On the other hand, history has repeatedly demonstrated we are intimately mind-to-mind connected through intuition, ESP, love, healing, prayer, and the collective unconscious. Lest we forget, it is good to periodically recall how connection, continuity, and a sense of belonging bring meaning into the lives of all of us, especially mourners. The ADC is capable of creating conditions for meaning-making, although its potential has yet to be recognized.

- *See also question 20*

45. What is an evidential ADC?

Having become interested in ADC phenomena, I occasionally am surprised at the wide range of experiences that take place. In particular, I am wondering about evidential ADCs and in what manner they take place. What does the word evidential *mean, and in what ways does this type of ADC occur?*

Evidential ADCs are among the most convincing of all ADC phenomena because they result in the survivors receiving information previously unknown to them. The word *evidential* is defined as "of or having the nature of, serving as, or based on evidence." It is used in describing ADCs that give information used in locating lost articles, deciding on new approaches to take in dealing with current problems, or providing actual evidence to assist in solving crimes. Christine Baumgardt received information through an evidential ADC after her husband was murdered in a robbery.

"They Help Me Get Through the Day"

I had this experience about three weeks after his murder. I started to dream about Jay. I saw him as vivid as life. He seemed happy and very healthy and peaceful. He never would come close to me, and this was one thing I didn't understand. I asked him questions in my dreams and he gave me answers. I asked him why I could not hold him or kiss him and his reply was that it was too soon and that I would have to be patient.

He would tell me he knew how frustrated we were that the case was not solved. He told me things about the crime scene. He told me things about the criminals and things that I had to do to help get the people responsible for his death. I was told who the killer was and who set up the robbery. I was given names as to the accomplices. The police thought they had an inside leak and wanted to know who was giving me this information. I then told them and since then, whenever I have a "visit" from Jay, any information I receive, I call the police and they act on it.

Our case is still unsolved, but not for lack of who or why, but because of lack of physical evidence. Yes, some may say it's all in my mind, the grieving widow who wants to believe her husband talks to her. Well, I now do believe that Jay is around us and I now get those hugs and kisses when we meet in my dreams. It may be my mind, and it may be hard to believe, but things that I have received from Jay's visits can never be explained to me, or anyone else as to where or from whom I have received this information. Only the people there and those who knew of the crime would have the details. Jay's visits help me to survive. They help me to get through the day one day at a time and sometimes one minute at a time.

Regrettably, as of this writing, the information received has not resulted in the hoped for ending. Christine's visits from her husband have provided much information and comfort, but have not led to the apprehension of her husband's killer because there is not enough physical evidence to corroborate the information that the authorities have and to stand up in a court of law. Nevertheless, these evidential ADCs have given her hope justice will prevail and have helped her deal with the tragic aftermath of her ordeal. Much anger is associated with this type of loss. Most important in coping with her loss is the belief her husband is not totally absent, he is still concerned and caring, something which adds immensely to her ability to deal with this senseless killing.

There are many dreams bringing the mourner information like Christine received. One of the most famous evidential dream ADCs involved the completion of Dante's *Divine Comedy*. After Dante's death, the final section of the manuscript could not be found until his son had the eventful dream in which he was told to look in a secret hiding place. Upon awakening, he removed the stone to the tiny chamber and there was the missing piece to the puzzle.

Evidential ADCs also take place in auditory and visual forms as well as through a third person who then relays the information to the primary mourner. I once had an opportunity to speak with a well-known radio announcer who had the following auditory ADC that resulted in a very happy ending.

"Look in the Inside Pocket"

My father passed away and my mother could not locate some valuables at their home. It was early in the morning, one day after his death, and I heard my father's voice, loud and clear, upon awakening. He said to look in the inside pocket of one of his jackets. Sure enough, the valuables were exactly where I was told to look. This goes to show that the spirit (or something) transcends death. Since it happened again, six months after his death, I believe the spirit remains long enough to clear up "loose ends."

There are many individuals, including caregivers and some ADC researchers, who believe that the evidential ADC is strong evidence to support the contention that consciousness lives on after bodily death. Opposing explanations would emphasize any information received came from the unconscious of the survivor and the voice of the deceased was nothing more than an audio hallucination. Still others might say the information is clairvoyantly obtained and therefore not an indication of an afterlife.

46. What are crisis ADCs?

When I have heard the word crisis *used as a description of an ADC, I'm suddenly at a loss deciding what "crisis" refers to. Who or what is in crisis? What is the nature and meaning of these ADCs?*

The crisis ADC is clearly one of the most meaningful and probably among the least common to occur, although a sufficient number have been documented by the Society for Psychical Research. When they take place, they provide great comfort and assistance to the mourner. Because the word *crisis* is somewhat misleading for people, let's define it as an ADC that occurs to the mourner before he or she has been officially notified of the death of the loved one. The term *crisis apparition* was first used by the early researchers in the major study of hallucinations conducted under the auspices of the Society for Psychical Research (SPR) in the early 1880s. It indicated the appearance of the person in the apparition experiencing some type of crisis twelve hours before or after the incident. The term has been used in describing ADCs that occur within twelve hours after the death, but before official notification has been given to the survivor. As you can well imagine, crisis ADCs are a skeptic's nightmare when it comes to trying to explain them away as hallucinations or illusions, because the recipient has no prior knowledge of the crisis.

The crisis ADC occurs in at least four ways:

1. The deceased may appear to the potential mourner in a vision or as an apparition sometimes saying he has died or he is okay;

2. The contact may come in an intuitive or sense of presence ADC, where the recipient senses that the deceased is close by;

3. It may occur in a visitation dream; and

4. Sometimes the contact may take place in an auditory event as occurred with Marilyn, whose story appears below, whose husband died unexpectedly at work.

"I Can Cope as I Think of This Event"

I came home from work on a Friday. My husband was not home, which was unusual, as he is normally home when I arrive. I was sitting alone and heard a voice say, "Pick up around the house, as there will be many people here." I thought about it for a while and decided to tidy up things and put dishes in the dishwasher. When they were done, I picked up his coffee cup (he drank out of a big cup), and put the cup in the cupboard. Then I heard a voice say, "That's the last time you will put the cup away." I called the college where he worked and received no answer. In about three hours a detective came to my door to tell me that my husband was found dead. I then had a house full of people. My friends rallied round me.

As I look back, I truly believe the voice was my husband preparing me. He always took great care of me and wanted me to be prepared. This experience helped me because I realize he helped me to the end. I always believe it was him and when I get depressed and wish he was with me—I can cope—as I think of this event and that he talked to me.

It is worthy of note, that without suggestions from others, Marilyn has already decided to use her ADC in times of distress—as one way of coping with her loss. The recollection of ADC experiences can provide comfort and a way to deal with normal reactive depression. The ability to focus on her husband's love and concern strengthens her resolve to reinvest in life.

The crisis ADC is of special importance and in need of careful study to determine how a contact can occur with information about the death of a loved one. How is such information transmitted? Telepathically? Through normal sensory perception? Or is it possible that we all have a faculty, yet to be discovered and verified by science, which operates outside of the commonly accepted space/time framework? No one knows for sure at this time; it remains one of humanity's great mysteries.

- *See also question 25*

47. What does the typical apparition look like as reported by the bereaved?

Given the fact that a large number of visions and apparitions have been the subject of endless debate over the years, I am interested in knowing what the deceased loved ones look like when they supposedly return to help the bereaved. Do they look like they did before they died? Do they look like ghosts that we see pictured in books and in movies? Do they look angelic? Please comment.

I'm really not sure there is anything like a typical apparition or vision. I do know that there are a variety of different descriptions that have been given by those who are convinced they have seen their deceased loved one. Here is an apparition that occurred to a man in his mid-thirties who has always been skeptical of any type of unseen phenomena, but was convinced his mother is "still here with me."

"It Was a Comforting Experience"

I awoke in the middle of the night; it was somewhere in the neighborhood of 3:00 A.M. I turned, sensing a presence and saw a diminutive woman standing next to my side of the bed. Although I didn't think it resembled my mother to any significant degree (although my mother was only four feet, ten inches in height), I felt in my heart it was her. I reached out to touch her and as my hand approached she dematerialized.

The next day, I didn't mention this to anyone, but when I returned home from work my wife told me that my mother was in the house last night and spoke with her aunt during the night. Now I don't have any idea what caused my experience. My only conjecture is that it had something to do with my wife's aunt who allegedly has a gift when it comes to communicating with the deceased. I am personally very skeptical, but I know I was awake and have no other rational explanation for what occurred. For me, the message was that to some extent my mother is still here with me. Although I had already worked through much of my grief, it was a comforting experience.

I had the opportunity to interview the aunt with the intuitive abilities and asked her how she learned of the presence of this man's mother and she responded with, "She just came to me. I was not trying to contact her." I also inquired about how she knew it was his mother and she said, "She told me she was Stanley's mother." Furthermore, the aunt said his mother wanted her to tell her son not to grieve for her anymore, she was okay and healthy, and to thank him for the yellow rose plants. As you may have already observed the above experience may also be classified as a fourth-party ADC because its confirmation came from an intuitive, was then conveyed to the wife, who then told the husband the messages her aunt had received. It is important to remember that the husband had not told anyone about his apparition.

The above is one of several types of apparitions that are experienced by some mourners. Let me list them at this time.

Two dimensional. Some mourners have reported seeing what amounts to a still picture of the deceased. This type of apparition may be of the head or the full body and their is no depth or fullness to the figure.

Three dimensional. In this type of apparition, the loved one appears as he did when alive. The figure is very clear and is often, though not always, wearing familiar clothing and is solid in form. Some authorities refer to this experience as a corporeal vision in which a physical body is seen. There is depth and fullness. In some apparitions, the person is described as having an aura around him.

Mist shrouded. In these apparitions the loved one appears to be surrounded by a mist or vapor and is not seen in the clarity associated with two- and three-dimensional apparitions. One woman I interviewed put it this way: "It was translucent; I can't explain it." Some people report being able to see through the apparition, others say the figure was solid.

Figure only. In this type of apparition the deceased loved one is not at all clearly identified (as in the opening example). The mourner reports that the figure observed was the deceased person, although she was in unusual clothing such as a gown or a robe and facial features could not be clearly distinguished. In some instances, although the face cannot be seen at all, the mourner is still convinced it was the deceased.

Angelic form. The final description I am aware of involves the deceased as being surrounded by white light and looking more like an angel, but with clear facial features.

The vast majority of apparitions reported by the bereaved usually occur in a context showing the deceased in good health and looking happy; they are usually two- and three-dimensional in nature, and prove to be strong resources to draw upon in dealing with the loss of the loved one. In a few instances, the deceased person has been seen as looking younger or at a younger age than when he died. In some appearances there is a regular conversational exchange while in others the deceased loved one speaks words of encouragement or indicates that he or she is okay. Not infrequently, an apparition occurs and no words are exchanged, yet the mourner is encouraged by the nonverbal messages received. In addition, many visions that occur when the mourner is around others, for example, in church, are only seen by the mourner and no one else.

F. W. H. Myers, one of the early researchers associated with the Society for Psychical Research and author of the classic *Human Personality and its Survival of Bodily Death,* believed crisis apparitions (apparitions occurring twelve hours before or after the death) were probably the result of the release of the dying person's consciousness just before or at the moment of death. These were usually full body or of the three-dimensional type. Other early researchers took the position that crisis apparitions could be explained by telepathy. As for apparitions that occur days, weeks, or months after the death, there are conflicting interpretations ranging from purely psychological explanations to the contention that the visits are real.

48. What types of ADCs have you found occurring more than five years after the death of the loved one?

It has been said by several authorities on ADC phenomena that most ADCs occur within several months of the death. However, I have read about people who had extraordinary experiences fifteen or twenty years after their loved

one died. What types of ADCs occur at such a late date and why do they
occur long after the bereaved have stopped grieving?

I want to make it clear that anyone may be "revisited" with grief at certain intervals for the rest of his life. Remember, the grief process is highly individual and progresses depending on many factors, not the least of which is the nature of the relationship between the mourner and the deceased. Furthermore, one may appear on the outside to have come to a resolution with the loss, but inside is still grieving. So the fact that a person believes he had an ADC ten or twenty years after the death of the loved one does not mean he or she had forgotten the person or still is not dealing with a painful relationship involving the deceased. Grief could be very much alive, although hidden from family members or the public. Conversely, there appear to be some individuals who complete their grief work and still have a contact experience many years later. One was Barbara, whose father died from alcoholism when she was twelve years old. On the fifteenth anniversary of her father's death, she had the following visitation dream.

"He Apologized"

Coming down the street is an old horse-drawn hearse. It stops next to me. I go over and open the glass side and realize it's my father. At curbside, my father says to me, "You were not able to attend my funeral; attending funerals is important so I have returned." Then I'm instructed to touch his body and observe the physical signs of death (skin color, no breath, etc.) The dream is very vivid.

Then I am at a roundtable in a house and he talks with me regarding his alcoholism and our relationship. He says he never intended to hurt me and was unaware how I was feeling. He apologized, saying that he wanted to return to tell me that he regretted his behavior. He said he was busy now in another life, with a sense of purpose in what he was doing, and had taken time to review his life. He likewise apologized to other members of my family, particularly in regard to his alcoholism and lack of awareness of how he was affecting us. The meeting closed. He said he needed to return to his responsibilities elsewhere, said goodbye, and left the table. The dream ended.

I spoke with Barbara about her dream and she said it was not merely vivid and clear in meaning, but it had a major impact on her despite the intervening years.

Here is another ADC dream that occurred many years after the death when grief resurfaced and the dreamer was in need of assistance.

"I Had Received Comfort, Peace, and Joy"

One day about five months ago I began crying because I missed my grandmother so much. She died seventeen years ago and we were very close. I asked the Holy Spirit to comfort me before I went to sleep. I had a dream early in the morning in which I saw my grandmother in heaven in her new body with no gray hair, not bent over, looking in perfect health, and wearing a new dress and shoes. I tried to touch her and yelled, "Grandma" and she moved her arms and acted like she couldn't see me, but I could see her. I started to cry and broke up and instantly a peace came over me as my crying woke me up. This feeling of total peace actually lasted for two weeks—it was a high. I had received comfort, peace, and joy in the midst of suffering. I could not believe how I felt and that's the only time anything like that ever happened to me. It was a gift from God. It helped me feel more peaceful, especially knowing to what extent God would go to comfort me. It's a pick-up when I recall it. I was blessed with a special experience.

I return to a fundamental fact. Even though many years intervene between the time of death and an ADC, the overall effect on the mourner may be as dramatic and useful as if it occurred shortly after the death.

49. What are the most intriguing ADCs you have come across?

I have read a number of the stories from people you have interviewed and I have heard you talk about others who have experienced some exceptional ADCs. You obviously have heard many accounts from mourners as well as from colleagues. What have been the most interesting or miraculous ADCs from your point of view?

There are several ADCs I am familiar with as having been instrumental in spurring me on to continue with the pursuit of the next experience. Along the way I have read many of the case studies in the Society for Psychical Research literature, which are well documented, and were literally captivating, to say the least. You can explore the literature for them. But in my own research three ADCs stand out.

The first came in a conversation I had with a colleague, Peggy Bruhn, whom I was having lunch with during a workshop we were attending. I later asked her if she would write it up for publication, particularly because of the profound effects it had on her daughter. Here is the account.

"Even in Death He Continues to Spread Cheer"

This event happened the year following my son's death. He died in an automobile accident at age twenty-one in June, 1985. The month was January and my daughter Jacqueline had returned to school in Maine for the spring semester. She had been in China for the fall semester, having left the U.S. in August. She arrived back in the States looking pale and exhausted and feeling sad, having once again contacted the grief around her brother's death. We received a call from her college telling us, in essence, that she was clinically depressed and needed to come home for a rest.

The night was stormy, with wind and pounding rain. We had asked Jacqueline to get a plane coming into one of the city airports since we were frightened of her arriving in a puddle jumper at our local airport. She agreed and took a late plane that landed somewhere around 8 or 9 P.M. When I saw my daughter, I realized how ill she was. Her color was yellow, affect was flat, and she had absolutely no energy. (This is a child who traditionally had energy to spare, red rosy cheeks, and a smile that could melt the world.) We drove home in horrible weather, indeed I remember being frightened of the elements. We arrived home late, as I recall somewhere close to 11 P.M. Jacqueline went upstairs to our bedroom, and as was their routine, I let the dogs out. At that time we had a German Shepherd and a Jack Russell, which is a small terrier, named Billy. Billy was a fearless animal. There was nothing in our world that frightened him or caused him to retreat. Though small, he thought he was also a German Shepherd. I straightened up downstairs, giving the animals time to take care of themselves, and eventually let them in and climbed the stairs for bed.

I would like to share with you the layout of our house in Port Jefferson. The back of the house is three stories high, with sliding glass doors on each level. The deck around my bedroom did not connect with any other deck in the house; it was a sunning deck for the bedroom. On the first floor was a deck that wrapped around the bottom of the house. The area between the two decks was about fifteen feet. Unless you were a kid—and very agile— who loved to climb, or if you had a ladder, there was no possible way to get from the first floor deck to the bedroom deck.

As I entered the bedroom, I immediately heard scratching on the outside door. I couldn't imagine what could be on the upper deck since there was no way of getting to it. I opened the door and there was Billy! He ran across the bedroom, tail between his legs, ears back, and left like a streak of light-ening. I had never seen Billy upset before. My husband, Jacqueline, and I stared in amazement. Then we started to laugh, and laugh, and laugh. In our hearts we knew my son, Jay, had somehow taken Billy out of the house and levitated him to the upstairs deck. I could almost visibly see my daughter's depression lifting. As a psychotherapist and nurse, I soon realized she would not have to go on medication. I had been contemplating a med check, but now knew it wouldn't be necessary. The week progressed and her mood continued to lift. She was back in school the following week with enough energy to complete the semester.

As you can only imagine, this is one of the stories the family tells over and over again. It is such a delightful tale, not only the event, but how my daughter was returned to health in a matter of seconds. This story and many others have helped us deal with the incredible loss we all still experi- ence around my son's death. We use it to let us know he is still around and up to his usual antics. He was such a joyous person that even in death he continues to spread cheer.

What is especially significant about this ADC is the immediate effect it had on Peggy's daughter and the long-term use of it for the good of the family. Its credibility is heightened by the credentials of the mother who has been trained in psychotherapy and the analysis of depression and posttraumatic stress disorder.

This next ADC has been one of the most intriguing for me because of the lasting long-term impact on the survivor: joy and peace, belief in survival of consciousness, and no fear of death.

"What I Now Know Is That He Will Be Waiting"

In November 1966, I was nine years old, approaching my tenth birthday. I was the youngest of four children. We lived in Queens, New York. I was so much younger than my siblings that they were practically part of a previous family. My oldest sister, Ann, had died at the age of eighteen when I was two years old (I have no recollection of an ADC following her death.) My brother Joseph was already married with a child, and the remaining sibling at home was my sister, Eileen, who is twelve years my senior. Although Eileen is the elder sister, she was the victim of polio and remains both physically and mildly intellectually challenged.

Since his early thirties, my father had been plagued with a "heart condition" and had had several very traumatic coronary events. When he died in 1966, he was forty-nine years old. Much of what I know about my father, of course, comes from family history rather than direct knowledge. By the time he died, my father had been virtually unemployable (and uninsurable) for over a decade. The prescribed lifestyle for people with "heart conditions," in those days, was a lot different than it is today. Consequently, most of the memories of my father are of a rather physically passive man who spent his days on the couch. Somehow, I never thought of him as sick at the time, as he appeared to be a strong, very animated man.

My ADC begins with a premonition—one I believe was shared by my father and myself. On November 29, 1966, just four days after Thanksgiving, my mother woke me up for school as usual. In September, I had been "skipped" from the fourth to the fifth grade and I was very pleased with myself and very excited by the new challenging work. I had always loved school—loved to read and the sunny, bustling classroom was such a relief from the usual somber mood of my house. I might add that I was pretty much a docile child and had somewhere along the way taken up the role as peacemaker in the household. This is why it shocked even me when I refused to go to school that day. My mother scolded and argued, but I wouldn't be budged. I didn't even have a reason, I just knew that I couldn't go to school that day. The feeling was overwhelming and I was willing to tempt my mother's anger to succumb to the feeling. Finally, my mother literally threw her hands up and left the house, late for work.

I remember sitting upstairs in my room when my house got quiet and thinking, "Why did I do that?" I couldn't understand what would drive me to such a strong negative feeling about leaving the house. Like any nine-year-old, I proceeded to take full advantage of the situation and prepared to spend the day goofing off. I don't even remember being aware of my father at this point, but I must have known he was still in bed downstairs. I don't remember exactly how long I played in my room that morning. I remember sitting in front of my vanity for some time, trying to get my cowlick to stay down. I had a general sense of unease and edginess and I even remember breaking into tears of frustration when my hair just wouldn't cooperate (which it never did). I remember that the house was very quiet and it was a pretty, sunny morning for November.

At some point, I did go downstairs; I think I was still in my pajamas. I remember glancing at my parents' bed and noticing that my father was still in bed. I think the notion had occurred to me that he ought to be up by now. As a child, however, you don't generally question what grownups do or don't do. So if it did occur to me that he was sleeping unusually late, I'm sure it would have been in a rather peripheral and matter-of-fact way.

The first floor in our apartment in those days was what would have been called a "railroad" flat. A straight path led from the kitchen through my parents' bedroom and then into the living room. Our apartment did have two bedrooms (one mine, one my sister's) on the next floor and the staircase was located off the living room (or parlor, as my parents referred to it). I plopped down into one of the upholstered chairs in the living room and became absorbed in the television. My father lay in his bed within my sight—probably about four or five yards away. I don't even remember looking at a clock but my sense is that it was later morning or early afternoon when I traversed the bedroom on my way to the kitchen. I had maintained a strong sense of foreboding all morning and this was heightened when my father called out to me as I passed his bed. His voice didn't sound right—too subdued. He motioned for me to crawl in bed next to him. I did this, but I found it extremely disquieting. After a child reached the age of five or so, my family's unwritten rules did not include displays of affection except in very formal circumstances. Frankly, my father's sudden breach of this protocol was somewhat repulsive to me and very upsetting. We lay still in his bed for a while. He had his arms around me. I remember feeling very uncomfortable and trying to determine the proper moment when I could pull away without hurting his feelings. This behavior was so out of character on my father's part that I later came to the conclusion it was evidence of a premonition on his part. The man I lay in that bed with was a very different man than the one I had come to know as my father. He was profoundly changed—in a way even a nine-year-old could sense.

Now, on top of the disquieting sense of dread I'd had all day, I was afraid to go near this man laying in my father's bed. I don't remember actually putting those two feelings together at the time, but now I know they were both present. Things seemed to take on a surreal quality after this, although more than thirty years later, details still stand out in glaring tangibility. I retreated to my room. I don't remember what I did there, but my sense is I found some sanctuary. If children have a gift of suspending themselves in space and time and simply removing themselves from a stress that is too big to comprehend—I am sure that is what I did. I simply went about my usual activities in my room—t.v., books, games, dolls. A familiar universe that as a practically "only child," I had long since cultivated.

I remember Mom's workday ended at 4:00 P.M. In some sketchy way I think I may have been waiting for her return before braving the dreaded downstairs again. I do know that what prompted my eventual resolve was that the bathroom was off the kitchen—through my parents' bedroom. So, ultimately, I quietly snuck back downstairs. At this point it was definitely afternoon; I remember how the golden light played off the walls. The t.v. in the living room was still on. I found myself sitting in front of it with a peanut butter and fluff sandwich. I couldn't tell you what was on television—but I can tell you that peanut butter and fluff sandwich has haunted me the rest of my life.

Quietly at first and then quite distinctly, a sound started coming from my father's bed. A gurgling—long and drawn out. I remember being thunderstruck. The sound was so unreal—so unlike any sound I'd ever heard a person make before. Of course, I now know it was the "death rattle," but at the time I only knew it was something consequential—I honestly wasn't sure what. I felt torn—I felt that some action was required of me but I didn't know what. I felt helpless and scared. I continued to eat the sandwich as though it would forever ground me to life as I had known it before. I froze. I ignored the sound as long as I could. Finally, it grew quiet. I don't know how long I sat there in silence; I think it was a long time. Eventually, I somehow propelled myself out of the chair and tentatively walked over to my father.

In a moment that will always be frozen in time, I had what I have now come to understand as an after-death communication. Slowly and fearfully, I moved toward my father's bed. He was on his back on the inside half of my parents' double bed. I remember the fingers of his right hand, so like my own, delicately curled up as if in sleep. I had to reach across the entire left side of the bed to touch him—but somehow despite my earlier fears, I was compelled to touch him. I remember reaching out with my right hand and touching his right arm just below the shoulder.

In that instant, two things happened. My hand reached out and touched his arm and my brain acknowledged that he was dead. The bare flesh of his upper arm was cold. Even at nine, I registered this as death. This was colder than a person should ever be. In the instant the feelings of panic should have overtaken me—this was my father and he was as cold as the kitchen floor—I was overtaken by a sense of utter peace. It was almost as though he were waiting for my touch. In that instant (I don't think my hand had even left his flesh yet) I had a clear communication from my father. His message was a simple one—it came and it went in a flash: "Everything will be all right." Simple and succinct, yet a moment in time and a message that struck my very soul with a profundity the likes of which I have never been able to re-experience in my entire lifetime. This message conveyed to me a very general sense of "okay." Not just that I would make it through this crisis. Not just that he was okay. Not just that my lifetime would be okay. "Everything"—every little thing in the universe was okay. Everything as we knew it and perceived it was "ALL RIGHT." It was how it was meant to be. And then he simply left. I would have to say that person

to person, regardless of our relationship and certainly our age difference—
our levels of experience—it was on joyful wings that he left.

One of the details that has always stood out in my mind about this
experience and has attracted me to many of the accounts of near-death
that I have read is this: My father's voice—and I know it was his voice—
did not have its source in or even near his body. Rather, his voice very
clearly and distinctly came from a spot where the right angles of the walls
met the ceiling in the corner of the bedroom. My father spoke to me from a
point that was many feet away from his body. Naturally, many times over
the years, I have relived this moment over and over in my mind. Was it an
audible voice? Was it telepathic? I'm afraid that I have still not reached a
conclusive decision. It seems to me that it was my father's voice but that I
heard it in my head rather than through my ears. Whatever, or however it
was, I have never been offered such a sense of peace again in my life.

At some point in the 1970s, I became aware of Dr. Raymond Moody's
work with people who had experienced near-death. These accounts frequently contained a description of the spirit (for lack of a better word) of
the person hovering around the ceiling at the time of death and watching
the activities around the body. Since then, I have always been on the look-
out for accounts that might come close to explaining my own experience.
Through my reading of near-death experiences, I have caught a glimpse
and through your latest book [After-Death Communication: Final
Farewells], I have "honed in" even further.

To finish my account of that fateful day in 1966, let me say that as profound as that experience was, I still had to deal with the world of "here and
now" and that wasn't a pleasant prospect. At around 4:45 P.M. my mother
came home from work. She opened the refrigerator door (maybe to install
a new carton of milk?) and said to me: "Didn't your father get up to eat
today?" Suddenly it occurred to me that no, in fact my father hadn't gotten
up all day. "ALL DAY!!!" Suddenly, the concept hit home: "If the man
hasn't gotten out of his bed all day, even to eat, then he's dead." In the
refrigerator was a plate containing the remnants of last night's dinner,
meant to be my father's lunch today—lamb chops, congealed in hardening
grease, green beans, potatoes, and mint jelly—a whole jar of it. To this day
the sight of lamb chops makes me sick.

Certain of my mother's question and certain of what I perceived to be the self-incriminating answer—I ran. I ran up to my room as fast as my feet could take me. It was at this point that my body collapsed. I remember hovering in a little ball on my bedroom floor. I simply did not want to deal with the aftermath. I got it. He was dead. Everything was okay. What else was there to say? My mother insisted on saying a lot. She called the ambulance. He'd been dead for hours—they called the coroner. It took six hours for the coroner to come. My father lay in the same position he'd been in when he spoke to me. Frozen in time—in the same posture as his last goodbye to me. It seemed a mockery.

As soon as my mother had ascertained my father's state, she talked me down from my room and installed me in my grandparents' downstairs apartment. She then enlisted her parents to accompany her upstairs to deal with the officials. Once again, I was alone, this time in my grandparents' apartment. I was sitting in the "front room" that looked out to the street. I still remember the television was showing "Joan of Arc"—a movie I hadn't seen before and haven't seen since. At some point, prompted by some noise between the buildings, I parted the front room curtains and looked out. The last glance I had of my father was when they wheeled him out to an ambulance zippered into a black plastic bag. Night had fallen.

I have never again sensed, heard, or felt the presence of death or foreboding that I felt in 1966—the day my father died. Nor have I felt the perfect joy and peace that I experienced on that same day. My father, to my knowledge, has never again tried to contact me, nor has any other soul. Yet, based on my experience more than thirty years ago, I believe that, in fact, we do survive after death in a way that I can only describe as blissful.

I refused to go to my father's funeral. I knew that the experience for me would be redundant—we had already said our goodbyes. This became just another source of guilt for me as my sister-in-law's friends tried and tried to convince me to go. My father will always be with me. I know that. His caring for me transcends any particular state of being. What I know now is that he will be waiting, my sister will be waiting, my grandparents and deceased friends will be waiting—their love will be waiting for me.

As you can well imagine, this experience had a great effect on Patricia's life. When she originally wrote to me about her experience, she emphasized how her craving to connect it to some larger framework had increased over the years. She told what had happened to her to three other people in her lifetime: one chalked it up to denial, the second was open to the possibility but had many stories more extraordinary, and the third tried to be accepting but actually came across as disinterested. In closing her story she said: "At the age of forty, along with all of the other things in life to assimilate, I find myself feeling somewhat estranged from other people—they can just never understand or appreciate what life is about—on a deeper level. Since I myself have a hard time understanding this experience, I certainly feel guilty about judging others. The conclusion I've come to is unless you have experienced this kind of thing firsthand, you have no basis for comparison." How true! How true!

This last ADC is best understood in conjunction with two other experiences that took place in the life of Fred Zimmerman of Lorain, Ohio.

Part 1. "I Saw Many of My Relatives Who Were Deceased"

In 1964, at the age of twenty-two, while swimming across Lake Mohawk in Tiffin, Ohio with two of my college buddies, I suddenly became aware of the fact that I was sinking. Even though I told myself to remain calm, I was moving my arms like an airplane propeller and kicking my feet like crazy, and still continued to sink under water.

Aware that I was choking and coughing, I suddenly realized that the light from the sunshine above was slowly diminishing while the water was becoming darker and colder. Definitely a bad sign! My two buddies were frantically searching for me with no results.

As I struggled under water I suddenly became extremely calm, the most calm I have ever been in my life. At the same time, I saw many of my deceased relatives all around me in the water. They looked as if they were a reflection in a mirror and I saw only their upper bodies. They were all concerned and comforting me. "Strange, what are they doing here?" was my immediate thought. My life passed in my mind as quick as a blink of an eye and was very vivid and real. I then realized I was out of my body and was watching this person six feet in front of me struggling for his life—and it was me! I could only watch and could not feel water on my face or hear splashing, only extreme calm and peace. My two buddies told me later that they searched for me for one to one-and-a-half minutes before grabbing the back of my shirt and towing me to a raft that was nearby.

In the meantime, as I watched the body in front of me fighting for its life, I heard a voice say "Fred, this is not your time to die." This was a definitive, authoritative, firm, and final message that left no question of its intent! I recall to this day looking over my right shoulder to see where that voice came from, but how could I do that when my body was six feet away from whatever I was in the water? It was as though my mind, or thinking process, or energy form, was watching my physical body struggle. When the voice gave me the message, I felt a gentle movement forward, back into my drowning body, and I could feel the water in my throat, on my face, and the coughing, choking, and struggling once again!

Both Jack and Jim said it was hallucinations, fright, etc. when I told them what had happened, but they were not sure either. It was ten years or better before Dr. Moody's book came out on near-death experiences. I read it and it reminded me clearly of my experience and that I would not be afraid to drown—it was so calm and peaceful. It was the greatest calm I had ever experienced.

Thirty-three years later, event number two occurred.

Part 2. "Eric Is Going To Die. Be Prepared."

On Sunday, November 30, 1997, our twenty-five-year-old son Eric Zimmerman was getting ready to leave our house to finish his last two weeks of training at the Ohio State Highway Patrol Academy in Columbus. Eric had been hired by the Bowling Green, Ohio, Police Department weeks earlier. His rigorous training lasted about fourteen weeks. Eric and I were as close as a father and son could be and he was the finest young man that one could know.

He and I were talking outside while he was standing on the sidewalk with the street light glowing behind him. It gave the picture of a halo of white light around his head. Eric was talking about Christmas presents and his graduation from the academy on December 12 and my coming down to see him graduate. I was thinking of a reply when all of a sudden my complete thought process went blank and a voice said to me telepathically, "Eric is going to die. Be prepared." It was definitive, authoritative, precise, to the point—and I got the impression there was not a thing I could do about it! It was not the same voice that told me years ago that it was not my time to die when I had the near-death experience in Lake Mohawk.

I did not want to scare Eric by telling him and I also felt that maybe because he was a police officer that it was a reaction I had because of the danger of his job. I hugged him and told him to be very careful at the academy, to drive carefully, and to take precautions. He said, "Okay Dad." And I knew he was a well-trained, competent, and capable person. I saw Eric at the graduation program on December 12, 1997, hugged him, and secretly said to myself, "Tell me that warning again. Give me some explanation." But to no avail.

A little over a week later, my wife Marilyn and I were in Jamaica getting ready to leave to come home after vacationing with two other couples. We had set the alarm clock for 7:00 A.M. At a couple of minutes after 2:00 A.M. on Sunday, December 21, Marilyn jumped up, got out of bed, and ran around the bed waking me up. I looked at the clock and said, "Its 2 o'clock, why did you wake me up?" She said something had awakened her. Eric's car accident and death was listed at 2:05 A.M. on Sunday, December 21, 1997! We woke up at the same time or very close to the time Eric died thousands of miles away.

We flew to the Detroit Airport and on the way home I asked Marilyn to call Scott, our youngest son, who had just come home from college the previous day. She called and he was nervous on the phone. So I asked her to call Eric at Bowling Green. She dialed the phone and asked for Eric. Ryan, one of his roommates answered and said, "Mrs. Zimmerman, Eric had a terrible accident! He is dead." Marilyn screamed, and as I looked over to her and pulled to the side of the road she was sweating on the left side of her face. Simultaneously, she was looking at her left shoulder as if someone had grabbed her on the shoulder. She said, "It's Eric. He said, 'Sorry Mom, so sorry'" and then he was gone. We were devastated! We managed to get some composure and arranged the necessary things for the funeral. Over one thousand people visited Eric at the funeral home to say their goodbyes to a wonderful young man. But as you will see, Eric was going to say good-bye to me in a wonderful way forty-five days after his accident.

Part 3. "I Love You Dad. I Love You Mom."

The crying and pain that we went through I would not wish on anyone under any condition. The support of many helped, but ultimately we still had a tough road ahead. The crying and grief can come up suddenly by see-ing a picture, hearing a song, or seeing a friend. The longing that one has is truly difficult, especially when one has such a close and loving family.

I had always believed there was a hereafter and that something still existed after death. But without proof, who knows?

Well, let me tell you, proof was on its way! On the morning of February 4, 1998, forty-five days after Eric's death in a car accident, I awoke at 6:45 A.M. along with my wife Marilyn. She got up to prepare for work as she leaves earlier than I, so I got up and prepared my computer for the day's work. Then I sat down on the bed waiting for Marilyn to finish drying her hair in the bathroom. At 7:15, Marilyn turned off the hair dryer signaling she was finished. I got up off the bed—fully awake and up for one-half hour. My mind was clear. I was not crying and not under any stress. As I took my third step toward the bathroom, I felt a tremendous squeeze and hug on both sides of my body that stopped me in my tracks. Eric appeared right in front of my face, smiling, and the whole room was full of energy. Its like the molecules, atoms, and air are all moving at a tremendous speed. It was forceful, explosive, loving, highly energized—the most exhilarating experience that I have ever had! I hugged Eric. I was hugging an energy force not a real physical body I kissed him on his right cheek and felt his beard/whiskers on my lips. He was moving so fast that I believe he had just passed through the bathroom and barely missed his mother. It was as though he was flying through the house. My mind was ecstatic, lucid, fully awake and aware of what was happening. I could see the tremendous love in the complete environment that Eric brought with him. I knew this was real, on purpose, planned by Eric as I could never have written or wished the events in this spontaneous experience. The force field, aura, and energy surrounding Eric was so strong and charged that it pushed me back onto the bed. It was not Eric's hands pushing me as I could not feel them on me. It was a moving energy of molecules that were traveling at an unbelievable rate of speed.

As I had my arms around Eric, his image and I were falling toward the bed. He told me telepathically, "I love you Dad. I love you Mom." His lips did not move. As we fell, he rolled over the top of me and I could see his whole body. He rolled right into the spot where we had placed his police uniform, leather coat, and hat in the middle of the bed. Marilyn and I placed his clothes there and slept with them for a week after his death because as a baby he and the dog would climb in bed with us. They would wrestle, Eric would grab the dog's hair, and be pulled off the bed. The clothes let us again relive his presence and we could cry and mourn over him together.

If I were asked to write a request for an after-death visit I would never have written this—it was wonderful. Eric Zimmerman was in full and complete control for the ten-plus seconds of his visit. He let me know positively that he was still alive in a fast moving energy force, in a different plane or dimension, which he was controlling with complete happiness and everlasting love. I saw a view of eternity and believe me it is a wonderful, loving, totally encompassing, joyful world.

I sell pharmaceuticals for a living. I could never reproduce the high, loving understanding, elated, explosive, forceful, molecular moving, ten-plus seconds with any drug or medicine!!! Never, never, never. I have tried to relive that experience, but I cannot raise my mind to a fraction of the degree of clearness, love, excitement or energy level that I was given by Eric's visit. Thank you son for allowing your Dad the opportunity to know beyond a doubt that we exist beyond the physical body and that a better life is yet to come to all of us.

Let me conclude Fred's ADC by sharing part of the letter he sent to me before my interview with him.

This three part personal experience of my near-death experience, my imminent death warning concerning my son, and my son's visit to me forty-five days after is intended to educate, inform, attest, and help anyone who reads this to believe that indeed there is life after the physical death of humans. I am fully open to take a lie detector test and answer any and all questions relating to the above information. I only hope that this information helps anyone who has a family member pass and is in their grieving process as we were in 1997 and for the rest of our lives. In memory of Eric M. Zimmerman, age twenty-five, a wonderful loving son, a responsible adult, a caring human being, a memory forever.

50. Are there any "negative" ADCs?

In reading about the near-death experience some people have said that it was far from being positive. In fact, it was scary for them. Can the same be said about ADCs? Do some people have "negative" ADCs and wish they did not have the experience?

What are referred to as "negative" ADCs can fall into three categories: those which call the survivor to task for something he should or should not have done, those which scare the mourner, and those which are misinterpreted by the mourner. Let's begin with the following experience that occurred in the life of Frieda Gardner of Henderson, New York.

"My Mother Was Still Teaching Me"

Some time after the death of my mother in the 1960s, my daughter, who was a teenager at the time, was very careless and broke the globe of a torch lamp that I valued highly. It had been a wedding present to me and my husband from a cousin with whom we had a close and warm relationship. I was very angry, lost my temper, and shouted at her. I generally behaved very badly and she ran up to her room crying. I picked up the pieces and went back to the kitchen sink to finish what I had been doing.

As I stood there at the sink I heard my mother's voice (this granddaughter had been a favorite of my mother) and she said, "Why are you making her so miserable over a piece of glass? That's all it is—it's only a piece of glass, and you hurt her little heart." After a few moments I went upstairs to my daughter, apologized for my bad behavior, kissed her, and she was forgiven. When I came back down to the kitchen I thought about it—my mother was still teaching me how to take care of my children.

Being chastised for one's behavior by a deceased loved one may or may not be considered negative depending on your point of view. In this instance, it was accepted in a positive way. However, there is a very interesting follow-up to this experience that helped Freida in her present belief that, what many would call coincidence, is something much more meaningful and thought provoking. As she later told me:

> During the next few days after this incident, I went to several department stores and then to lamp stores, trying to find a new globe to replace the broken one. None of them had anything that would fit. Finally the salesperson at one store explained to me that this lamp had been made in the 1930s and that since then the sizes and patterns for such lamps had changed so the present-day globes would not fit the neck of my lamp. I gave it up as a total loss and went on with other things in life.
>
> About a month later, an organization in which I was active asked me to make the rounds of other members to pick up contributions of household things for a rummage sale that was going to be held to raise money. At one member's house, after she had put her contributions into the trunk of my car, she mentioned she had something that had been cleared out of her mother-in-law's apartment after her death. It was a globe that her mother-in-law had saved from an old broken lamp, but what good was it for the sale since nobody would buy it without the lamp base? She brought it out to show it to me. Not only was it the right size for MY torch lamp, but it was even more beautiful than the one that had been broken. I still have it on my lamp to this day.
>
> You said that evening at Border's that "nothing is a coincidence." And I believe that too.

On many occasions, dreams are also the vehicles through which the dreamer may be chided by the deceased loved one. While some individuals like Florence are taught important lessons by deceased loved ones, others are sometimes frightened by the experience. I recall a young girl, ten years of age, who saw an apparition of her grandfather beckoning her to come toward where he was sitting. She was so frightened she ran out of the room. How can we account for her behavior when most recipients of an ADC are comforted and happy if they are given such an opportunity?

One common answer has to do with nurturance. That is, how the one who perceives fear in the ADC has been taught about the world in which he lives. To illustrate: consider how television deftly portrays the unknown in inauthentic but commercially profitable and frightening ways, and how parents, who themselves portray nonphysical reality as nothing more than ghosts and goblins. The child who is not given information on the normalcy of ADC phenomena can easily create fantasies and images that spawn fear of apparitions, visions, and other hard-to-explain experiences.

Faulty interpretation based on past experiences is often the cause of the relatively minute number of "negative" ADCs reported. Also, as in the following instance, failure to share the experience with another can prove to be damaging. I once was taken to task by a middle-aged woman at a book discussion I was conducting on ADC phenomena when I made the statement that the ADC experience invariably results in positive outcomes for the mourner. To refute my statement she gave the following account of her "negative" ADC.

"I Was Fearful"

I was nine years old when my mother died and it was a terrible loss to deal with. One night, shortly after her death, she came to me to offer comfort and solace. Her appearance scared the daylights out of me. From that day on I was fearful of this type of thing happening again and this fear was with me for many years until I got older, matured, and the way I looked at life changed. So you shouldn't say that ADCs always result in positive outcomes.

I immediately asked her, "What did the adults in your life say about your experience?" She replied, "I never told anybody." Her negative view of the experience, spawned by her lack of knowledge about extraordinary phenomena and having kept it to herself, caused her much pain over the years. It is regrettable, at such a young age, she did not have someone with whom she felt she could share her experience and receive guidance and understanding. What form should that guidance have taken? Essentially, to let her know that her mother came back because she loved her daughter so very much. Also, adults need to provide an environment in which the child can be given an opportunity to express her feelings about the death and her ADC experience.

The preponderance of "negative" ADCs that are reported are often the direct result of misinterpreting the messages or meanings conveyed in dreams, or choosing the negative for secondary gain. For example, many dream state ADCs occur when the recipient refuses to interpret the experience in a positive way. In an earlier work, I described the wonderful dreams my father had of my mother, who would appear smiling and wearing the beautiful dress he loved to see her in when she was alive. Nevertheless, he would fail to see the message that she was happy and whole, but rather chose to lament the fact that when he woke up, he realized she had died and was not with him. This would devastate him every time it happened. Let us keep in mind that deceased loved ones who are allowed to enter the dreams of survivors, or be recognized in other ways, are there for positive reasons and not to bring additional stress at times of great sorrow.

51. What do you mean by direct ADCs and indirect ADCs?

Dr. LaGrand, I have frequently heard you use the terms direct and indirect in referring to ADC phenomena. Could you give definitions of these terms or explain how you use them in referring to specific ADCs?

Essentially, these two terms are used to refer to ADCs that either directly or indirectly involve the deceased loved one and the mourner. For example, a direct contact would mean the mourner believes he has heard, seen, smelled, sensed the presence, or been touched by the beloved. The indirect contact includes all other ADCs where the deceased loved one or a Supreme Being is believed to be somehow responsible for the contact. Below are listed the ten classifications of ADCs according to whether they are considered direct or indirect.

Direct ADCs	Indirect ADCs
Auditory	Symbolic
Visual	Third-Party
Tactile	Fourth-Party
Dreams	Birds and Animals
Intuitive	Olfactory
Olfactory	Dreams
Out-of-Body	

Symbolic ADCs are most frequently referred to as indirect ADCs because they involve objects, natural or manmade. These objects are signs or indicators to the bereaved that the deceased person is somehow connected to or the reason why the symbol presents itself at a specific time and place. Having noted I include olfactory and dream ADCs in both columns, let me explain why. First, the olfactory ADC. On some occasions, the mourner reports smelling an odor directly associated with the deceased such as body odor, cologne, or perfume. Or, the odor comes with an auditory or sense of presence ADC. On other occasions, the odor is representative of something the deceased liked, such as roses, or a favorite food when none of those items are around.

Dream-state ADCs can be direct or indirect (third-party) depending on who has the dream. Obviously, if the mourner has a visitation dream involving the deceased, this is direct contact. On the other hand, a person who is not a primary mourner or did not know the deceased could have a visitation dream intended for the primary mourner. This would be an indirect contact as far as the mourner is concerned. Here is an example: Fourteen years prior to the following dream, three teenagers who had been drinking were involved in a massive collision with another truck. Patrick died at the scene, Chris was thrown from the truck the three were riding in, and Willy was burned over 75 percent of his body. He was taken to the county medical center, admitted to the burn unit for treatment, but died the next day.

Dana O'Toole, who had the eventful dream and was in high school with all of the boys, including the person for whom her dream message was meant, picks up the account.

"His Eyes Filled with Tears"

In the fall of 1994, I dreamt I was in a sort of terminal or large entry way. As I look up, walking toward me, is Willy. (Now Willy had not been a close friend of mine in real life. He was more or less an acquaintance.) Patrick, who had died at the scene of the accident, was really my friend. Anyway, when we make eye contact, Willy comes over and hugs me and says, "You have to do me a favor." I agreed. "Go tell Brian I'm okay. He has to let it go." I agreed. I knew he was talking about a childhood friend of mine.

A few days passed. I told my sister about the dream and she said I should go and tell Brian, whom I hadn't seen in years. Of course, I was hesitant to go, but I stopped down at his house, and luckily he was just coming home from work. We exchanged greetings and small talk and then I told him of my strange dream. His face fell and his eyes filled with tears. He then told me he had been crying at Willy's grave the Sunday before. I was relieved that I told him.

This was a vexing, but important, dream for Dana, and especially important for Brian. He obviously had been deeply affected by his friend's death for fourteen years. Diana's message from Willy brought comfort and relief to his long internal vigil. This is an example of the ADC dream being referred to as indirect.

I classify the out-of-body ADC as a subgroup under dream-state ADCs.

52. How can dreams be considered an ADC when we dream every night?

It seems to me as though I dream just about every night and when I talk to friends, they say they dream most nights, too. Dreams of all types are extremely common, or so it appears. Therefore, how can you classify dreams as a source of ADCs?

You are correct in assuming that all of us dream every night even though large numbers of people do not remember their dreams and think they do not dream very often. However, over the years, science has discovered that dreams are important to the health of the physical body. Dreaming is perhaps the most common example of an altered state of consciousness that, of course, is not completely understood by science. Nevertheless, much is known about this altered state. For instance, it is well documented that several cycles of REM (rapid eye movement) sleep occur during a typical seven-hour night's sleep and such rapid eye movements are related to the dream period. Consequently, it is commonly accepted by dream researchers that we dream anywhere from four to seven times each night. In addition, it appears as though dream time lengthens as the night wears on into morning. Most interesting for our discussion is the fact the dream state offers a one-of-a-kind frame of reference. This is because it has no space/time boundaries and it frequently provides much creative material as well as information from which problems can be solved during our waking hours.

But that is only the beginning. Let's not forget, according to the great books of religion, and for centuries before their existence, dreams have been a means of communication between humanity and the Divine. Germane to your question is the work of researchers Montague Ullman and Stanley Krippner at the Maimonides Dream Lab in Brooklyn, New York, who demonstrated that dreaming was a highly psi-favorable state. Specifically, telepathic information was shown to be introduced into the dream world of the dreamer. Though yet to be documented in a laboratory setting, precognitive dreams have also been reported by many individuals who had no previous knowledge of the event or information they received. The point is that dreams are clearly a viable avenue for receiving information of all kinds. Many stories, songs, and other creative endeavors have appeared in print and enriched our lives essentially as a product of dreams providing fertile ground for insights leading to inventive creations. Where all the information comes from is another issue of contention among prognosticators. Is the information always there and we just need to tap into it? Does it come when we are ready for it and in need? Do we have to ask for it? Who sends it? And why? These are only some of the ponderables that, in the final analysis, you and I have to decide for ourselves. But one thing is obvious: there is much evidence to show that dreams have been a source of comfort, healing, advice, warning, creativity, and even admonishment.

With the foregoing in mind, there is every reason to include visitation dreams as a classification of ADC phenomena. Consider the healing and comfort that occurred in the following ADC dream that helped Deirdre deal with her first Christmas without her mother.

"I Was Able to Let Go of Some of the Hurt"

This ADC happened nine months after my mother's death. It was December and I was having a very difficult time dealing with Christmas without her. I dreamed that God let my mom come home for Christmas. Dad and I were outside decorating a house for Christmas. It wasn't my father's house and it wasn't my house either. We had just finished when mom appeared and said, "That's not the way I would do it." We were so surprised and happy that she was with us. She had us move the decorations and then we all went into the house. I asked mom if she was busy in heaven and she answered that God said she could come down for a little while. I asked her if she was teaching in heaven like she had done when she was alive. My answer was a vision of her sitting in a room with a child on her lap and other children around. At first I thought they were our children, her grand-children; but then I realized they were too young and I didn't recognize them. I sat next to her and the children and I felt so good to be with her. I felt such love coming from her that I just wanted to sit there forever.

Mom smiled and said she could only stay a little while.

I woke up and I was crying. I told mom that I loved her and then I went to find my husband to tell him about the dream. At first, I felt bad about the dream because it just seemed to make me miss her more. But, then I started feeling better. I knew mom's love was forever and she was watching out for me. I was able to let go of some of the hurt and enjoy Christmas with my family.

The fact that we dream every night is not necessarily relevant to the fact that the dream state is a marvelous receptacle for communication. It is common knowledge among ADC researchers, in some manner or other, that many mourners make contact with deceased loved ones through the visitation dream. Such contact assists mourners in accepting the death of their loved ones and gives them courage to live their lives; dreams also give information about one's progress in the process of grieving. Mourners receive immeasurable consolation through the ADC dream. This type of phenomena—psi phenomena—occurs repeatedly in dreams the world over. It appears to be an integral part of the human condition. Although some people are more open to it than others, at the same time we have to recognize that, for reasons not yet known, not everyone seems to receive parasensory information in their dreams. But regardless of how dreams are accepted, there is no dismissing the wisdom and reality of the ADC visitation dream when it occurs. That is why I have included it in my classification and continue to pursue the dream experience in my research on ADCs.

In *The Power of Dreaming,* author D. Jason Cooper writes:

> Within our dreams there is a wisdom that can advise us, guide us, and
> make our lives more fulfilling if we will but listen to it. Dreams open to
> us a world of instinct to a symbolic life that is richer, more fulfilled, and
> more successful then we could imagine. More than that, dreams open a
> path to spirituality that leads to the road of initiation.

Our culture tends to minimize the importance of dreams as a resource
to live a wholesome existence, when in fact those who pay attention to
their dreams find a wealth of information for choosing a new road in life.
Those who have joined dream groups for exploring this option readily
attest to this fact. Dreams are another dimension of reality brimming with
insights.

PART

, 4 ,

The Experiencers and the Messages

Questions 53 through 66
Characteristics of Experiencers • Celebrities •
Children and ADCs • Hospice Staff • Atheists and Agnostics •
Types of Messages • Misinterpretation of Messages •
Related Questions

It is not only permissible to doubt
the absolute validity of space/time perception;
it is, in view of the available facts, even imperative to do so.
—C. G. Jung

53. Who reports experiencing ADC phenomena?

Dr. LaGrand, much of the early literature on ADC-type phenomena appears to focus on widows. I am interested in finding out if there are other subgroups that seem to have the experience and whether religious groups and church-goers are more apt to report the phenomena?

As I mentioned in question 32, there is a total lack of standardized terminology among ADC researchers because it is such a young research topic that few are interested in pursuing. Likewise, the research on the topic of ADC phenomena from the point of view of the mourner is at best sparse (almost nonexistent) when it comes to accurately determining where the data is coming from and who has the experience. I am not implying the existing data is not valid, but rather there is little information on groups and subgroups in our society who have the experience. Consequently, I must admit I can only provide some educated guesses toward answering the question you pose.

In my own experience it is safe to say ADCs occur to the rich and poor, the secularly anchored hard-nosed types and those who live in the spirit, men and women, the old and the young, the educated and the uneducated, as well as people from all races. In short, it appears to be a universal experience. My interviews have included individuals representing a wide range of occupations: secretaries, teachers, law enforcement, businessmen and woman, counselors, social workers, nurses, and people in a variety of trades. In my opinion, there are no groups or subgroups who do not have some members who have experienced the phenomena.

Although bereavement counselors were among the first to report widows and widowers often talked about ADCs in counseling sessions as well as support groups, those same counselors are now willing to admit the experience has been brought up in sessions by young children and adolescent siblings, fathers and mothers of deceased children, and friends and relatives of deceased loved ones. Adult children have frequently reported ADC phenomena involving their deceased parents. A number of these individuals have reported multiple contacts.

In terms of ethnic and religious groups, Bill Guggenheim, author of *Hello from Heaven,* has suggested that in his research he has found three groups whom he believes tend to report more ADCs than others: American Indians, African-Americans, and Mormons. There is no indication that those who are members of organized religions or who regularly attend church services are more favored for receiving an ADC.

As a forgotten group, I would like to suggest that the elderly often seem to receive many contacts. If there is another forgotten group, it is young children. Their experiences are all too frequently dismissed as totally imaginative, yet it seems that sometimes children's ADCs are third-party contacts meant primarily for their parents. This was the case with Margaret S.

"The Lady That Sits on My Bed and Plays with Me"

On January 16, I dropped my daughter Samantha off at my sister-in-law Cathy's house. She agreed to watch my daughter while my mother-in-law, father-in-law, and I went to the hospital where my husband was going to be undergoing back surgery. After several hours of surgery and recovery, he was finally taken to a room where we could go see him. It upset me very much that he was taken to the same room in the hospital where my mother had died several years before. But I was finally convinced that my husband went to this room so that my mother could watch over him.

Leaving the hospital late that night, my mother- and father-in-law took me back to Cathy's house to pick up my daughter. Then they drove us home and my father-in-law helped us into the house. He made sure we locked the door behind us.

I was taking my three-year-old daughter upstairs to bed and walking down the hallway to her room (she was looking over my shoulder as I was carrying her) when very happily she said, "Oh, who's there?" I got so scared being all alone with a small child I turned around and looked—and sort of nervous and scared—I said, "There's nobody there." Then, all excited with a smile on her face she said, "It's the lady." I was so scared for a split second and then something said to me, "Oh my God, that's my mother." I said to my daughter, "What lady? There's no lady." And she said, "Yes, the lady that sits on my bed and plays with me." I was so stunned I didn't say another word.

About a week later, my husband and I were questioning Samantha about the lady that sits on her bed. We asked her what she was like and what she looked like. She used the words "pretty" and "nice" in describing her and then she pointed to the picture on the TV. "That's the lady, that's the lady that sits on my bed and plays with me." At that time, my daughter did not have any idea that the lady in the picture on my TV was my mother, her grandmother. I thought she was too young for me to explain that her grandmother had died and that she was my mother.

The way I interpret the experience is that I was worried about my husband and I had also been thinking about my mom since her birthday had passed a few weeks before. I always felt it would have been nice if she could have seen her granddaughter. I feel she was looking after my husband and had met her grandchild. The message was my mother would always be with me no matter what, she was looking out for us all, she did meet her grandchild and loved her very much. More than anything, I always regretted that my mother never saw her grandchild, and I feel strongly in my heart that my mother was the lady playing with my daughter. I know she would have been crazy about her and my daughter seemed so happy when she said, "Oh, it's the lady."

It is easy to dismiss these experiences as simply the ramblings and musings of an infant; it is quite another perception when you are there undergoing the experience, can read the nonverbal behavior of the child, and possess a deep heartfelt awareness of the intent and love of your mother.

54. Have any well-known people reported having an ADC?

It appears that many people have ADC-type experiences and most of them are the average person you would meet on the street or in the grocery store. What about those who are considered well-known or celebrities? Have they had similar experiences and if so why don't we hear much about them?

When it comes to ADC phenomena celebrities are no different than you and I. However, I have always said that even though there is much more talk about extraordinary phenomena in general, there is still much secrecy that shrouds the ADC experience. And it is easy to see why. Many people do not want to be labeled as "having serious problems" or "losing it." Consequently, much discussion of the phenomena is not initiated by those who have had an ADC. Many tell only a selected few they think they can trust. When it comes to celebrities, more than ever, they want to maintain a good public image and are especially careful about letting their story get out. Some, however, have shared the experience.

There are a substantial number of celebrities who have experienced ADC phenomena. Omitting here the large number of historical figures in the world religions, we begin with Winston Churchill, who reported an apparition of his dead father. At the time, Churchill was in his studio copying a portrait of his father when he turned and saw him sitting in a chair. They spoke about politics and various changes that had occurred over the years, and as quickly as he had appeared, he vanished.

Carl Jung heard celebratory music, as though he was at a gala wedding, when he was riding home on the night train after being informed of the death of his mother. This experience eased the pain of his grief as he could only think she must be in a happy place. Psychiatrist Elizabeth Kübler-Ross, who played a major role in introducing the plight of the dying person to the American public with her groundbreaking book *On Death and Dying*, experienced the visual presence of one of her former patients whom she also spoke to at some length (see *Death is of Vital Importance*, pages 95–98).

C. S. Lewis sensed the presence of his departed wife. After his death, he was a "visitor" to J. B. Phillips, Canon of the Episcopal Church and translator of the New Testament in Modern English. Charles Dickens had a visual ADC of his father, and Otis Williams, founder of the singing group The Temptations, likewise experienced his best friend in the same manner.

Three of the most moving and beautifully written ADCs occurred to David Morrill, the award-winning author whom you met when reading question 37. In his book, *Fireflies*, he writes not only of the beautiful experience he and twelve other friends and family members had involving a mourning dove, but also about two contacts when he was alone with his grief.

The first occurred the night after his son's death when he had completed writing the eulogy and was on his knees in the darkness of his bedroom, overwhelmed with the prospect of facing the future without his beloved son. Suddenly the room was filled with fireflies of various colors. Allowing for the dreadful feelings he was dealing with, he was sure this was no mirage, no imagination at play. Out of the hoard of fireflies he sensed the presence of his son and carried on a conversation with him—a two-way conversation. His son made it clear he was at peace, there was no pain, and he wanted his dad to let him go.

The second ADC occurred the next evening after the visitation at the funeral home while he was visiting the church to make final arrangements for the funeral the following day. Once again, he heard his son's voice, just as so many before him have been allowed to share thoughts of assurance through the voice of the loved one. Like the previous evening, his son gave him a similar message that has been relayed by many deceased loved ones to those in the throes of grief: I'm happy, I'm okay, don't mourn for me.

These and other ADCs occur to the rich and famous just as they do to the not so famous. A short list of others who have shared their experience with the outside world would include: Marianne Williamson, Theodore Roosevelt, Wayne Dyer, Michael Crichton, Norman Vincent Peale, and Maurice Gibb.

55. Can an ADC be initiated by the mourner?

Assuming, as you have stated previously, the ADC invariably results in bringing comfort and relief to mourners, it would follow that many individuals would want to have such an experience. Therefore, is it possible to initiate the experience in some way? Has it been tried and what were the results?

This question opens up the issue of receptivity to psi phenomena in general. That is, how can one develop such an ability, if it does exist, as the literature on the paranormal suggests. Before we get to that, let's deal with the fact of the matter: many mourners have tried to initiate a contact. It is not unusual for people to beg for assurance that their loved one still lives and is safe in another existence. In fact, those who have received the gift of an ADC usually come away from the experience with just such assurance and are better off for it. Most people would be better able to deal with their personal loss if they had the conviction that their loved one lives on and they will meet again.

Without a doubt, people have tried to invoke the presence of their deceased loved ones. Some plead for a sign by asking their loved ones to do something to show they are near. Others have tried to meditate in order to set the stage for a possible contact. Still others will go to a counselor who has purportedly had success in helping the mourner obtain assurance that their loved one lives on. (I once had a conversation with a therapist who practiced in the Midwest. She and her client had felt the presence of the spirit of the deceased loved one during a counseling session and she felt that she could create the conditions where this could happen again.) You may want to go back and read the answer to question 10 on internal communication and guided imagery.

Because I am inclined to believe that the ADC is a singularly exclusive spontaneous experience, I find it difficult to see it as something that can be turned on and off at will by anyone. In my view, the ADC is not a controllable phenomena to be induced; its unfolding is directed by an outside source. This does not mean one cannot prepare oneself to be more open to and hope for the phenomena—to catch it, if you will—and ultimately receive the satisfaction that accompanies the experience. But there are absolutely no guarantees, as those who have tried will readily tell you, although it does help to persist. So how does one prepare for the possibility? There are several valid approaches that have been used for centuries to open oneself to a greater awareness of the world of the unseen and utilize the psi ability.

1. **Desire it.** At first glance, this condition may seem obvious. However, the urgency to get immediate results often tempers the most fervent desire you can muster. Over time, desire wanes and the state of mind—so important in achieving any goal—crumbles. With it goes the motivation to continue the search for insight and understanding. Passionate, on-fire, unbending desire must be ongoing and mixed with a generous portion of faith that your goal will be met. Desiring it implies daily attention to opening oneself to the expectation that good will come from the search. I emphasize daily attention and positive expectation. This means imaging and voicing—either aloud or to yourself—your expectations daily. You will receive an answer; it will come. Not necessarily when you want it and perhaps not in the form in which you would like to have it. But it will occur. How will it come? You may get a flash insight, a

sign, even an ADC. But if you persist, you *will* receive an answer. Remember: attitude is everything. This leads us to the second necessity, which is an integral part of desire.

2. **Believe.** Believe you can open yourself, especially your heart, to a new awareness of the unseen. This implies accepting the place of psi and intuitive phenomena in your worldview, and possibly receiving an ADC. Believe in what you are doing, as hard as it is to go against cultural dictates. There is too much evidence to discount the unused sixth sense we all possess that can help us deal with many problems, including our loss experiences. Jung and many who have followed have consistently stressed the importance of belief in the pursuit of individual development, especially in areas where we have little knowledge. Find others who are open to your way of thinking and who are willing to provide mutual support. There is power for commitment and development when those who band together hold mutual beliefs. Look back in your past life when you had so-called coincidences and hard-to-explain good things happen. Use them to reinforce your belief in unseen reality.

3. **Relax.** Setting the stage on a daily basis for opening to the unseen means setting aside time to withdraw from the hurry-up life we so often live and giving ourselves a daily stress break. The quiet receptive mind has long been considered a prerequisite for experiencing nonphysical reality. This is an essential state in order to utilize our sixth sense and gain awareness of our transcendent nonlocal mind. Here is where meditation can be employed to open our hearts and minds to a different world, one we all have access to and can use in the development of the intuitive self. If meditation is something you have trouble with (not everyone likes or can use this approach), then use music or nature or the sounds of silence to bring your mind and body to a different level of receptivity. A major factor in daily relaxation is taking the time and sometimes the energy to find a place conducive to peace and quiet. On occasion it can be hard to find a place where you will not be disturbed, where you can conveniently retreat for release and change. Finding one is a big step toward your goal since we all need quiet space and time.

Remember too, the unseen and our intuitive faculties cannot be forced. We have to set the stage and let it happen. Letting it happen is the hard part because of our need to see results. Attempting to be patient when in need is an essential task. Place downtime on your daily schedule today, at least twenty minutes of it. It will help you reach your goal of receiving an answer and a secondary benefit will accrue—stress release at a time when it is most needed.

4. **Open to Your Spiritual Self.** In as much as the ADC and intuitive or psi ability springs from nonphysical reality, and those who experience ADC phenomena invariably connect it with a spiritual universe or source, let me suggest that it will be most helpful if you will consider developing an openness to spiritual reality. If you have trouble with the word spiritual, substitute an openness of heart instead. In either case, our spiritual or heart side is grounded in pure unconditional love that never empties and is always there for the asking; it sets the stage for an awareness and receptivity that escapes all other mind sets. F. W. H. Myers, the English essayist, well known for his investigations with the Society for Psychical Research, believed love was a "kind of exalted but unspecialized telepathy." Love does not recognize the space/time barriers in our physical world. Many who claim special intuitive (psychic) ability believe that love is a major factor in their work to help others.

If we can focus on that invisible power consistently, we create an attitude that translates into an external environment that paradoxically comes back to change our inner world. Spirituality is all about our inner life and how we project that inner life to everything we touch. Unconditional love facilitates the communication we all so desperately seek and fail to recognize. It's amazing how miracles seem to hang around where love abides. Only the mourner—no one else— knows the deep emotional investment, the spiritual connection, existing between him and the deceased. This is why an ADC event, seemingly irrational to the casual observer, can be a meaningful sign for the bereaved. The spiritual bond is a connection—a one-of-a-kind language—that never dies. It is a basic criteria for understanding and interpreting whatever sign, literal or symbolic, which may occur. Developing your spiritual life and openness to the unseen provides the mindset for hope to flourish. Whether consciously or unconsciously held, no one lives without hope.

5. **Pray.** It has been said that prayer is often the last thing people turn to when in need; it is often considered the last resort by some. But if we look closely at the history of prayer—it is easy to see it works and is not the act of the desperate. Those who pray believe prayer is talking and listening to God as a loving friend—its a partnership! In this context, prayer becomes two-way communication where we not only speak, but more importantly, we listen. That demands an all together different attitude. Listening is part of what theologians suggest is the highest form of prayer.

Prayer may take place in four ways. Perhaps the most common is called prayers of petition. That is, we solicit, plead, even beg for something we think we need. At the second level is intercessory prayer, where we ask for help for someone else who is in need; we are asking for a healing or for strength for them to persevere. The third type of prayer is prayer of thanksgiving, gratitude, and praise. Here we acknowledge the goodness of the Creator and all that has been given to us.

Fourth is two-way prayer. It demands so much more from the pray-er because one frequently has to discern the answers in the world around him (or within him), be vigilant and open to people, places, the inner self, and spontaneity. The answer may come in a dream or an intuitive flash, not necessarily immediately but after what seems to be a long delay. Two-way prayer is challenging, time consuming, and causes us to slow down in order to listen. When we spend as much time listening as we do talking, new insights come into the heart and mind and we can learn to accept answers we weren't looking for. Silence and stillness favor connection to the world of the Great Unseen, so how you pray must be guided by what comes from your heart, not by any manmade formula. Remember, speaking and especially listening are all part of praying. Most importantly, be vigilant. God can send you a message through anything in the world or outside of it. Anything means nature, people, symbols, your inner voice, coincidence, imagination, chance, or a mystical experience. If necessary, an ADC. As Tennyson wrote: "More things are wrought by prayer than this world dreams of."

I said earlier that prayer works. There is even scientific evidence prayer works. (See *Healing Words* by Larry Dossey.) Many studies have shown how prayer has influenced a broad range of physiological parameters from blood pressure to antibody activity; it has resulted in the reduction of medications and mechanical devices needed by those who are ill and has been shown to have startling effects on other forms of life such as bacteria, plants, and animals. Miracles of healing abound, although dismissed by medicine as spontaneous remissions or misdiagnoses. Miracles happen; ADCs happen. An active prayer life is highly recommended in the search for understanding and receptivity to unseen phenomena and the possibility of a sign or reassurance concerning a deceased loved one.

What am I telling you with these five approaches to accessing your intuitive abilities and possibly receiving an answer concerning deceased loved ones? Try them! Practice diligently! Put five key words for the above on a card and paste them on your mirror to remind you. This is an incredibly powerful approach to implementation. And above all—most importantly—give yourself much time to let the process unfold. Persist!

56. Do children ever have the ADC experience?

All of the written accounts of ADC experiences I have read deal with adults although indirectly children are sometimes involved. Are children the direct recipients of ADC contacts and, if so, in what contexts do they occur? I am wondering if children might be more open to the phenomena.

Children report receiving visits from deceased loved ones, angelic beings, and other divine figures. In particular, a substantial number of children have had ADC experiences involving grandparents who have died, as well as parents. This occurs with adult children as well as with young children. One of the first examples of adult child contact I came across was with a college student who had both a tactile and auditory experience involving her deceased father. Most of these ADCs are dramatic and comforting, and in some cases play a major role in helping the child cope with the immediate grief period following notification of the death.

This is exactly what resulted from the visit fourteen-year-old Christy Tozzo received from her father. Both had denied his impending death in different ways: she by overlooking his ongoing four-year illness, and he by keeping the painful details and dismal prognosis closely guarded secrets. Though her mother lived in a world of honesty and fact, at the insistence of her husband she worked diligently to keep the truth from the children. As the only girl in the family, Christy had a special bond with her dad, who watched her practice gymnastics with great pride and satisfaction. She later realized it was his love for all the family that drove him to keep his silence, as damaging as it would eventually become.

It was a cold November morning when she opened the door of her bedroom and found her mother crying in the hallway. At that moment the paramedics were working on her father who was having difficulty breathing as life slowly ebbed away. He was whisked away to the hospital after each of the three children kissed him goodbye. Shortly after, the dreadful news came of his death. As Christy put it, she felt "overwhelmed by the need to run—run from the truth." She went to her bedroom to sob and deal with the searing pain. "Suddenly, I heard a voice call out to me. A vision of my father appeared before me. He was smiling and reassured me he was okay. He told me he was in heaven with his father and grandparents. He spoke of a beautiful white light. 'Everything will be fine,' he said. 'Please tell Mom I will be playing baseball again and, remember, I love you all.' Then he was gone."

A complete change enveloped Christy. No one could understand her acceptance and composure even though she shared her treasured experience with many. They dismissed her response as nothing but sheer denial in the face of overwhelming trauma. "God had allowed me one final denial," she said, "the denial of death as the final separation."

Christy experienced what many children of all ages must deal with: adults who dismiss the ADC experience as simply a figment of the imagination or, at best, a dream. Some writers have even suggested that children are natural hallucinators. There are few parents who, on hearing a young child say they talked with a deceased loved one, would not dispatch the notion as untrue or perhaps another way of getting attention. And why not? Young children often invent imaginary friends because it is well-known how fantasy and magical thinking are characteristic of early childhood. Their inventions may help them deal with loneliness. But talking with someone who has died? This is exactly what happened to Janice's grandchildren after the death of her husband. Here is the account.

(Christy's full account of her visual ADC can be found in the *Sarasota Herald Tribune*, March 23, 1997, p. 1E.)

"Tell Him That She Loves and Misses Him Too"

I have two grandsons, Darren, five, and Dennis, seven, who were their grandfather's pride and joy before his untimely death. Darren had been getting up after his grandpa died and waking my daughter to ask her about heaven. He was upset with the thought of something happening to his mother and her going there and leaving him and his brother. The questioning about heaven went on for about four days. He and Dennis never were told about death and couldn't understand the death of their grandfather. Then one day in the car the questions about heaven began again with, "When will we have to go to heaven?"

It was time to start finding out who was telling them about heaven and death. So Tina sat down with Darren while Dennis was at school and tactfully inquired about who was telling them about heaven. "Grandpa," he said, "he tells me and Denny about things in heaven. He kisses us goodnight Mamma, and sometimes Denny falls asleep before Grandpa leaves. But Grandpa says that's okay because Denny has to get up early to go to school. Grandpa misses us all and he misses Grandma a lot. He knows that you and Grandma cry for him." Well, my daughter thought this was some story and couldn't believe her ears. No one had talked to them about heaven and they had not gotten a TV at this time.

Tina waited that day for Dennis to come home from school. She decided she would question him alone and see if the boys had made up the story. So when Darren took his nap and Dennis came in from school, she asked him the same questions. He gave the same answers as his brother, so she did not push the issue. About four hours later she asked,

"Who comes to visit you and Darren at night?" Dennis looked to Darren and said, "It was a promise. We were not to tell that Grandpa comes to see us at night. Will he be mad at us, Mama?" My daughter told them he wouldn't be upset with them and that she was glad they can talk to Grandpa, and when they talk to him again, to tell him that she loves and misses him also.

Although skeptical at first, Tina was convinced her children had been visited by their grandfather and it was a good experience for them. Equally important, she did not try to discourage the boys in their beliefs about their grandfather's visits.

There are also a number of children who have reported ADCs involving angelic beings. One of the most interesting in this regard is the encounter Eileen Elias Freeman (editor of *The Angel Watch Journal* and author of *Touched By Angels*) had when she was five years old. Her angel came around ten o'clock one evening, three days after her grandmother's death. Eileen had been very fearful of her world as a child. Not having attended her dear grandmother's funeral was another reason for her to conjure up the worst fantasies of what it must have been like to attend, as only a child can do. Terrified of death and sure she would soon be death's next victim, she fought trying to sleep. But on the third night, out of what she could only describe as a beautiful unearthly light, emerged a strong masculine figure who dashed her twin fears: that her grandmother would be food for worms and sleep was the prerequisite to death. With the words, "Do not be afraid, Eileen. Your grandmother is not in a cold and dark grave. She is happy in heaven with God and her loved ones," Eileen was well on her way to freedom and her ever-deepening interest in angels.

Eileen's mother dismissed her experience as a dream. Nonetheless, let me emphasize that a significant number of adults have reported seeing their guardian angels as children.

Even though adults often disregard children's enthusiasm for the reality of their ADC experiences, there are too many of them that culminate in positive life-long changes for the child to be summarily dismissed. With regard to the question of whether or not children are more open to ADC-like experiences than adults, I have heard some adults who argue convincingly the opposing viewpoints on this issue. There is really no research to point the way in resolving the issue. The variables are many.

However, it is clear children can learn much about life and death from adults who treat ADC angelic encounters and nonphysical reality as a part of life and not apart from it. Many lessons about love, hope, caring, and wisdom are inherently an integral part of these experiences.

- *See also questions 49 and 53*

57. Do many people receive more than one ADC or does it run in families?

With all the talk about the variety of ADCs that occur, is there any indication, like so many other characteristics that appear to run in families, that some families have the experience more than others? If there is a pattern, why do you think it happens when the phenomena is so unpredictable?

Many individuals who experience a deceased loved one appear to have one or two ADCs early in their period of mourning, use them to help in accepting their loss, and never receive another contact. This may be due to their no longer needing additional assistance, using the ADC as a final farewell, not looking for additional signs, or the plain fact that no other contacts were initiated.

Others seem to receive a series of ongoing signs and contacts for a long period of time that may include several different types of ADCs, ranging from sensing the presence of the deceased to symbolic contacts, all apparently coming from the same loved one. There are still others who seem to have a life sporadically filled with events associated with friends and family members who have died. For example, seventy-nine-year-old Rosalind Hill-Tandy, a direct descendent of the first governor of Massachusetts, comes to mind. Some months ago she had attended a lecture I gave and subsequently agreed to be interviewed in her winter home in Venice, Florida. Description of three of the many ADCs she has had over her lifetime are presented here.

The first occurred at age thirty-eight, after the sudden death of her brother-in-law, Al Martin.

"I Was Allowed to See Him"

Al was hit and killed by an automobile whose occupants were both drunk. He had come in from Ohio where he worked for the New York Central. My sister had pneumonia and he came in that afternoon and everything was fine. To help out, he decided to go grocery shopping and that's when he was killed. The night he was buried, my husband had gone to bed earlier, and later I finally joined him. As I was laying there in bed, I wasn't asleep, I heard our front door open and I said to myself, "You locked that door." I could hear the dog also and I could hear Al's step and I knew his step and the dog walking in the living room, then in the long hall, then turning left to come into the bedroom, then right along side of my bed. And I just thought, "What's going on?" Then all of a sudden I opened my eyes and I'm seeing the bottom part of Al. And I'm thinking, "Well it can't be." And then I put myself up and I saw him entirely and I went, "Al, Al." And he disappeared. But I still heard him turn and go with the dog, all the way back out, the same steps, and out. So I poked my husband and I said, "Coley, Coley." And he said, "Yes, Rose?" "I heard Al." And I said, "Did you see him?" He said, "No." And I said, "Well, I was allowed to see him." And I begged Al to come back and tell me. I felt he wanted me to do something for him that wasn't finished. I've never been able to find out why Al came to me that night.

The next ADC involves Roz's second husband, Vince, who died of lung cancer.

"I Feel He Was Alerting Me"

Vince died August 12, 1991, and my most memorable experience took place here in the South on the following November 1. I was sitting on the couch. I walked in the door first and thought I smelled a little bit of Brut. Eh, no Brut here for a couple of years. (That's the after-shave he always used.) Then it seemed to get stronger and stronger and I was thinking, "What's going on?" I was wondering where the smell of Brut was coming from. I did not see anybody. I did not feel him standing here or touching me or behind me. But all I heard was, "Roz, there's no time to waste." I didn't get scared or no feeling came over me that something was very wrong ... I feel he was alerting me to just be careful and watch and make sure you don't lose any time. Do what you have to do immediately.

The third experience was a tactile ADC. It occurred in church and involved her son Jerry, who had committed suicide.

"I Knew It Was My Son"

I was at St. Mark's down here (in Florida) on Easter. I was sitting in the pew and decided to move all the way over to the wall to make sure other people could get in. There was no space between me and the wall. All of a sudden, I felt an arm and I knew it was my son Jerry. He didn't say anything or do anything but he was there. People used to wonder when I was alone up in the house in Clinton Corners if I felt scared being alone. So I always tell them no. I have three people with me. I have my husband, I mean Coley, and I have Vince, and I have my son. When we were kids we were all taught as children and grandchildren—ours was a very, very close family—grandparents, great aunts and all this, always together. We were never afraid of death because we were shown it. We never went to the funerals, but we were shown the death because the people were always in their homes just as though they were still alive in a way, until they were taken out to be buried.

Roz has had other ADC experiences, and so have a number of her family members and in-laws. However, although there is a history of experiencing extraordinary phenomena in the family, including Roz's mother, there are an equal number of family members who have not had a single experience—nothing even resembling an ADC.

At this point in time, there is little credible evidence to conclude that the ability to receive a sign or experience a deceased loved one is genetically based or a function of family social patterns. However, it can be said with certainty that there are a number of families in which more than one family member has had an ADC. One reason may be some family members are more open to the phenomena, look for it, and embrace a belief system that is accepting of the possibility of these events occurring. To read about another family who has experienced several ADCs see questions 16, 62, and 75.

58. Do those who work with the dying and the bereaved look at ADC phenomena differently than the general public?

Dr. LaGrand, for years I have marveled at those who work with the dying, whether in a hospice or in an acute care setting, and having been in a support group, I admired the leader for her sensitivity and insight. Do those who are involved in this type of work hold views about ADC phenomena and death similar to or generally different from the public they serve?

In the past twenty years I have had the opportunity to meet and in many cases work with a large number of hospice volunteers and nurses, bereavement counselors, and funeral directors. Invariably, these individuals were always dealing with people who were dying or mourning the death of loved ones. Their interest in serving others and their commitment to go beyond the call of duty are salient features of their roles. Significantly, their attitudes toward dying and death contrast markedly with those in the general public. There is some research that suggests those professionals who are death-accepting, as opposed to death-denying, tend to interact with the dying and the bereaved in more healthy and helpful ways. This implies they have dealt with their own death fears and come to terms with their own mortality. In my judgment, this is one reason why hospice programs have been so successful throughout the country—caring volunteers and professional hospice staff view death more as a final stage of growth rather than as an enemy to be fought. Much good comes from being around those who will promote living in your time of dying.

To better understand the attitudes of those who work with the dying and the bereaved (and their attitudes toward ADC phenomena), allow me to make a few comments on the philosophy of the hospice movement and explode some myths. To begin with, hospice is not a place where people go to die. On the contrary, it is not a place, it's a program, and it is not where people go to die, it's where they go to live. One's last days can be the most meaningful in life. Most of the time the person with life-threatening illness can be cared for in the familiarity of the home surrounded by loved ones—both family and nonfamily members alike—who give the most precious commodities of all: time and attention.

Time and attention translate into three major goals in the care of the dying. First, pain management. Pain can be controlled. Second, to eliminate the perception of isolation that so often in the past has been the plight of the dying person. Loneliness is stressful and can be every bit as painful as anything one must face. Third, to allow the dying person to be in control of his dying and the decisions affecting his care for as long as he wishes. In accomplishing these goals, volunteers learn to become good listeners, and are trained in helping the dying person dress, get up, change positions, soothe with lotion, support good nutrition and relaxation, and, most of all, be there with their healing presence. At the same time, they also provide support for other family members. In this context, love manifests itself in the most tangible ways.

How then do those who work with the dying and the bereaved view death and the unseen? I have no reservation saying they often see death as a friend, an integral part of life, an event bringing motivation and meaning to existence. This does not mean they are not saddened and in need of people to talk to about their feelings at times. Nor are they completely free of anxiety about death. Very often they look at the death of one in their care as a new beginning for that person. They have witnessed patients who have experienced death bed visions or told of other NDEs, and heard numerous accounts of the bereaved who have had ADCs. As the years wear on, these experiences can have a deep impact on a belief system. Obviously, their attitudes toward the ADC are invariably positive—whether they personally believe in the phenomena or not—because they have seen the positive results of the experiences: fear of death diminishes or is eliminated, while the bond between the living and the dead is strengthened.

59. Have you ever experienced ADC phenomena?

Dr. LaGrand, I hope this question is not too personal, but I feel it may have some bearing on how you view some of the ADCs you write about. I would think as a researcher if you have experienced an ADC it could be a motivator in your work as well as a potential hazard in making judgments about authenticity. In any event, it would be interesting, if you had an ADC, if you would share it with your readers. How about it?

I know that many people who pursue knowledge in certain areas of study are usually motivated to do so because of a personal experience that piqued their interest and started them on a long but enjoyable journey. I have a surprise for you! That is not the case in terms of my interest in ADC phenomena. My mother died of a massive heart attack in her mid-60s. I was with my father when he took his last breath in his hospital bed. My older brother died of prostate cancer and my younger sister from anorexia nervosa. My only daughter died a SIDS death. I am telling you this because I would have liked very much (and still would like) to have had some sign or visit. That has not been the case. I have never had anything remotely resembling an ADC.

On the other hand, I have had more than my share of daily miracles. Many of them, I regret to say, occurred when I was younger and I took them for granted. However, I am still receiving them: strength and endurance when really needed, perfect timing, a job when I wanted it, another book published just at the right time, a loving family, and the ability to teach and counsel. These miracles and others have left a mystical resonance in my life that seems to be at constant battle with disbelief and my scientific enculturation. But most of the time I believe I am winning the battle.

Would I be influenced or biased about ADC phenomena if I had had the experience? I probably would, although my interest in this phenomena has sprung primarily from the wealth of experiences occurring and the absolutely amazing good things accruing to those who are fortunate to have one. So in a way, it may be good that I have not had an ADC because if I had the experience it may well have influenced me to the extent that I might lose whatever credibility I currently possess with those who are familiar with my work. Believe me, I am still skeptical at times.

- *See also question 16*

60. Do atheists and agnostics have ADC experiences?

I have a problem regarding the ADC being a spiritual experience. So I'm wondering if atheists and agnostics ever report an ADC. If they do, how do they respond to the experience? Does it change them in any way?

Atheists and agnostics are subgroups in the population who do have the same types of ADCs (and they also report NDEs) as those who are professed believers. How many have the experience in comparison to the general population, no one knows. Nor do we know why any one particular person has the experience and someone else who seems in even more need of reassurance fails to have one. All anyone is sure of is that the experience does happen frequently to people who are grieving the death of a loved one, including atheists and agnostics.

An interesting story of an atheist turned believer in an afterlife is the following account from Geri Wiitala, author of *Heather's Return,* an absorbing book that chronicles the series of ADCs she and her husband experienced after the premature death of their teenage daughter. Having read her book, and knowing of the change in her husband's beliefs, I asked her if she would ask Walt to respond to my request to write about his experiences. First, Geri provides some background material.

> *Walt's parents are both agnostics or atheists. His mother comes from Finland and his father from Canada. He was raised in a home where he only spoke Finnish until he entered the American school system when he was seven years old. He was never taken to church and God was an unknown entity to him. Although they celebrated Christmas and Easter, it was more of a cultural event than a religious one and he never connected them to religion. Because Lutheranism was the state religion of Finland, his aunt urged his mother to have the boys baptized when they were about twelve years old as Finnish Lutherans. He did not understand what it meant and associated it more with Finnish tradition. Finnish tradition was the most important thing in their home. When he became a teenager, he never understood why other classmates talked about religion or believed in God.*
>
> *When we began to date, I was a student in college at a time when "God is dead" was a popular philosophy. So, when we married, we were both considered atheists. Three years later, I became involved with the Jehovah's Witnesses (I was raised a Catholic at a time when the Masses were in Latin and I didn't understand it very well either). When I became a Jehovah's Witness, Walt was very upset and confused by all this, since he did not understand it and it was now taking a lot of my time. It became a sore issue for us and I had to wing a lot of this on my own. This is where we were when we had our separate ADC experiences.*

Here is Walt's experience.

"I Will Be with Her Again"

I never believed in God and I never understood what the big fuss was all about. I attended a few funerals and remember the phrase "from dust you came and to dust you go." That's what I thought happened. It didn't bother me and I hardly ever thought about it. When Heather died, I believed that was the end of her and I would never see her again. I could not understand Geri's obsession at all. Heather was dead. Gone. That was it. I was very sad and missed her greatly. But, it never occurred to me I would ever see her again. I was shocked by what happened to me when she came to me. Just that one time convinced me that Heather is in a spirit form. I believe she did and can communicate with us, to show us that she is alive in a different form. I don't know how this all works, but I know when I die I will be with her again in a spirit form. I know that it is not my time yet. But when it is, I am so looking forward to being with her again. I believe we will all be together again, but in a better place.

Other atheists and agnostics have had similar experiences that caused major changes in their worldviews. Most dramatic of course is the change in belief about death being the absolute end, to death being a door to a new existence where "we will all be together again."

61. What are the types of messages received?

If millions of people have experienced one or more ADCs, there must be some data available to suggest the kinds of messages that are received. Is there a particular pattern or message that accompanies one type of ADC as compared to another? Or are there a variety of messages without regard for the type of ADC?

Thornton Wilder said, "the highest tribute to the dead is not grief but gratitude." Of course, the attitude or habit of gratitude has also been shown to be health promoting as Hans Selye reminded us in his classic work *The Stress of Life*. Although Wilder's observation is an apt reminder of what we all need to show loved ones during life, it is equally important to speak of it when they die because of the insight they continue to bestow. In fact, the deceased (or?) often appear to continue to play the roles they played when alive. At times they are comforter, motivator or protector. At other times they can be teacher, advisor or messenger. Oh yes, on occasion, they can also play the role of chastiser. They have been observed playing one or several of these roles by those who are mourning their absence and receive a contact or a reminder. Here is an example of just such a reminder as experienced by a young woman in an eastern state a few days after the death of her mother.

"I Truly Believe My Mother Led Me to the Box"

My sister, my father, and I were going through my mother's clothes when I realized we had not found the family christening gown. I was in a panic because I remembered she always kept it in her lingerie drawer and I had quickly cleaned that drawer out when I was getting the clothes for the funeral director. We went through everything again and could not find it. I felt terrible!

During my mother's illness, I had taken over cleaning their house and I continued to do that for my father. One night before I was going over to clean their house, I had a dream. In the dream I was at my parent's house and I was kneeling in front of what I thought was a large box or trunk. When I opened the trunk, I found the missing christening gown.

When I woke up, I felt let down because it was "only a dream." Anyway, I went over to the house and started to clean. When I got to the den, I was on my knees in front of a large armoire where my mother kept all her extra towels, sheets, and tablecloths. I suddenly had this overwhelming urge to open the doors and look inside. Way down at the bottom I saw a corner of a box sticking out. I pulled out the box and opened it. Inside was the missing christening gown! I truly believe my mother led me to the box in the armoire; she knew I felt bad about losing it and she helped me to find it.

Messages may be implicit or, as in the example, implied. Sometimes they appear to be associated with a particular type of ADC. Obviously, the messages received are highly individual perceptions of the experience based on the relationship that existed between the mourner and the deceased when alive. Thus the same type of ADC could deliver a different message to two different mourners. Although I hesitate to suggest the most frequent interpretation of the ADC by the mourner, if I had to make an assumption based on what they have told me, it would be that the mourner is convinced the loved one is okay and lives on. But that is only part of the story. There may literally be multiple messages that one receives after he is able to sit down and think about what happened. As I have noted elsewhere, the ADC is a universal message of love. Most mourners who have had the experience would tend to agree if you asked them about it. Within that one observation, however, are many additional messages the mourner is grateful for.

Here is a short list of the kinds of insights that are gleaned from the ADC.

1. He's okay, it's all right to let go.

2. The deceased is no longer in pain.

3. Her spirit will always be with me.

4. I had an opportunity to say goodbye. (Some people use the ADC as a form of closure, a way to say goodbye, while others use it as a continuing bond.)

5. I received courage and reassurance that I can assume my new duties.

6. I now know from experience that spirit does not die with matter.

7. My loved one still cares deeply.

8. The experience made me feel much more positive.

9. I found peace and comfort.

As you can see, these are very individual interpretations of ADC phenomena. In many instances, there is no direct verbal communication in the ADC. However, the mourner interprets messages from the experience based on the background of having known the deceased, and on his conscious and unconscious beliefs about what is real.

62. How are messages conveyed?

There must be a variety of messages conveyed through the ADC, but I would like to know just how one can interpret a particular message based on a single experience. In particular, when a person receives a sign or a symbolic contact, just how is the message conveyed and understood?

Messages come in a variety of ways and are interpreted in many ways. What we need to initially understand is that the way a message is conveyed and how it is interpreted are two different questions. So let's focus on your interest in the way messages are sent.

Verbal. A number of ADCs involve what is believed to be a verbal response from the deceased loved one. Not infrequently a mourner may hear a deceased loved one call out his name or hear the voice say, "I'm okay, it's all right to let go." In some instances the deceased is seen as an apparition and also speaks similar words of encouragement or comfort. There are also occasions in which an apparition takes place and a two-way conversation ensues. Two-way exchanges also are common in dreams. Sometimes the mourner hears laughter that is thought to be the way the deceased sounded when alive.

Nonverbal. These messages appear to occur more frequently than verbal messages. Several kinds of messages may be conveyed through the clothing worn by the deceased in an apparition or dream. A special piece of clothing can refer to an event only the mourner fully comprehends and finds meaning in. Of course, facial expression can send a host of messages, as can the overall appearance of the deceased. The context in which the deceased is seen gives insights, whether he appears in a natural setting, in mist or wisps of vapor, or surrounded by a white light. Skin color and health are also markers that convey messages for some mourners.

Telepathic communication. Sometimes an apparition occurs and the message is conveyed in telepathic form without speaking. A mourner will say he understood a message without the loved one moving his lips or making a sound ("We didn't need to talk, we could read each other's minds"). Many authorities believe dream messages are based essentially on telepathy. Numerous parapsychologists believe most ADCs can be explained by telepathy and are not spiritual experiences.

Music. Another modality that provides much comfort and information is music that is heard, particularly when there is no source to be found. On other occasions, a particular song will be heard at a point in time that coincides precisely with events in the life of the mourner, or is a reminder of a past experience involving the deceased. It provides the sign or symbol that sends a particular message to the mourner, a message others cannot fully appreciate.

Intuitively. There are some mourners who report sensing the energy of the deceased, and in doing so, assume it to be a sign from the loved one. Others will say, "She sent me energy." Intuitively, they pick up information that for them is fashioned in a way that only they can fathom as a form of communication. It is difficult for them to explain, yet they have no reservations about the intent or meaning of the intuitive flash.

Symbolically. Symbolic communication is an inherent part of life. We have many symbols that provide specific messages such as the eagle, skull and crossbones, butterflies, and the flag of our country. Symbolic messages can also be received through inanimate objects within the house that have special meaning to the mourner and the deceased, as happened with Terri Kaczmarczyk whose sons were killed in an automobile accident.

"When My Husband Came Home He Said This Was Really Impossible"

On May 7, 1997, my son Tommy's birthday, he would have been sixteen if he had lived. I was very sick. I wanted to go to the cemetery and put flowers there for Tommy, but I just couldn't make it. Mom and Dad said they would go and do it for all of us. But it wasn't the same.

I was all alone in the house, except for Michaela, my granddaughter. I had to get up to get a drink, and as I was walking down the hall to the kitchen I heard one of the clocks ticking. I have two little wind-up clocks in the kitchen, over the glass doors. They were the ones Tommy would always wind for me. They hadn't been wound since he died. In fact, the one that was ticking was missing its pendulum. I called my Mom to tell her. We couldn't believe it. She came running over to see for herself. When my husband came home he said this was really impossible. The clock ran until about 10:04 then stopped. My husband said for the past couple of nights he heard the alarm on Tommy's wrist watch, which is in his bedroom, go off a few minutes after ten. We don't know if the time had more meaning, or that Tommy just wanted me to know that he was there with me and it was okay that I was too sick to go to the cemetery.

Other sounds. Finally, a number of messages are conveyed by sounds like church bells when there are no churches in the vicinity. Or it may be sound like wind chimes and the wind is not blowing and the mourner's home, or those near it, have nothing that could make the sound as clear and meaningful as it comes through. In other instances, mourners have heard sounds associated with favorite birds at unusual times, like at night. What is important to remember in all of the situations in which symbolic means of communication occur is that the message conveyed is only in the eye of the beholder, no one else. That is why it is so easy for us who are on the outside looking in to dismiss this form of communication as nonsense. As Blaise Pascal wrote: "We know the truth not only through our reason but also through our heart. It is through the latter that we know first principles . . . " The mourner knows through his heart. All of us can use an educated heart.

63. How do ADCs change the lives of mourners?

Whenever I think of those I know who have had the good fortune to have an ADC experience, I am struck by the fact that although there are similarities in how they respond, there are also real differences. How does the ADC translate into behavioral changes in the lives of mourners?

The ADC experience culminates not only in changes in behavior for the mourner, but it has an equally strong impact on his emotional disposition. Moreover, depending on the individual, certain beliefs are either strengthened or new ones supplant the old ones. Again, I must emphasize here the changes that ensue from the ADC experience are highly individual and occur according to specific needs and circumstances. Therefore, the changes I will list below are not applicable to all mourners. In addition, other specific changes occur that are not mentioned here and are unique only to the individual mourner.

1. **Changes in worldview.** One's paradigm of reality is often affected to the extent that the person believes life is eternal and death is not the end of existence. I need to remind you that for some, the nature of the ADC experience is dramatically inspiring; temporarily they are in a state of wonder and awe by what has transpired. Their view of life and reality broadens to include the world of the unseen in ways that motivate them to change as never previously considered. They are more open to their immediate world, more sensitive, and embrace a more positive approach to life. Here is an example from a young woman whose boyfriend died unexpectedly. She had two ADCs involving him over a three-day period.

"I Have Greater Faith in God"

Because of my encounter with Tom on the evening of his death and also two days after his funeral, my life has changed. Not only have I become more spiritual, but I have fewer fears in my life . . . I moved 3,000 miles to pursue my dreams to work in TV and film; I am more insightful of my feelings and the feelings of others; I have greater faith in God and a greater sense of the universe, as corny as that may sound. I was so sad to have never known Tom well in life, but I was so happy that my own encounters with him had resulted in such an unbelievable, spiritual encounter. To this day, I have difficulty repeating this story to anyone because it is so profoundly odd and incredibly emotional.

What anchors this narrative and highlights one of the universal themes of most ADC experiences is this: one is brought in close proximity to the spiritual side and to the broader implications of looking at the world through the lens of a spiritual encounter. All of this often includes changes in priorities as one suddenly sees a bigger

picture and is more willing to begin the task of assimilating the loss
into life, thus regaining the balance so desperately needed.

2. **Emotional changes.** These may occur immediately, be gradual
   and sustained on a long-term basis, and/or become an integral
   factor in the search for meaning. Although all deaths do not bring
   forth the need to find meaning and make sense of the why of the
   death, those that are sudden or unexpected invariably do. Finding
   meaning in the death of a loved one can be an important grieving
   tool. Although many mourners do not have success in their search,
   those who have an ADC usually do. The experience tempers their
   emotional disposition allowing them to begin to integrate the loss
   into their lives as they find a sense of continuity in a life after death.

   In one way, the ADC becomes a teaching tool in which dormant
   beliefs are awakened and revitalized. One is able to let go of the
   feelings of emptiness and despair built on the assumption "she is
   gone forever." The transformation comes in the new awareness that
   "we will someday be together again." The deep emotion of sadness is
   gradually replaced by hope of reunion or a sense of peace from the
   conviction the loved one is happy. Based on their ADCs, mourners
   respond with, "It made me feel much more positive," or, "It has
   made it easier to cope with my feelings." For some, the reassurance
   associated with the ADC tempers the fears (sometimes the panic)
   that often has to be dealt with when one is thrust into new roles
   and responsibilities.

   Last, but certainly not least, love is made manifest through the ADC.
   It is love that is the major force for sustaining the endurance-like
   journey back to living in a world without the deceased. Reinforcing
   the bond of love in a different configuration is the hidden force that
   allows the bereaved to deal with the additional demands placed on
   them by the new roles they must assume.

3. **Behavioral changes.** The behavioral changes that occur following an
   ADC are clearly a result of the emotional change preceding them and
   the rethinking of the world in which the bereaved find themselves.
   These changes are not necessarily always dramatic or noticeable by

those who are in the social circle of the mourner. However, they are tangible and comforting to the mourner. For example being able to rise in the morning and greet the day with a more optimistic outlook can be a monumental step forward for someone who has been deeply depressed. Or being able to go to familiar places that previously were painful reminders of what one had lost, can be equally pleasing. The internal changes, particularly moments of inner peace, old feelings of warmth and comfort, and dwelling on happy memories are the building blocks for some of the more external behavioral changes.

Much more noticeable to those giving support to the bereaved is the willingness to interact with others, to slowly reinvest in life. One may be more inclined to talk about the death and obligingly reach out to others. Significantly, those who experience an ADC are much more open to unseen phenomena in general and to speaking with those who have had similar experiences.

In summary, the ADC is a motivation to action for the mourner to reinvest in life. There is a renewal of energy in many instances. One has less difficulty finding the strength to go on. Depending on the solace and validation provided by the person's support network, the overall benefit from an ADC can be a major factor in motivating and accepting the new routines that have to be structured and followed in the absence of the deceased.

64. Are messages ever misinterpreted?

Whenever I think of the phrase after-death communication I have a little trouble with the idea that in most cases the message received, whatever it might be, is crystal clear. Yet, maybe I see a problem where there is no problem. From your vantage point, are there misunderstandings and misinterpretations or are exchanges pretty well accepted and understood by the mourner?

The circumstances in which the ADC takes place are such that it is difficult for the mourner to be too far off the mark in interpreting what the experience is saying. We are not dealing here with the usual encounter that we all have many times a day where we sit down and talk with someone for a length of time. This type of exchange is always subject to the misinterpretations inherent in human communication. If we are practicing good communication techniques we seek feedback to be sure we are understood whenever there appears to be a question. However, the background for the exchange in an ADC is the knowledge of death of the beloved. Most ADCs do not present the luxury of extended conversations, which automatically reduces the possibilities for misunderstanding what is being said. In fact, most messages are rather short, clear, and to the point making it difficult not to receive whatever was intended. And when there is no verbal exchange, the signs or visual cues need little or no explanation.

We have to remember also that interpreting the meaning of the ADC is often based on nonverbal and symbolic forms of communication that characteristically have a specific personal meaning only to the mourner. Of course, most of the time the mourner is really the only one who is in the best position to make a decision on meaning. He or she knows the deceased like no one else can. This personal meaning does not preclude the possibility of someone else making alternative suggestions—as usually occurs in dream groups when interpreting the symbolism in a particular dream—so the mourner may view the experience from a different perspective. Sometimes this can be very helpful in seeing multiple meanings in the ADC and the mourner finds another memory to add to the one he already possesses.

Are mistakes made? Do mourners misinterpret what they hear or see? Yes they do! I say that only because of the conditioning that some are subject to early in life that causes fear, disbelief, or self-doubt when they encounter the world of the unseen. I'm not talking here about misinterpreting whether or not one has had an ADC, but seeing fear in an ADC, or questioning one's sanity after the experience. However, the highly individual nature of the ADC, the spontaneous and clear meaning of the event, and the usually bone-deep conviction of the mourner as to its authenticity, leaves little room for misinterpretation. Dream state ADCs are vivid and clear; auditory and visual ADCs are short and to the point; indirect ADCs are subject to a wide variety of interpretations, all of which are unusually positive. Misinterpretations, if and when they do occur, are few and seldom harmful to any extent.

65. If you have an unusual experience involving a deceased person, when you receive a message for someone else, how can you be sure it is authentic and decide whether or not to tell the survivor?

It must be a very perplexing experience to have an ADC with a message for someone else. But when it occurs, one can also be in a quandary with regard to deciding on authenticity and whether or not to say something to the primary mourner, or to dismiss it. What are the guidelines for making a decision on these questions?

Actually, it isn't difficult to decide on either of these potential problems. When you are not the primary mourner, and do not have the deep emotional turmoil to deal with, deciding on authenticity usually is not a big concern. Those I have talked with who have been the third- or fourth-party involved in relaying a message have never reported a concern about what they experienced. It was clear: they had something happen that involved the deceased and the big question was always, "Should I tell the mourner(s)?" The third- and fourth-party messages usually come in hearing a voice, having a dream visitation, or seeing a vision. What is heard or seen has an authenticity all its own. There is no question about it. It happened, but was it important enough to tell the person who was closest to the deceased? Don't let me give you the impression that the person who carries the message is not awed by the experience, even sometimes confused. They are at a loss to tell you why they were chosen and are moved by the implications and meaning of the ADC.

In authenticating any ADC if you happen to be the person who receives a message to be passed on, it is essential to go through the usual procedures of ruling out natural causes or misperceptions. Look for normal explanations before exploring the more unusual ones. Depending on the type of ADC, examine circumstances that you could have created—such as medication you are taking—that could influence your judgment. Look for light reflections, wind caused phenomena, or illusions caused by heat, distance, or water.

Deciding to tell the mourner what occurred usually hinges on two major considerations: Can it help the mourner better cope with his loss, and will it provide an avenue for finding meaning in the death? In most instances, the answer is obvious. It's the thing to do and it will help the mourner. Nonetheless, preface your remarks to the mourner by saying you must tell him something that ultimately only he can judge as significant, that you feel obligated to share it with him, and that you are doing so hoping it will help in some small way. Then provide as much detail as possible in laying out what you experienced.

66. What kinds of messages from the deceased do people receive through dreams?

So much has been written about dreams and their symbols that I am wondering about the kinds of messages that are received in the ADC and how someone would go about deciding on what the message actually is. Are dream messages different from those received in other forms of ADCs?

After a discussion on dreams about the deceased, a young woman wrote me the following optimistic view. "When I dream of people who have died that I love, I feel so nice when I wake up. It's like I was just granted a visit. It's very pleasant." This illustrates an important factor in the interpretation and use of dream messages: the attitude of the mourner toward the dream is the essential element. So much of the good that comes from dreams of the deceased has much to do with the way mourners choose to accept them. ADC dream visitations are commonly vivid and clear. The mourner has a wealth of information to assimilate, since the dream can usually be interpreted literally. Not having to deal with symbols and metaphors makes for an easier understanding (and often acceptance) of the dream contents. The literally interpreted dream content makes more sense to the dreamer since he needs clarity and immediate answers to his stressing problems.

What do dreams convey to the mourner? Or, put another way, what does the dream messenger say? The answer to this question can range from seeking forgiveness and saying, "I love you," to believing our loved ones can communicate with us through dreams and the deceased came to give consolation. Whatever can be said in normal conversation, when two people have been separated in real life situations and meet again, can be said in a dream visitation. Let's consider the dream that Bridget had about her deceased uncle.

"The Dream Helped Me Know He Was Okay"

I dreamt I was at my aunt and uncle's house (he had recently passed away). My extended family was also there and we were all eating. We were all gathered for something and I was sitting on the top step of the stairs leading to the bedrooms. We were all talking, when all of a sudden, I turned my head to the left to look down toward the bedrooms, and I saw my uncle and one of his grandsons playing chess; they were lying on their sides. When I looked at my uncle, I said out loud, "Uncle! It's Uncle Joe!" He looked a little younger. He still had salt and pepper hair, but darker. He had on a gray sweater-like shirt and beige pants with a belt. He looked good. It was weird, because at first it felt like I knew he was gone, but then I felt that he had just returned from being away somewhere. It's kind of hard to explain. It was such a nice feeling.

Without speaking, he said he was okay and that the reason why he "came" to me (I was the only one who could see him) was because he knew I would tell everyone. I was offended at first, because I thought he was implying that I had a big mouth. But then that feeling left. I felt both sad and relieved to know he was okay. Then I started to cry a little bit when I felt my mother console me. At that point, everyone knew he was there.

The next thing that happened was like from the movie Ghost. *I went up the stairs and saw my aunt and my cousin (my uncle's daughter) in my aunt and uncle's bedroom. When I looked in I saw my cousin hugging her dad from behind. There was a glowing white light around my uncle. They were rocking back and forth; then all I saw were her arms in "hug stance." I didn't see him but I knew he was still with her. Then it was as if he left her and went to my aunt. While she was holding him closely they started to slow dance. My uncle still had the white glowing light around him. Again, at first I saw his image, but then all I saw was my aunt dancing with her arms folded upward and close to her as if she were leaning on his chest. Finally, I was sitting next to my mother, when my cousin came to us, knelt down and told us that my uncle was with my aunt upstairs, and that she and her dad had made an appointment to meet again. He was going to come to her again; she was so excited.*

In the final analysis, only the dreamer is in a position to decide what the dream messenger is saying by his or her appearance. In this instance, I asked Bridget how she interpreted what happened and what messages she received. Her response was: "I interpreted the dream as my uncle telling us he was okay, not to worry. Also, an explicit message for me was not to be afraid of death. I have to say that, combined with the other experiences the rest of the family had, the dream helped me know he was okay, no longer suffering, and I realized for sure there is a hereafter." It is important to note the clarity of the dream and Bridget's positive unequivocal belief her dream was a visitation from her uncle.

The messages in this dream are common to many visitation dreams among mourners: there is an afterlife, my loved one is there and in good health, death is not to be feared, the dream is a valid form of communication, and we will meet again. Keep in mind, if you are heavily into dream work, I am not talking here in terms of the wide variety of messages associated with symbolic dreams long after grief work has come to an end, but those dreams where people are still actively mourning and in need of support. To summarize, ADC dreams may provide any or all of the following for the mourner: reassurance, reconciliation, a continuing bond with the deceased, guidance and support, and in some instances helpful advice.

PART

، 5 ،

Positive Influences

Questions 67 through 88

Changes in Worldview • Dream Interpretations •
Providing Support • Unconscious Effects • Accepting Death •
Unfinished Business • Spiritual Changes • Symbols of Hope •
Therapeutic Benefits • Educational Program • Related Questions

The mind, which sometimes presumes to believe
that there is no such thing as a miracle,
is itself a miracle.
—M. Scott Peck

67. How can an ADC help someone heal?

Dr. LaGrand, obviously there are many people who claim their extraordinary experiences involving a deceased loved one has helped them heal the wounds of grief. Could you give some specific examples of what they mean by healing? Are we talking here about physical healing as well as emotional healing?

Healing from an ADC experience may occur in a variety of ways, not the least of which involves a physical dimension. I'm not talking here about miraculous healings from major illnesses, although I would not be surprised to some day come across someone who was grieving and desperately ill and as a result of an ADC experience made a startling recovery. In order to clarify what I am implying about physical healing, let me digress a moment to emphasize a dimension of the grief response that is commonly overlooked.

Grief is often defined as the normal emotional and physical response to any meaningful loss. Most fail to realize that grief is as strong in the physical demands on the body as it is with its emotional demands. Looked at in another way, we all tend to forget a major factor in dealing with the stress of life, namely, for every thought and emotion there is a corresponding physical manifestation of that thought or emotion. This fact of life has long-term implications for health and well-being, yet it is forgotten by many in the conduct of daily affairs and the consideration of the stress of mourning. What continually dwells in the mind—what we choose to focus on—is animated in the life of our cells.

For many years, those who served the bereaved were well aware that prolonged grief often resulted in sickness and poor health for the mourner, not merely because of poor diet and little rest, but because the immune system was compromised when grief was forever ongoing and strong. Recently, researchers in the blossoming field of psychoneuroimmunology, or PNI for short, (the study of the relationship between the nervous system, the endocrine system, the gastrointestinal system, and the immune system) have gathered scientific evidence suggesting the devastating effects that one's thought-life can have on his physiology. In short, the body mirrors the mind. The implications of this concept are profound and need careful study by all. Why? Because life and grief are inseparable and ongoing, while loss and change are conditions of existence. Growth and maturation—from birth to death—is a series of losses that must be mourned.

Can the ADC make inroads on the insidious effects of the stress of grief? Anything that can change the nature of emotional turmoil—from deep despair to hope for the future—will affect the physical body. If we look at the impact of intense guilt, deep depression, and suppressed anger on the mourner, we see they can take a significant toll on the health of the person and whatever energy is available. Healing through the ADC occurs when any of these emotions or unfinished business is resolved, or at least managed in a healthy way. Remember: thoughts affect biology either for good or for bad, whether we are grieving or harboring these intense emotions for whatever reason. Despairing, hopeless, and fearful thoughts trigger a cascade of chemical changes in the body that if prolonged will eventually cause damage. If those thoughts can be replaced by thoughts of peace, acceptance, gratitude for what the deceased has given and taught, and the belief that "love lives on between us," they can speed emotional healing and promote physical health. Our body knows how to create health if we will only feed it healthy thoughts. Thoughts of continuity, meaning, and the conviction the world can still be a friendly place rekindles hope not merely in the mind, but in the entire body. Candace Pert—one of the pioneers in the PNI movement—calls this process of exchange the mobile brain. The informational exchange that is continually going on within the body between the immune, neural, hormonal, and gastrointestinal systems can be affected in a most positive way by the ADC experience.

Consider the emotional disposition of Arlene Brown who was fortunate to have had several ADCs (tactile, dream state, and symbolic) that convinced her of her mother's love and brought a change conducive to healing.

"It's Not a Figment of My Imagination"

When I would least expect to hear from my mother I would have an unusual contact. I always feel she's close; she loves me. I'm at peace about her and me as we were not as close in life as I would have liked. I was her caretaker and she was controlled by others. She had been a widow almost fifty-five years. Yet she was seventy-eight when she died of cancer. My experiences have helped me because I know she lives on. I knew she would before she passed over, but she has continually let me know she loves me and lives on. It's not a figment of my imagination, because things too unusual for me to expect occur, and it happens at times I least expect. I just know she's loving me now because she couldn't, or wasn't able to, when alive.

Finishing unfinished business, coupled with a renewed sense of love, created an internal environment for Arlene that was health promoting. In most instances, the ADC affects both the emotions and the physical well-being of the recipient. The degree to which healing occurs depends on the content of the ADC experienced and the belief system of the mourner. Mind-Body medicine as a separate discipline and intensive training using the biopsychosocial-spiritual model have yet to address the ADC as a viable healing experience for the bereaved because these disciplines are still emerging. Nevertheless, the principles of Mind-Body medicine are directly applicable to the ADC experience and healing does occur.

68. I have had several dreams of my father since he died a year ago. How can I decide if any of them are ADCs?

I have hoped for some kind of sign that my father is okay after his sudden death. Nothing like I was looking for has happened, but I have had several dreams in which he spoke to me. I have never thought much about dreams as being of any particular importance. Actually, I think most of my dreams are rather odd and make no sense. Now I wonder if I have received what I had hoped for, but I have failed to recognize it. How can I decide?

As you may already know most people dream of their deceased loved ones at some point after the death. Sometimes the dreams are not remembered, but most of the time, at least part of the dream of the loved one is remembered. Generally, let me say that if you had an ADC dream, it would be convincing, you would note its clarity and detail, and you would not dismiss it as insignificant. In the case of an ADC dream, most dreamers generally report specific characteristics about their dream scenario.

1. **Dream Clarity.** ADC dreams are most often described by dreamers as being bright and vivid, not like their usual dreams. They are able

to describe the scene in which the dream occurs in considerable detail. The deceased loved one and other people in the dream are clearly seen in terms of clothing worn, which is readily described by the dreamer. Although the face of the loved one may not always be seen, the dreamer has no doubt that it was the deceased loved one. The entire dream scene is alive and rich with information.

2. **Specific Message.** In most cases, the message or messages from the dream are specific and there is no doubt about content or meaning. Frequently, the deceased in the dream will speak to the dreamer and make it clear that all is well, not to worry, and that he is happy and whole, free from illness. Sometimes these messages are inferred by nonverbal signs or mind to mind (telepathic) communication.

3. **Strong Feelings.** Feelings and emotions are most important indicators of authenticity. As the dream unfolds and develops, the dreamer often reports strong emotion associated with the content being experienced. This emotion may be joy, love, happiness, or specific feelings that are part of the unique relationship that only the dreamer and the deceased had previously experienced in real life. Some dream content may evoke feelings one is not proud of or happy with, depending on the nature of the relationship. It is not unusual for the dreamer to wake up and feel a previously unknown sensation of deep inner peace and freedom that lasts for a long period of time. Relief and new meaning may also be experienced, all depending on the individual needs of the dreamer and the nature of dream content. Dreams in this sense are most trustworthy.

In the following dream, one not as spectacular in addressing immediate needs as many ADC dreams are, sixty-three-year-old Frank B. was able to find exceptional meaning and strong feelings about his father who had died several years previously.

"I Know That My Father Loves Me"

On January 18, 1991, I dreamed I was driving an old Auburn four-door car. I could see every detail of the car including the huge dashboard. As I came to a sharp curve in the road, I lost control and the car went into a field, rolling over many times. As I lay in the front seat, upside down, my father pulled me out and asked if I was okay. As we walked down the foggy lane, I noticed he was wearing his usual clothes—gray pants and green sweater. We walked hand in hand.

I always felt my father was a protector for me. He was always in the background, more or less watching over me. I know that from this dream, my father will always be near to me, much closer now than when he was alive. When trouble occurs in my life, I know I'll have help in solving it from my father. I know that my father loves me, probably more now than when he was alive. Also, when I get involved with home projects, I am helped by my father in getting them solved.

From the above dream, I know my father lives on.

The detail and events in this dream obviously had a strong impact on the dreamer. It fit perfectly into his image of his father before he died and it brought forth strong feelings of connectedness and being loved, meeting the deepest of all human needs.

4. **Comfort.** As one replays the dream scenario over and over again upon awakening, it provides a deep sense of comfort, a sense of completeness. One finds an unexpected resource has burst on the scene, something to hang on to, as the work of grief still has to continue with all of the adjustments demanded in the "year of the firsts." Recalling the dream can be energizing and telling it to others a therapeutic release.

In reviewing the dreams you have had of your father, first find a quiet place where you will not be disturbed. Take a few moments to relax by taking some deep abdominal breaths. Once you feel your heart rate and breathing quiet down then slowly, from beginning to end, recreate each dream in your mind's eye. Here is where you will have to get in touch with your intuitive self, with your heart, to help you interpret. If you believe in God, ask the Holy Spirit for assistance with your task. Tertullian (ca. 160—ca. 230), Roman theologian and Christian apologist, said that God works through dreams.

It will also be helpful, if you have not already done so, to write down each dream in as much detail as possible. Make two columns on several sheets of paper, the one on the right twice the width of the left hand column. Fully describe the dream, with specific messages, in the right hand column. In the left hand column list all emotions and feelings during the dream and when you awakened. Look for differences in feelings between dreams. If you experienced different feelings, ask yourself how you can explain them. What do they mean to you? Also look for similarities and continuity of emotions in all of the dreams. You may find much meaning in them, but your early negative conditioning has simply not allowed you to see them as a possible communication form. Relationships always live on after one dies and dreams are often one way we continue to honor our relationships with our loved ones. If your dreams were of the ADC variety, you will get the "click" or that "aha" feeling that something good has transpired. Only you can decide after recreating each dream in a quiet setting, looking at your dreams on paper, and the written clues (especially in the emotions and feelings column) that will give you valuable insights into your experiences.

69. Have you ever heard of someone who has had an ADC but essentially was over their mourning?

In your work of interviewing people who claim to have an ADC experience, have you come across anyone who says a deceased loved one came to her for reasons other than to ease the pain of grief? That is, in your estimation, have some individuals who were dealing with other problems in life ever had encouragement from deceased loved ones?

First, let me comment on the phrase "but essentially was over their mourning." The idea that people should get over their mourning is to imply that everything should return to normal or the way it was before the death of the loved one occurred. This is a myth that has a long history in our culture. People do not magically get over the death of a loved one. When a person we love dies, a part of us changes, perhaps dies. We are not the same persons we were before the death; we will continue to cherish their memories, be reminded of them on special occasions, perhaps cry again, and reconstruct our lives. The process of reconstruction does not bring us back to who we used to be. One is now a widow or widower with all of the social ramifications that state in life entails. Another is now childless. Someone else no longer has a mother or father. We are changed because of the experience and getting back to where we used to be—as the phrase getting over it suggests—is a myth. We are able to accommodate it and go on with our lives, but we have learned and grown through the experience. We are at a different place in our journey.

With that aside, what you are asking about is actually the type of scenario that frequently transpires in many near-death experiences (NDE). A person thinks he is dying, has an out-of-body experience (some have the OOB experience without the circumstances or belief that they are dying), eventually meet a loved one or loved ones who have predeceased him, and is given reassurance about some pressing issue being faced. Now if we take away the OOB experience and substitute a set of circumstances commonly found in the ADC experience (the person is mourning), or in the situation suggested in the opening question (the person is not mourning), we have essentially the same type of assistance being given. There are a number of people who are convinced they have received a visit from a deceased loved one having little or nothing to do with the mourning process, but was helpful in reducing the intense emotional trauma they were facing. As with ADCs, the circumstances surrounding these extraordinary experiences vary considerably from person to person. Here is an example from Judy L. who lives in Fort Meyers, Florida and received a "visit" and reassurance from her deceased mother at a much needed time.

"Ruth Will Be All Right"

Three years ago this December 26, our only daughter, Ruth, called to tell us that in two days she would be in the hospital for a modified radical mastectomy. Dan, her husband, is a nuclear submarine commander and they are stationed at Pearl Harbor. They had known for ten days, but would not tell any member of the family until Christmas was over. We were both shocked, and I felt like the floor was going out from under me. Our only daughter! Why couldn't it be me instead?

Dick and I were at our son's home in North Carolina when we got the news, and it was a very somber ride back to Fort Meyers. My son and our daughter-in-law had just had their first baby in October, so in January we were invited back to Raleigh for the christening. This was three weeks after we had received the news about Ruth. We left Fort Meyers that Friday morning, January 13, traveling north. As we approached I-95, north of Jacksonville, we had car trouble and lost two hours of time in a garage. By the time we got to our motel it was 7:30 P.M., so we immediately went to a restaurant to have dinner. Returning at 9, I knew Dick was tired and wanted to go right to bed, but he did not object to my watching TV until 10, which I did.

By 10:15 P.M., I had turned out the light and went right to sleep. At 11:20 (digital clock) I suddenly awoke and sat right up in my bed with my whole body shaking. I did not know what was happening to me, and I turned my head to the right in the direction of the bed where Dick was sleeping. Between the two beds—my mother was standing—and she said five words to me before disappearing. "Ruth will be all right." I lay back down in my bed, but it was a long time before I could get back to sleep. When Dick awoke the next morning, I told him what happened. It never occurred to me to awaken him earlier, as there was nothing he could do, and I felt he needed his sleep.

People have asked me what my mother looked like: she appeared elderly, as she was when she died in 1968, and she was dressed in yellow. (My mother never wore yellow, but I have since been told that it is a very spiritual color.) Of the four ministers I have confided in, two told me that I was dreaming: I do not accept this. My personal view of this episode is that the Lord knew how upset both Dick and I were with Ruth's illness, and He sent someone to me that I loved and respected to offer me comfort. And I can honestly say, those five words got me through the last three years.

On the other hand, a dear friend and Navy chaplain and I were walking on the following Easter Sunday morning when I told him the story. His reaction was completely the reverse of the other two ministers. Standing on the golf course on Ford Island, he took both my hands, thanking the Lord in prayer for sending my mother to me to ease my worry. In my own mind, I know it was not a dream, and I so appreciate that I could experience this event. I eventually told Ruth the story, and I believe it was some comfort to her also. We have had encouraging news from her. In June, on her regular three month check-up, the doctors were so pleased with her progress that they told her she need not come back for six months. We still have two more years ahead of us, and we know we are not out of the woods yet. But we feel we are going in the right direction and are cautiously optimistic.

It is interesting to note the support this experience provided for Judy and the importance of validation for anyone who has an extraordinary experience. Also, her belief in its authenticity was not thwarted by the two ministers who said she was dreaming and when she found a minister who validated it, she was given additional power to cope with her anxiety about her daughter. If you talk to those who are familiar with ADC phenomena, as well as those who counsel others, you will come to find people who were not grieving, yet have had experiences similar to Shirley's in which comfort was given and received. Incidentally, this type of experience can and does happen by way of a dream messenger as well as a visual or auditory event.

By definition, this is not considered an ADC because Judy was not actively mourning. However, this question concerning people having extraordinary contacts with deceased loved ones after the mourning process seems to be over is valid and interesting. It brings forth the observation that many people who have what they believe to be a contact with the deceased interpret it as though the loved one will always be there to watch over them.

70. Have any of your beliefs about life or death changed since you have been doing research on ADC phenomena?

Dr. LaGrand, I have thought about people like you, who have worked with and researched the unseen and topics that are not culturally sanctioned and approved, and I wonder if they have arrived at new ways of looking at life or death. Have your experiences in dealing with others had an impact on your personal beliefs, or have you adopted any new beliefs about life and death?

I once was asked this question by a woman who sat in the back row of a large gathering of professional counselors and educators at a national conference in Washington, DC. She was very sincere and interested in my response, and I have to say in anticipation of such a question, I had made some notes and have since continued to grapple with the way the topic of nonphysical reality has changed or reinforced my beliefs.

In the last few years, more and more, I have found myself telling others there is no such thing as coincidence. Of course, this reflects my being influenced by the many individuals I have talked to who were mourning the loss of a loved one and suddenly received a sign or a message totally unsolicited. Being in their presence is a powerful, convincing experience. When people receive so much help from unexpected resources time and time again, it becomes difficult for me to hold on to my old belief system that cranks out the cultural dogma of chance and coincidence. The positive results of these supposed coincidences reach far and wide, compelling me to believe they don't just happen. They happen for a reason and a purpose as a result of a design. I regret to say, I do not possess the insight to fully explain the design. I only know, without a doubt, it is not a chance design.

As part of this same design, I am also sure that we all possess the ability to transmit and receive information by means other than those to which we are normally accustomed. Specifically, we all receive information in ways of which we are completely unaware and rationalize it as coming from our unconscious or subconscious, from deep memory, or from a grieving mind that is fully capable of conjuring up vivid images. That is a comfortable way to deal with phenomena that is mind boggling to the point of defying explanation, but for me its mystery is one of the most intriguing of all unseen phenomena. When people report that they knew a person had died because they received an apparition or sensed his presence—before they had been actually notified by authorities or relatives—I am unable to accept the explanation of probability theory. For me, that type of experience has to be occurring through means far from our ability to understand at this time in human history. There are other means of communication that are instantaneous and not a product of the way we currently perceive and process information. But it is clear: it happens.

As a result of the overwhelming positive responses of mourners who have had an ADC experience, my belief in the power of the experience to assist in coping with the death of a loved one has changed substantially. I am convinced that friends, relatives, and others who give support to the bereaved—including counselors—need to become aware of the frequency of the event and its potential to be an integral part of the coping repertoire of the mourner. The single obstacle to utilizing the ADC as a powerful resource is the belief systems of those who have never had the experience, who dismiss it as an aberration or a product of a confused mind. The failure to take advantage of the ADC experience is to miss a golden opportunity to emphasize connectedness and what gives people life when they are engulfed in feelings of isolation and despair.

Specifically, and this is a fourth belief change I have undergone if you are counting, there are spiritual forces that come to the aid of people who are in need in all sorts of situations, whether they are looking for help or not. Spirit touches everything: people, places, things, and, yes, even the ADC experience. What these forces do is reinforce what most people already know, but have forgotten in the confusion and pain of their problems—to remind them that they are still loved. In the immortal lines of Whittier, "Love can never lose its own," and that very love reminder—manifesting in a variety of different forms—is at the heart of the ADC as a resource for enduring massive change. Many people who are mourning the death of a loved one and experience an ADC regain a sense of belonging, a basic need we all share and that has deep emotional significance. There is meaning and continuity in a simple experience that, in most cases, only lasts a few seconds. Love is the motivating force behind nonphysical reality.

With the benefit of hindsight, I must say that diversity has taken on new meaning for me. I am talking here about the diversity of people who have the ADC experience as well as the diversity in how they interpret what happened and why. In particular, I am amazed at the very personal and unique messages that evolve from their ADCs because of the one-of-a-kind relationships they had with the loved one who died. Although we are all similar in our many needs and desires, we are immensely diverse in how those needs and desires are met. As much as diversity expresses itself in the results of the ADC, it also brings me back to the realization that we are all in need of mystery, of something outside of and greater than the self, that can quench the yearning for a fulfillment we all crave.

71. If you are providing support for someone who has had an ADC-type experience and is not sure how to interpret it, how should you respond?

As someone who often has to provide support for those who are mourning (I am a volunteer, not a professional counselor), I have a feeling and a little fear that eventually I am going to meet someone who has had an extraordinary experience. However, my concern is what to do when the mourner asks me about the experience and about whether or not I think it was real. Are there any guidelines for responding to someone who is not sure of his experience and wants your feedback?

Whenever you are helping someone who is mourning the death of a loved one it is essential to begin with the premise that it is their grief, their loss, and they should be given the dignity to be in charge of how they wish to deal with it. I am not implying that everyone wants to assume charge or control of how they grieve and the decisions to be made. If that is the case, for a time, you may have to step in and take on tasks that, as soon as possible, should be turned back over to the mourner. While recognizing some mourners need someone to step in and take over, be careful of how you assume those responsibilities and for how long, so you do not reinforce the victim role. Whenever someone feels victimized, the tendency is to become immobile and believe nothing can be done by himself. Deciding how to intervene in the victim role, and when to discontinue your daily assistance, is of special concern. But that's another issue for other books.

Whether or not you have assumed many responsibilities for the mourner, the way to begin to answer the question of authenticity is for you to ask questions of the mourner. Examples follow:

1. What were the detailed circumstances surrounding the event? Where, when, and how did it occur? Ask questions until you are sure you understand exactly what happened. Do not ask questions in such a way to imply that the person may have misjudged the experience. Show sincere interest. Your nonverbal communication, including your tone of voice, will be important to the mourner in judging if you think he is losing touch with reality. Here you wield great power to strengthen the mourner's belief in your support efforts by your manner of inquiry.

2. Ask the mourner how he felt during and after the experience. Was he encouraged? Discouraged? Was there a feeling of peace, however fleeting? Has it helped the mourner in any way? Does he feel good about it? Was he scared? The essential test is the test of peace. Has the ADC brought peace or has the experience, whatever its nature, produced agitation and more anxiety? If the latter, the experience may well be self-induced or, as believed by many in an ancient tradition, the work of an "evil spirit." If the former, you can assume it has come from a good source or a "good spirit."

3. Ask the mourner how he interprets what has happened in terms of meaning and messages. Was there a specific message, either symbolic or explicit?

4. Finally, ask the person how he feels about the experience deep inside. I usually say something like, "How does it feel in your heart? Deep inside? Is this the kind of thing your loved one would do? Allow your deep intuitive self to help you decide. What's the feeling?" I believe it is safe to say the authentic authenticates; deception is conspicuously absent.

Once you are convinced the information you have received is valid, then remember your validation is critical to the mourner in terms of helping him use it to deal with his loss. I strongly recommend emphasizing how one feels deep inside about it, and inquiring about the peace it brings. Emphatically tell the mourner that this is meaningful—but the only person who can ultimately decide is the mourner. Remind them to not let anyone else tell them what to believe about their experience.

What should you do if you simply do not believe in ADC phenomena? Gently make it known to your friend that you are not a good person to be asking for an opinion about this experience because of your personal bias. If you allow the mourner to go through a lengthy discussion and then tell him there is nothing to his experience, it will add to his stress and the isolated feelings he has about himself. Do not take away his hope. Recommend someone else whom you know has experience with the phenomena. Finding a resource person of this kind is something you, as a volunteer, should do as soon as possible, especially if you have no experience with ADCs or are adamantly opposed to the concept they represent. A resource person with ADC information should be available and known to all volunteers. All of this is done with the interests of the mourner coming first, for you may have to ask someone else to help you in order for you to help the mourner.

72. Why should a person who has an ADC, which is so personal, share it with others?

Most ADCs appear to me to be very intimate and personal experiences. If I had one, the last thing I would want to do is broadcast it to others. The experience would be a private thing between me and the loved one. Why is it important to talk about it and share it with others?

There certainly are people who believe the ADC experience is so personal they tend to guard it very carefully and are especially cautious about sharing it with anyone. I can appreciate and respect this belief. However, sharing it can potentially bring forth greater possibilities for healing for others, as well as for the recipient, and for normalizing the event. Normalizing the grief process in general, and the ADC in particular, is an important piece of work for anyone who gives support to those who are grieving. Reactions to loss in our culture are often stigmatized to the point where a mourner tries to respond to his loss in a way that is dictated primarily by those in his family or community. He often stifles true feelings and the need for expression of emotion. The stigma is even greater for those who experience an ADC.

In a nutshell, there are basically two reasons for one to share the ADC experience: it can help the person who experiences it and it can help others. How? By sharing the experience with someone who is trusted, the mourner receives reinforcement in his beliefs about the event and the deceased loved one. We all receive additional support and satisfaction when we are around others who share our beliefs. We want to share our joy. The solidarity created feeds into our need for community, recognition, and enhanced self-esteem. The sense of belonging that ensues, so critical to reestablish when coping with loss, reminds the mourner he is loved. Encourage sharing the ADC with special people in the life of the recipient. Also, remind the person who has experienced an ADC that it is likely someone he shares the experience with will not be accepting of it. Be prepared for the event; it will lessen its impact. Remind them that those who have not had the experience are often undergoing emotional responses associated with the loss, have beliefs diametrically opposed to the unseen, and are unable to accept anything of this nature as being possible.

Although it will generate mixed responses, sharing the ADC within the family may result in helping other family members who embrace a more open view of the hard-to-explain. Sometimes, other family members have had an ADC but are unsure about it or feel they should not share it out of fear of the reactions of others. When they hear of someone else's ADC, they are more open to sharing their own experience and discussing the implications of both events. The discussion will often generate unspoken (sometimes spoken) thoughts of when and how they felt the love of the deceased in happier times. Reconnecting with those moments from the past can be comforting. It reawakens a sense of meaning and continuity in life. That is, she loved me then, and she still is showing her love now.

73. How can you use the dream ADC to deal with your loss and grief?

Because there are so many people who are mourning the death of a loved one and have a dream ADC, can you tell me how to use the experience to deal with the loss? It would seem as though it is more difficult to take a dream and use it in a way to help deal with the loss. What can I do to help someone who shares his dream with me?

Using the dream ADC to help cope with the loss of a loved one is not too much different from taking advantage of any other type of ADC experience. As a matter of fact, dreams are considered to be highly reliable sources of information about all types of events, including the death of a loved one. If someone were to do a history of how dreams have helped humanity, he would be inundated with so much data it would take months to classify. Dreams are enormous sources of insight and understanding. It's a shame we don't do a better job of educating the young on the importance of dreams in learning about the self and achieving that elusive goal of happiness.

The first thing to do as a helper, once the dream has been explored and verified (and the mourner is satisfied with its authenticity), is to highlight it as a gift to be accepted and utilized in the coping process; it has a message and a purpose. Notice I used the word *process.* Doing the work of grief, dealing with all of the changes that occur in one's life because of the death, is an ongoing process, not something that has a specific time limit. Grieving and coping is not time bound. Therefore, the use of any coping technique may be spread out over months or years depending on the individual circumstances. This is exactly applicable to the dream ADC; it can be used indefinitely.

Help the mourner firmly establish all the details of the dream in his memory. You can do this by asking him to repeat parts of the experience and asking questions with regard to messages and meanings received. Also recommend writing it down in a diary or notebook. If possible, and you feel confident in doing so, you might even want to suggest additional ways to view the dream, perhaps from the point of view of other people. Objects in the dream can also be looked at in different perspectives. At the very least, reemphasize what the mourner has already said to you about the meaning of the dream. This reinforcement is significant for the dreamer in terms of both his perception of you as a support person he can trust in his struggle, and in his belief that you understand what has taken place in this experience. Saying back what you have heard is simply another way to check out your own understanding of events in the dream. This is an important active listening strategy to help the mourner.

At some point bring up the subject of how the dream can be used. Or at an appropriate time, suggest the mourner recall the dream when he feels particularly low or is having a difficult time dealing with loneliness. Loneliness is the greatest enemy of the elderly and often of those mourning the death of a loved one. The dream ADC, with all the love it conveys in the eyes of the mourner, can be called upon to remind him how the beloved still cares and wishes him to go on with his life. Let's look at an example of how this can be accomplished with the following dream, shared with me by a woman in her sixties, who gave me permission to present it here.

"I Believe My Husband Was Trying to Console Me"

I dreamed that my husband was lying next to me. I said, "Joe, you look great. How are you?" He smiled and said, "I'm fine, hon, I'm okay." He looked very strong and solid. I asked, "Where are you?" At that moment he leaned over to the right side of the bed, as if to pick something up off the floor. As he did I noticed a large bruise on the back of his left arm; it was reddish, black, and blue. I immediately thought, "Oh, I know how that happened. That's probably when they were preparing him at the funeral parlor." As he turned back to answer me, my daughter, in my dream, opened the bedroom door, he disappeared, and I woke up.

I believe my husband was trying to console me. I had been extremely upset because it had been exactly a month to the day of my husband's passing. I was so emotional that I was unable to go to work that morning. I believe that's why he came to me in my dream that night, to let me know how he was and where he was. The message I received from this dream was that there is life after death. This experience only served to reinforce my belief that our departed loved ones can communicate with us. My husband was a very spiritual man who believed in life after death. I definitely feel he was passing along a message to me.

This experience greatly helped me in my grief. It served to comfort and console me. The dream reaffirmed my belief that my husband will continue to communicate on a spiritual level.

Because of the strong beliefs about the messages received in the dream, this woman has several resources to turn to in times of duress. She can find consolation again as well as recall her conviction that he is safe in an afterlife. She can focus on the possibility they will be together again. With her belief that he can communicate with her on a spiritual level, she can nurture hope. In helping someone who shares his dream with you, look for the salient points that give meaning to the mourner. Remind him of the tool he has to deal with sadness that lingers too long. In using this dream to help the mourner, I would emphasize recalling it especially on those days the person singles out as significant, such as the one month anniversary of his death or the two month and so on. Birthdays and religious and secular holidays can be times when the dream is shared with significant others as reminders of his life and death.

74. How does the ADC bring hope to the person who has the experience?

Hope can be an important factor in the life of the bereaved. It can mean the difference in trying to pick up the pieces and go on with life, or retreating and becoming a recluse. What would you suggest in trying to use the ADC as a tool for strengthening hope in a world in which the loved one is gone?

Whenever the subject of hope surfaces in articles or books, one almost always finds a suggestion or a concept that has sprung from the experiences of psychiatrist Viktor Frankl. The survivor of Nazi concentration camps, Frankl saw many people lose hope, give up, and shortly die. He soon noted that those who never gave up hope lived longer. The opposite of hope—despair—had a powerful influence on shutting the body down, bringing on sickness and eventual death. Of course, what was the destroyer of hope in the concentration camps is the perpetual destroyer of hope for most people: a belief that there is no future. All productivity, all strong relationships, all conquering of problems are cast in the seconds, minutes, hours, or days ahead, and when one is convinced there is no future—and refuses to live in the present moment—one has set the deadly time clock of despair ticking. Hope, then, is that something outside of and bigger than the self that can get us through anything.

Despair may surface in individuals who are in the throes of grief or who are dying, as those who work in hospice programs have witnessed. When it comes to the bereaved who have had an ADC, I see a wonderful opportunity, depending on the specifics of the experience, to plant the seeds of hope and combat despair. The task of planting hope is one anyone who provides support for the bereaved should not take lightly. It is one of the many responsibilities of the journey we take when we choose to come to the aid of those in need. Each of us, mourners and nonmourners alike, need ways to invest our lives with new hope, which we often find in ritual, specific celebrations, and holidays. When we dwell on hope, suffering is diminished. We cannot think two thoughts simultaneously. Stuart C. Brush of Woodbury, Connecticut found hope in what he said was "something too coincidental to be a coincidence."

"I Was Reminded in This God-Moment That Caterpillars Are a Symbol of Resurrection"

My name is Job and my wife is Jobette. At least that is what some people call us as a result of many disastrously bad things that have happened to hopefully good people! In a little farm cemetery on the Canadian border in Vermont are buried our two sons: Dean who was senselessly murdered two days after his twenty-first birthday while delivering pizzas in Bridgport, Connecticut; and Jon, his younger brother, who never recovered, became despondent, telephoned to say goodbye, and hanged himself. Their young lives were snuffed out, and these grieving parents search for the meaning of their lives and their deaths.

For us, our pets became part of the healing process, among them being our pair of lovable miniature wire-haired daschunds, Hannah and Willie. Unfortunately, as they became aged and infirm, my wife Laura and I became convinced that it was time to show compassion by allowing them to fall asleep. As the veterinarian administered the lethal injection, Laura held Hannah and I Willie. It was peaceful but sad.

Lovingly, I took the lifeless remains to Vermont and buried them between the two boys, including in their shallow graves a tennis ball and their plastic hamburger. Then, going over to the lilac tree that had been planted in Dean's memory (it was September, and I wanted to snip off the dead flowers), I noticed something too coincidental to be a coincidence: On the lilac tree were two caterpillars, one being blond like Willie and one being black like Hannah! And I was reminded in this God-moment that caterpillars are a symbol of Resurrection, being as they are transformed into butterflies! I knew then that Hannah and Willie would be at home with Dean and Jon, and that some day we would all be together again.

Stuart's hope was replenished with his brief encounter with the caterpillars.

There are two types of hope for the future we should be cognizant of: other-worldly hope, which the ADC directly addresses, and this-worldly hope, which is essential for maintaining health and vitality in the recovery process. Do not emphasize one at the expense of the other; most mourners (and you and I) need both. Life has to go on. As the mourner attempts to rekindle or maintain both kinds of hope—with your help—the focus has to be on living in the present, getting through this hour, this day. That is what this-worldly hope is all about. Your willingness to talk about the ADC at the precise time the mourner needs to talk about it, and your skill in bringing the topic up at the right time are parts of maintaining hope in getting through the ordeal of change. Your continued presence is part of the process of building the hope for the mourner that "I can make it through this." Consistent human presence provides a spiritual orientation that is part of building this-worldly hope. Being comfortable in the presence of pain is your major contribution to your bereaved friend.

Here are some specific things to do when using the ADC to help the mourner maintain hope.

1. Emphasize the spiritual aspects of the experience, especially those the mourner has already recognized. This would include such concepts as the reality of an afterlife, that the loved one lives on, and that she cares. Remember, the ADC itself gives hope; it is a sign that there is a future. You need to tap into it, and make it clear to the mourner it is perfectly normal to turn to others for assistance when hurting and in need. We need each other.

2. Based on the ADC, ask the mourner how he thinks the deceased would want him to deal with the loss. Once the information is clarified, then suggest small immediate goals that can be set up. Hope is tied to achieving an end, a goal. This means helping the mourner decide what he really wants first. The question, "What do I want?" is a crucial one we all need to address many times in our lives in order to set meaningful and reachable goals. For example, should the mourner start dealing with financial matters now? Or the goal might be deciding how to deal with getting through the day when something occurs that brings painful memories. You may have to partially assist the mourner in meeting some goals. At some point you may also want to suggest to the mourner, if appropriate, to consider what actions or behaviors he could initiate that the deceased would be proud of him for doing.

3. Emphasize the relationship has not ended, but it has to change and a new relationship needs to be established. Here is a major challenge for you: be creative in helping the mourner establish that new relationship with the deceased. In particular, how can the ADC be used to remember the deceased in a healthy way? How will the deceased be memorialized? Can the ADC be used in any rituals of memorialization? Most ADCs can be utilized for the purpose of memorialization.

People and their love are major sources of hope for others. People who can provide options for dealing with the changes imposed by loss bring added hope for the mourner. It is my guess you will be doing many things for the mourner, including some of those listed above, that bring hope. However, you may not recognize the results because you do not see great changes in behavior. Persist and be patient. In fact, these are the very same attributes you must encourage and recognize in the mourner and give him credit for practicing. While anything that offers hope has the potential to bring healing, recognize you cannot compel a mourner to be hopeful, but you can create the circumstances so that hope will blossom.

One more thing: it is easy to misinterpret helplessness for hopelessness. When a mourner exhibits helplessness, the approach must center around restoring feelings of power and control. Believing one is "in control" can have positive effects on immune function and assist the mourner in the long-term struggle to adapt to the massive changes in his life. No one can ever have complete control over everything in life, but it is the belief that you have control, even when it is questionable, that brings significant results. Gradually establishing and meeting goals helps lead to reclaiming a sense of power and control. Above all, never forget that one of the most important sources of hope for the bereaved is the consistent unspoken assurance of human presence—your presence. Accept the numbness, the mood swings, and the sadness of a friend in pain. This is part of your contribution so the mourner can build hope. Real hope is mirrored in facial expression, in manner of relating, in one's total behavior—not merely in what one says. Be there! It is easy to overlook the fact that the least influential part of communication and hope-building is verbal.

75. How should I respond to the child who reports an ADC experience?

Although the major focus of ADC research is on adults, you have said that many children have also been the direct recipients of ADCs. If one of my children comes to me with an unusual story, what is the best way to check out what I'm hearing her say? In particular, what attitude toward her story should I convey?

To set the stage for my answer let's look at a visual ADC that occurred to Terri Kaczmarzcyk's granddaughter. You first met Terri in question 62.

"No Make Mommy Cry"

My older son Rocky, who was nineteen when he died, is the father of Michaela, my granddaughter. She can see him and Tommy, my fifteen-year-old, who was also killed in the crash. She was only about seventeen months old when they died. But it started almost immediately: she would sit on the couch and turn and say, "Not now, Tommy" or look to the corner of the room, and with a big smile on her face, look up and greet either Tommy or Rocky. She was always looking around a corner for them, like she was playing hide and seek. Or, in her bedroom, when she was ready to go to sleep she would tell Tommy, "Not now, Tommy, I'm tired."

On my Mom's birthday, Mom was so sad that day, April 22, 1997, Michaela and I were getting ready for my Mom's birthday. Michaela was brushing her teeth, standing on a stool in front of the bathroom sink. All of a sudden out of the blue, she looked up and behind her in the mirror and said, "Look Mommy, Rocky's flying."

But the best one that I can't forget is the day I was sitting in the kitchen and I started to cry. Michaela came into the kitchen and asked why I was crying. I told her that I missed Rocky and Tommy and sometimes it makes me cry. It is important to explain to a child the reason you are crying or she might think you had been hurt. At that, she turned around and pointed her little finger, shaking it and said, "No make Mommy cry!" Apparently she knew they were there. We often feel their presence when we are sad or crying. She still talks to them even now, over a year since their deaths.

My remarks here will assume that someone in your family or someone at your child's school has recently died. Let's begin with the understanding that every child needs unconditional love and a sense of personal worth if she is to develop an identity that will carry her through all of the pitfalls and changes life has to offer. For any adult who is responsible for a child, love and worth must translate into a belief within the child that "someone will always be there for me." There are few traumas more devastating for a child than the belief that she has been abandoned or isolated by those she thought could be trusted. So many of the problems of life as adults are tied to issues of abandonment and isolation that have never been resolved.

With the above in mind, the child who comes to you with a story that seems out of the ordinary, or which may be a possible ADC experience, should be given the same basic respect that would be offered any adult. Your open attitude toward the child with a story is critical because it will show in your nonverbal behavior. Never forget that children are astute readers of the nonverbal. An open, respectful attitude will be essential in maintaining communication long after this particular situation has been addressed. It will set the stage for the child being willing to come back, talk again about death, and ask other questions about feelings and emotions.

Processing the potential ADC experience with a child should include the following:

1. Do not expect the child to respond as an adult who has had a similar experience. Children can be expected to be more animated and descriptive in relating what happened. This should not be misconstrued as their overactive imagination. In this vein, never immediately invalidate the experience and lose the opportunity to gain valuable information about what and how the child is thinking regarding the death.

2. Begin with the teach-me-about-your-experience approach. That is, allow the child to direct the flow of conversation, to tell you what it was like. Do not interrupt to inquire about specifics until she has given a complete description of the experience. Then go back and fill in the gaps as you see fit. Ask open-ended questions as opposed to yes and no types to encourage a more detailed account of the

event. "What was it like?" "How did she look?" Remember that children are literal in their thinking.

3. Make every attempt to get into the flow of feelings that accompany the telling of the event. Watch facial expressions and gestures, as well as body movements. Is the child saying, "I miss my brother" or, "I need to know someone is still here for me." Normalize the expression of emotion. Is the account of the event told in matter-of-fact terms with little show of emotion? If so, try to determine further whether the experience has had any effects that have caused this void by asking how the child feels about what happened.

4. Determine the meanings associated with the experience. How does the child interpret what happened? Does she want you to reinforce anything she is saying? Can you? Was it a positive event and helpful in dealing with the loss? Ask the child if she has any questions she would like to ask you about what happened.

5. Always give the child the benefit of the doubt. Begin to ask questions about where the event took place, at what time, and how it began. As you do this, show signs of interest, understanding, and acceptance. Ask yourself if the child had previously regressed and whether or not the experience has brought her back from some of her regressive behavior such as wanting to sleep in the same room as the parents, thumb sucking, or not wanting a parent to go anywhere without her.

6. If the experience is obviously healthy and benign, ask the child what the most important idea or insight she received was. Does the experience have the potential to bring peace and provide understanding about death? If peace and meaning are inherent in the experience as it has been told, pursue and build on that feeling. Has the child been helped by telling you and by your reaction?

7. Tell the child she can always come to you with questions, to talk about her experience, and that you are happy she told you. Ask her if it is all right if you tell others or if it is to be kept confidential. Use the occasion of this conversation to tell the child that she will always be loved.

76. Are there unconscious effects of the ADC?

Although the study of ADC phenomena is in its infancy, I wonder if there is any consensus on how the experience might affect a person on the unconscious or subconscious level. Could this phenomenon have positive or negative effects on individual behavior based on changes in unconsciously held beliefs?

Nearly a decade ago, I wrote to the late Willis Harman, who at the time was the President of the Institute of Noetic Sciences, a nonprofit education, membership, and research institute founded by Apollo 14 astronaut Edgar Mitchell. Among other things, the institute offers opportunities for members to bring "diverse modes of knowing to the study of consciousness, the mind, and human potential." In my letter, I asked Dr. Harman how one can become aware of unconscious beliefs that affect behavior. I was fascinated with the idea that what we are not consciously aware of could have an impact on how we deal with the world in which we live. Here, in part, was his answer.

> I find the most important step in discovering one's unconscious beliefs is simply the recognition that they are there and they play a commanding role in perception, values, attitudes, and behavior. Furthermore, they can be changed.
>
> You find out what the unconscious beliefs are by inferring them from all you say and do. Since you are intent on deceiving yourself (and have lots of practice), relationships with others are especially important—you don't fool others the way you fool yourself. However, some of the beliefs are shared by most of the people around you, so they are especially difficult to become aware of. Travel to another culture is one of the time-honored ways of learning about these.
>
> Affirmations and inner imagery . . . provide the most powerful yet safe way to reprogram the unconscious beliefs.

Beliefs, both consciously and unconsciously held, power everything we do. The way unconsciously held beliefs are formed is basically the same as how we come by our consciously held beliefs—through what we hear and say and the images we create to accompany our experiences. We think constantly by way of the images we create. What we hear and image, of course, is dictated in part by our experiences, our significant others, and the culture in which we live. After all, things told to us often enough in childhood can become part of our unconscious beliefs for the rest of our lives—unless we do something about it. Therefore, with concerted effort one can influence the unconscious beliefs shaped by earlier life experiences, the dominant cultural mores, and the social community.

The priceless resource that we call the unconscious can, as Dr. Harman put it, be reprogrammed by conscious effort. We can and do change our unconscious beliefs without our awareness simply by repetitively placing ourselves in certain circumstances and using the same thinking patterns over and over again. In doing so, we ultimately affect our behavior. The unconscious mind is always open to suggestion. Therefore, we can develop fearful negative beliefs about unexplained phenomena like the ADC, and shun anything that seems mysterious or inexplicable, or we can be open to the unknown. Let me emphasize that negative beliefs about the unexplained and the unseen can be deeply imbedded in the unconscious. Thus interpretations of ADC experiences can be colored by the lenses of the unconscious mind and affect behavior.

How can one consciously begin the process of conversion of long held unconscious beliefs, to rid oneself of earlier views? By using affirmations (positive statements) and visualizing in detail the behaviors associated with the new beliefs to be adopted. In addition, self-talk, pictures, tape recordings of your voice, writing in a diary—any mode of expression that carries the new belief messages to your mind—assist the process. Self-talk, especially, is an automatic process that can change the quality of life as well as challenge the inner critic we all carry around with us. We constantly talk to ourselves throughout the day and the unconscious mind is always listening, it never sleeps. Thus, choosing one or a number of the above approaches becomes a matter of personal choice. But making a plan and consistently following it is essential.

Now let's enter the ADC into the program. Does the ADC experience affect the mourner on an unconscious level? As with any other experience in life, we know it is imprinted in the unconscious. That is a given. How it is utilized and what it means to the mourner will determine what changes it will induce on an unconscious level. It is safe to say that the impact the ADC has on the person often changes his behavior for the better in accepting his present circumstances and making the best of them. Sometimes the changes are emotional and very sudden. At other times, the changes occur slowly, both emotionally and behaviorally. If you question the mourner about the role the ADC plays in how he feels and what he does, the answer will vary in terms of current needs and degree of impact. How much can be attributed to unconscious changes? No one really knows. There is no research I am aware of on the subject.

On the other hand, there is no doubt the ADC affects beliefs. Just ask the mourner who has the experience. Beliefs about the presence of the deceased, her condition, the afterlife, a reunion, life, and the meaning of the vast universe in which we live are in part recast based on the experience. The degree of change occurring on an unconscious level depends on how frequently the mourner replays the event and thinks about the meaning and implications for continuity in life and after death. As noted earlier, we are constantly talking to ourselves as we face the world each day. It is meaningful repetition and self-talk that plays a major role in our belief shifts consciously and unconsciously. Because we have somewhere in the neighborhood of nearly sixty-thousand thoughts a day—many of which are repetitive during each day and from day to day—we can begin to imagine how some thoughts can be translated into cultural beliefs and become deeply programmed into the unconscious mind.

One reason I tell those who have had an ADC to tell others about their experience, and repeatedly play it back in detail to themselves, is for the potential effects it will have on the unconscious mind. I want them to develop lasting unconscious beliefs that their loved ones are okay and they can go on with life. Furthermore, if the ADC fits into their belief system, they may accept the idea of reunion in the future. This may help them presently and, hopefully, as the years go on. Perhaps the most important and dramatic belief change that occurs and can be nurtured is that death is not the end. Reduction of the fear of death is not uncommon. It is also likely the ADC may help some mourners deal with suppressed feelings toward the deceased, particularly the feeling of anger. At the same time, the ADC may change one's view of the self ("now I know I am capable and willing to deal with this difficult change") and in doing so affect a whole range of behaviors including reaching out to others, joining the workforce, or returning to school to further one's education.

Repetitive ADC imagery and self-talk regarding messages received can help accomplish the task of imprinting beliefs on the unconscious mind. In like manner, the ADC can be used in conjunction with advance rehearsal, an important coping technique in which the mourner plans on how he wants to respond to any anticipated situation involving the absence of the loved one, long before it occurs. In this vein, the ADC is not merely a gift to cherish; it is an active means of coping with loss and adjusting to change. In conjunction with a friend or counselor, the mourner can explore imaginative ways to use the ADC as a tool in advance rehearsal. The imagination is a powerful ally, if one can overcome the negative image that it wrongfully bears. The mourner may also wish to assign a word or title to his ADC to trigger a playback at times when it is most needed. Let's consider an example. Kay Ramie's twenty-five-year-old son was killed instantly in an automobile accident during a snowstorm outside of Lake Placid, New York, on April 8, 1996. Five days later she had the following experience.

"Come On Tom, Do It Again"

I had had a previous contact experience with my mother so I knew Tom would send me a sign when he could. The first one happened on Saturday, April 13. His funeral was held on the 12th and my two daughters were still at home as we, along with my husband, were going to Lake Placid on Sunday to get his personal effects and see the scene of the accident and the car.

We had been talking about funny things the three of them did when they were kids and we were laughing. I said, "It seems so terrible to laugh, but we can't cry twenty-four hours a day. Tom must know how much we loved him." As I finished saying this the smoke alarm in the dining room gave one long tone. (This was a new alarm and had never gone off. It also wasn't the short tones it gives if something on the stove smokes.) We were all startled and exchanged glances. I said, "Now you can't tell me that isn't my son. Come on, Tom, do it again." We received a second long tone. My daughter Vicki said, "Way to go Bro"—a third tone rings out. After the third tone Vicki asked that there be no more as I think we all had the hair on the back of our necks standing up at that point. The smoke alarm was silent until I heard from him again a week later. I suppose this would be referred to as synchronistic timing.

My husband, who never believed in this sort of thing, also witnessed this event. Coupled with seeing an apparition of Tom in our bedroom, he now realizes that these things do happen.

If highly significant events impact the unconscious mind, then certainly Kay's experience must be placed in that category and will go a long way in strengthening her belief on both a conscious and unconscious level that her son lives on. If she chose to use the experience as a form of advanced rehearsal to deal with the pain of his absence, she could decide to give the experience a name such as "Tom," "tone," or "love" and begin to image the ADC in conjunction with the time and stressor that is most difficult for her to manage. For example, if it is most painful for her when she cleans his room or comes home and he is not there when he normally used to be there, then that is the time to trigger the ADC experience and relive her belief that he lives on (or whatever else is applicable). Simply suggest that she pair the ADC with her confrontation of those painful episodes as a way of coping. Encourage her to use her creativity in this regard.

One of the significant characteristics of the unconscious that Carl Jung suggested was that it is driven by the propensity toward personal growth and well-being for the individual. It may well be that those who have had an ADC are much more aware of other means by which the unconscious manifests itself to the mourner, namely through dreams, greater self-awareness, and intuitive flashes. You may want to remind the person that the unconscious mind can utilize the ADC just as much as his conscious mind. In summary, there is no consensus on the effects of the ADC on the unconscious mind. My belief is that it can have a major impact for the better, and on a rare occasion for the worse, depending on how it is treated not only by the mourner, but by those who provide support in the mourner's inner circle. You, the support person, will touch the mourner on an unconscious level.

- *See also question 28*

77. Does the ADC experience strengthen one's belief in the concept of immortality?

Is there any evidence to suggest the ADC can provide one with information to support the belief that we are immortal beings? In particular could you comment on what types of experiences appear to be most conducive to accepting a belief in immortality?

There is evidence galore of an anecdotal nature that points toward immortality. However, anecdotal or experiential evidence is not accepted by the scientific community as valid. This does not mean that subjective and experiential evidence has to be considered useless. There are too many positive results that were spawned originally by information normally rejected by the scientific method to simply abandon it because it fails to meet certain manmade criteria. I am assuming you are using the term immortality to imply unending life or to suggest that consciousness survives bodily death.

Many writers have dealt with the subject of immortality, although few from the point of view of ADC phenomena. Let me say outright that to those who have had an ADC the question is ludicrous. Everyone lives on. In fact, this is a common conclusion, based on the very nature of the ADC. Let me give an example, one of many, by a certified grief counselor and registered nurse. Highly grounded and trained in the scientific method, Shirley Scott was able, after experiencing her ADCs, to integrate them into a belief system that accepted the obvious: there is something else after the death of the body. These accounts are especially significant because of the belief changes that occur among professional counselors who have the experience. Shirley does not stand alone in this regard.

Experience 1. "His Hopeful Message Helped Me"

We had been married forty-five years when my husband, Hal, died from cancer on January 7, 1992, after an eighteen-month illness. I was beginning to reach the full depth of grief by the following fall. One early afternoon in November 1992, after a very difficult and tearful morning, I decided to take a short nap in the hope I would do better after some rest. I fell asleep quickly and woke up thirty minutes later still feeling terribly sad and desperately lonely. I looked at the clock, turned over on my right side, and decided to rest just a bit longer—maybe then I'd feel better. Immediately I felt Hal's presence as he pressed against my body, spoon fashion, his arm around me from behind. He said very soothingly and clearly, "It's going to be all right." I felt myself relax as a wave of peace flowed through me. I looked again at the clock. Less than a minute had gone by. I know I was not asleep; it was not a dream. His hopeful message helped me get through that day and many more that followed.

Experience 2. "I Felt Peaceful and Hopeful"

In April 1993, I was still having some pretty bad days from time to time. On one such day I took a nap in the early afternoon, again hoping I would wake up feeling less sad and lonely. After about twenty-five minutes, I woke up to the sound of a small music box on my dresser playing "Lara's Theme" from the movie Dr. Zhivago. The box was closed (it should only play when open), and it had not worked for several years. I listened for a minute or so, felt Hal's presence briefly, and said out loud, "Okay Honey, I know you're still looking out for me." I got up, opened the box as the music continued to play, and then closed it. The music stopped and I have never been able to get it to play since that day.

I looked up the words to the song. The phrases that struck me as most meaningful were "Someday we'll meet again, my love" and "Somewhere there will be songs to sing"—I had done very little singing since he died, something that I had previously loved to do.

Again, I felt peaceful and hopeful following this experience.

Experience 3. "It Made Me Feel Good He Could Still Try to Comfort Me"

On February 9, 1994, Hal's birthday (the third since his death), I had a very difficult day. I had scheduled a number of things for the day so I would be very busy, but I felt very depressed all day. After dinner alone, I finished up my paper work from my job. I still felt depressed and also agitated. Following my usual pattern, I called a friend just to chat for awhile to distract myself, but she was not home. I decided to write out my feelings in my journal.

A minute or so after sitting down to do this, I heard "beep . . . beep . . . beep . . . beep." I had to stop and think what the sound was and finally realized it sounded like the alarm clock in my bedroom. I went back to the bedroom and looked at my radio alarm that was not making a sound. The beeps came from Hal's travel alarm clock on his night stand on the other side of the bed. I walked around the bed and saw the time was 9:02 P.M. The alarm switch was in the OFF position, but the beeps continued. My first thought was (and I said it out loud), "Well, Honey, I guess you know how awful I'm feeling and came to let me know it will be okay!" Then I picked up the clock (which I had not touched since I had dusted the area a couple of weeks before), turned the switch to "ON," and it stopped beeping. I turned the switch back to "OFF"—no more beeping. At that point, I burst into tears, a much needed release for the pent-up feelings of the day.

A bit later, I was thinking more rationally and started to question the event, beginning to doubt it as a "sign." But then I remembered the time, 9:02; 9 is his birth day and 02 is the month of February—it had to be Hal! It made me feel good he could still try to comfort me, just as he had many times over the years we were together.

Experience 4. "Hal Was Still Looking Out for My Best Interests"

In June 1996, I was debating whether to continue a relationship with a man I had been dating for several months. I was in my bedroom changing clothes to go for my evening walk, adding up all the pros and cons in my head. There were many more "cons" than "pros" on the list. I was somewhat agitated, knowing the relationship was not the best thing for me, but dreading going back to the loneliness of not having someone to date again. Arguing with myself aloud, I finally decided to go out with him just one more time. At that moment, Hal's travel alarm started to beep. Again, the switch was in the "OFF" position.

My immediate response was to laugh aloud and say, "Honey, I guess you're telling me that's not a good idea!" Information I received the next *day confirmed this. Hal was still looking out for my best interests. By the way, in the almost six years since Hal's death, the travel alarm has not had a new battery and continues to record accurate time twenty-four hours a day. The only time I touch it is to dust the area. I think I keep it there just in case he wants to let me know he's still concerned about me.*

In all of these contacts I have felt comforted, peaceful, thankful for the contact. Before my own experiences, I had heard of other people having ADCs, but I felt a little skeptical. Were they just dreaming? Or having an hallucination? Or just wishing so hard for the contact they convinced themselves it was real? In the past I had had many conversations with my friend Bill Guggenheim, author and ADC researcher, concerning the events people told him about, but I guess I had to have the experiences myself before being completely convinced they could happen.

As you have observed in these four ADCs, the experience itself is one that provides information to strengthen one's view of immortality—but the convincing piece of the puzzle is to feel the experience, to go through it. It is one thing to talk about ADC phenomena from a theoretical perspective. It is altogether a different thing to experience one. Anecdotal or subjective experience may be rejected by science, but it is solid enough proof for one who has experienced an ADC. Or as Mark Twain put it: "I do not wish to hear about the moon from someone who has not been there."

Millions of people have had experiences similar to Shirley's. She has been fortunate to have had more than one along the arduous path to adjusting to her husband's death. It is obvious she believes life continues on, and that consciousness survives bodily death, just as so many others have believed through the centuries, despite the denial of the reigning scientific and naturalistic paradigm. Although there will always be further discussion on the question, it will likely end in the proverbial stalemate. Perhaps the only way the final answer comes is through faith or a subjective experience involving the unknown, which not everyone is given.

The most convincing type of ADC to support the belief in immortality usually depends on the perception of the mourner, although visual and auditory ADCs seem to be most convincing. For the outsider who has not had the experience, the most credible ADCs appear to be the reports of visual, third- and fourth-party types, as well as the crisis, evidential, shared, and protective ADCs.

- *See also questions 6 and 27*

78. Can a single ADC be interpreted in more than one way?

When several individuals have ADCs that have very similar features, is the interpretation of the event generally the same? It seems as though a case could be made for different interpretations. What has been your experience in this regard?

Many years ago I heard a woman with many years of experience teaching on the graduate level make the following statement: "We see with our eyes, but we perceive with our brains." She then when on to explain that although we all may look at an object or a person and see the same thing, we tend to interpret it differently. For example, if a teacher were to walk into a classroom, hop up on the desk and start tap dancing, all the students would see the event. However, some might say to themselves or others, "She's a good dancer." Others might say, "What's wrong with her?" Still others might be concerned about the safety of such an act. Succinctly stated, viewing the same action or object often results in perceiving it differently. Perceptions are the personal meanings we give to our experiences, How we perceive has an awful lot to do with individual backgrounds. Our core beliefs shape our perception of reality.

In addition, perceptions are based on such things as values, current needs, self-esteem, hometowns, threat, fear, and significant others who have influenced us. For example, on the college level, people perceive the professor in one way when they are taking a class from her (they need a good grade), and often quite differently when they are no longer taking the course. Similar perceptual differences are found in interpreting the same type of ADC. Two mourners may have separate visual ADCs of a loved one. One may interpret the experience as bringing much peace and comfort, while the other may focus on the implications it has for seeing the person again in another life. Someone else hearing the two discussing their experiences could easily perceive them as being in need of professional help because of his perceptual background. Beliefs weigh heavily in how we perceive the ADC.

Dream state ADCs may also appear to be similar in the way the dream messenger (the deceased) appears smiling and says he is okay, however, the dreamer's interpretation of the experience depends on current needs and other individual factors. This is not to say the dreamer is necessarily locked into that interpretation. He may also be open to more than one interpretation. Both may bring the solace and comfort inherent in the experience. That is why it is important to discuss the ADC with others: to obtain input that may broaden the meaning and depth of the experience for the mourner. Just as grief itself is an individual process with great variability in emotion, thoughts, and feelings, so too is the ADC experience and the personal meaning inherent in it.

79. Does the ADC help one deal with feelings of isolation?

You have said that the perception of being alone and isolated is one of the most damaging factors in the stress response associated with mourning. Also, those who are mourning need time alone away from the crowds so they can think and sort out their feelings. Can the ADC ever be used to deal with feelings of isolation? If so, how?

Not only do mourners who perceive themselves as being alone and isolated face a major hurdle in dealing with the stress it creates, but the same dilemma is common with anyone who shares that interpretation of their current state in life. Most people like to be alone at times, but no one chooses to be lonely. Once again, using the ADC to deal with isolation is a possibility depending on the characteristics of the experience that occurred and its creative use by the mourner. A friend, relative, or counselor could also suggest ways to use the ADC to deal with feelings of isolation when they crop up.

To begin with, I would not recommend relying too heavily on any ADC to deal with the perception of isolation. Doing so may minimize the critical importance of human presence in time of loss. Rather, if you are providing support for the mourner, I would recommend patiently drawing the person back into life by your loving presence and by furthering interaction with others in one's social circle. The ADC can be used as an adjunct to this process, but a strong social support network is both health promoting and most useful in adapting to any loss or massive change. Let's examine an ADC and see how it might be used in terms of coping with isolation.

"I Felt Such a Deep Relief That This Was My Dad"

My father, Samuel Porter, passed away suddenly on October 12 at age sixty-eight from an aortic aneurysm. Needless to say, my entire family is devastated and each member is grieving in his own way. I live in Massachusetts, but the rest of my family live close to each other in Southern California.

I returned to Massachusetts a few days after the funeral. On the morning before leaving, I went to the cemetery and took a rose off my father's grave. I stuck it in a book I was carrying back with me. When I got home, I remembered the rose and reached up into my bookshelf, opened our family bible without taking it down, and stuck in the rose thinking it would be safe there. I was having an extremely hard time with my dad's death and would cry and beg him to show me a sign that he was okay. A few days later, while in my room crying and talking to my dad, I reached up and pulled down my bible. I opened it up to where the rose was, and it was in a chapter called Samuel. I was a little surprised and showed my daughter, telling her of the coincidence. Then I looked a little closer, and the rose itself was bent over. The bottom part of the bud was resting on and highlighting the sentence "Now Samuel died." All of a sudden I felt such a deep relief that this was my dad letting me know he had died and was indeed okay—and able to reach out and send this message.

I would like you to know that I never went to church much as a child and have never read the bible. It was a wedding gift from my mother-in-law. I did not even know there was a chapter called Samuel. My father, however, was well-versed in the bible, having attended Catholic schools all his life. I have shared this with my family members, hoping it might help them with their grief, and have received different reactions from them all. My brother said he could see dad laughing and wondering if we'd get it. This is how my dad made us find answers to things. He was extremely smart and would make us search for answers.

Although I am still having a very hard time, this has helped me because I know he is okay and was able to reach out. He wanted me to share this with my family.

It is noteworthy that the nature of this ADC was indicative of the way the deceased did things when alive and that Susan's brother brought that point out when he learned of his sister's experience. These were important factors in the meaning Susan drew from her experience. She had been begging for a sign and received one. How can the sense of isolation be dealt with in such instances? I would suggest the following if I was providing support. In fact, in a conversation I had with her recently, I made these suggestions to Susan.

1. Anyone in the family who believes as Susan does that her experience was a sign from their father should be utilized as a special resource on occasion. The subject should be brought up again, as a normal part of conversation.

2. Susan should also look for friends she can trust to share the experience with and again use those who are accepting as special resources.

3. I also suggested she look for information about this type of experience by going to her local library or bookstore to find anything in writing to strengthen her own beliefs and to learn that many others have had similar experiences.

4. I further recommended she seek out leaders of support groups in her area, including bereavement coordinators at hospices, to discuss the subject of ADC phenomena and/or attend their meetings.

5. She also should do everything possible to locate someone else who has had an ADC and talk about each other's experiences. The type of discussion that can grow out of such a meeting can be highly supportive and help break the chains of isolation.

6. This ADC experience is also an opportunity for Susan to get back in touch with and strengthen her spiritual beliefs. As her partnership with a Higher Power grows, inner peace will make great inroads on

the sense of isolation. Emphasizing the spiritual aspects of the experience is something the support person should assess in view of the type of experience and the mourner's openness.

Through her ADC experience, Susan has a reason to reach out and interact with others; it has been a pivotal factor in her coping repertoire. Most individuals who have the experience are eager to find out more about it as well as about others who have had similar experiences. That interest is a wonderful asset to use in order to help the person deal with a sense of isolation and abandonment, and to interact with others. Prolonged social isolation is a major problem for the grief-stricken. Extensive investigations have shown profound alterations in immunological and cardiovascular responses leading to what has commonly been called the "broken heart" syndrome. Thousands of people die every year because of their inability to adapt to the death of a loved one. Of course, Susan can also be encouraged to use the ADC as a reminder that her father lives on. Much good can come from her ADC if she can continue to find validation, because this is the type of experience that is often shunned as meaningless by those who have never had an ADC or are not knowledgeable of the wide range of experiences that occur. Yet the ADC can be a device that stimulates many interpersonal transactions and a medium through which new relationships are established.

80. How does the ADC promote the acceptance of the death of a loved one?

I have been told that accepting the death of a loved one, especially on an emotional level, is critical to reaching some sort of inner peace and dealing with life again. Is it possible to help promote acceptance of the death of a loved one through the ADC?

On an intellectual level one is able to acknowledge the death of a loved one in a relatively short period of time ("Yes, I know my father is dead'). However, coming to accept the death in terms of emotions, expectations, and feelings ("I can't believe we will not be going fishing as we did every year" or "I can't believe she won't be there when I walk into the house") is usually a much more difficult and long-term process. In fact, it is much longer than our culture likes to admit, since mourners are often expected to return to their jobs in a few days, assume their normal work load, and perform at the same level as prior to the death—something few, if any, actually accomplish in those early days after the funeral. Once more, friends and work associates expect the individual not to show emotion and "get on with their life." That is easier said than done for most, depending on several factors, not the least of which is the nature of the death. Sudden unexpected deaths are especially difficult to deal with because there is so often unfinished business with the deceased. Those who are grieving children or loved ones who died in accidents or by violent means can go for many months or years before they reach some state of realization that someone "is gone and is not coming back." Emotional acceptance is elusive at best.

The ADC can aid in shortening the time factor for acceptance or reduce the intensity of pain along the way, or both. The emphasis for using the ADC for this purpose must hinge on the message received and the recognition that communication through the means used is, ipso facto, an indicator the loved one has died and yet lives on. The emphasis in this instance is on the idea that the ADC does not occur unless it comes from an other-worldly source. Here is an example that occurred through a child's experience that was reinforcing for her father and is narrated by the child's mother.

"My Husband Was Happy"

My daughter Jessica was playing in our yard. Jessica was two years old and my son was ten months old. Suddenly Jessica said to me, "There is my grandfather. Don't you see him mommy? He's standing right there." And she proceeded to point to a section of our yard. I asked her what he looked like. She said that he had white hair and a white beard. My husband's father fits the description. He died in 1988 and I personally had never met him. She said that he lives in the red house.

The next day, my husband, my daughter, son, and I were driving to my husband's sister's wedding. Suddenly, Jessica announced from the back seat that she was going to see her grandfather today, the one with the white hair; and that he was going to pick her up today. I don't know what it means, but my husband was happy to think that his father "spiritually" would be at his sister's wedding.

Once the mourner recognizes that a contact has occurred, and embraces the idea, support persons can utilize the event to relate to the loved one as having died, but living on in another dimension. "He has died, but he still cares." You as a support person have to carefully decide the choice of words and the timing of your supportive endeavors in this regard. You must be sure of the mourner's beliefs about the ADC experience. To promote acceptance, one may find the following useful.

1. Refer to the deceased in the past tense, not as though he is still physically alive as is common for mourners to do. This is especially important when talking about the deceased and the mourner's ADC.

2. Do not use euphemisms when referring to death or to the person as having died. Say "died" or "death" instead of departed, expired, passed away, gone, left us, etc.

3. Emphasize the basic meaning of the ADC: the deceased is saying he's okay from another place, wants you to know that and deal with it, and he is helping you manage your grief.

4. Use discussion of the ADC to allow the mourner to express his emotions about the loss and the meanings he attaches to it. The ADC is often an excellent topic through which one can engage the mourner to reflect on other good things the deceased has done, show gratitude, and review the relationship with the deceased. The review of the past relationship by the mourner is a demanding but integral part of the process of reaching emotional acceptance. Emotions associated with the ADC, and those associated with past experiences involving the deceased when he was alive, can be compared and discussed. This can take a long time and can be repeated on many occasions when the topic of the ADC surfaces again and again. It will also mean many tear-filled sessions, good therapy for the mourner and his long process of facing the pain of adaptation.

Standing by someone who is struggling with accepting the death of a loved one will take unusual patience and understanding on the part of the support person. Your persistence will pay off over time, if you realize the person you are helping must be allowed to grieve at her own pace. Refuse to put a time frame on the process and keep in mind that helping the mourner face the pain—through the review of the relationship and your patient listening—will assist in the task of acceptance.

81. Can an ADC help someone who has unfinished business with the deceased?

If sudden unexpected deaths often leave people with unfinished business because they didn't get a chance to say goodbye or say, "I love you," then there must be a lot of people who have to deal with the dilemma. How would you use the ADC to help in this regard?

You are correct in saying there must be a lot of people who have unfinished business when a loved one dies, because there are an increasing number of deaths due to accidents, fires, and violence. These traumatic deaths result in what counselors call complicated grief, reportedly on the increase. I am happy to say that many people who have an ADC and are dealing with complicated grief find the ADC provides some relief from their pain. In some instances it even removes the stigma of unfinished business. Sometimes the ADC is dramatic and addresses the unfinished business directly. At other times, the ADC can be seen as a way in which the deceased is saying, "I understand and it's okay that you weren't there or were unable to say goodbye." On some occasions, by appearance alone, the ADC implies the relationship is mended.

Here is a dream state ADC experienced by a young woman who had a poor relationship with a friend who was dying. On the night he died she had the following dream that resolved her unfinished business.

"I Felt Very Peaceful"

I dreamt about Jim Norton. I knew that Jim was dying from liver cancer, which was diagnosed in January 1991. In my dream Jim looked very healthy and bright. I remember his face being very white with a warm light surrounding him. In the dream, I asked Jim if he believed in reincarnation. He laughed and said, "No, it is not reincarnation but pathy." I did not know what pathy meant and I was afraid to ask him out of fear of scorn. I remember saying to myself I would look the word up when I woke up. I also remember that Jim and I were friends, although in my conscious state I detested him. We had not been on good terms for the last eight months of his life. In my dream, I forgave him. I felt a strong sense of peace.

When I awoke, I told my husband about the dream and that I felt very peaceful. I also told him how odd I thought it was that I could feel so peaceful with a person in my dream, who in my conscious state had caused me so much pain. Two hours later, Mr. Barton, my boss, telephoned to tell me Jim had died during the night.

This ADC dream was actually a crisis ADC, with the deceased appearing in the dream and the dreamer not realizing the person she had unfinished business with had died. Nevertheless, her experience gave her peace of mind. In any ADC the appearance of the deceased, or any contact, may serve as a sign that the person still wants the relationship to be a positive one, to heal it if necessary, or he wouldn't have bothered attempting to communicate.

As a support person, after studying the ADC and understanding the way the mourner has viewed it, you should tactfully suggest several things. First, the contact is indeed healthy and meaningful. Second, the deceased is strengthening the relationship by making a statement through the contact: he forgives or he wants you to let go of your guilt. Third, depending on the nature of the unfinished business, one may also suggest that from the point of view of the deceased loved one, whatever the supposed unfinished business, it is not a major problem for him, so let it go now.

You as a friend or counselor may say, in referring to the deceased based on the ADC experience, "From your description, he appears to be so happy with you. Perhaps you have read too much into what you were unable to do. He understands or he wouldn't have appeared so happy." Or one may say, "It appears as though he has clearly forgiven you. He knows you had his best interests at heart at the time. You did what was humanly right at that time." You are planting the seeds of acceptance and/or forgiveness. The task of the support person is to analyze the possible meanings that can be deduced from the ADC, then emphasize parts of the ADC that do not suggest negative feelings as assumed by the mourner. The ADC is essentially a positive experience. Communication—whether verbal, nonverbal, or symbolic—is a means of maintaining continuity, mending, and preserving relationships. You may need to help the mourner see her ADC in this way.

82. What can you say to a person who has been hoping for an ADC experience but has not received one?

How do you handle a situation in which someone very close to you is mourning, knows that others have had an ADC, and asks you why it doesn't happen to her? My friend is in a great deal of pain and needs some reassurance that her loved one lives on. I am at a loss to give her an answer, other than to tell her to continue to keep hoping for a sign.

Obviously, everyone does not receive the kind of reassurance they are looking for when a loved one dies. Nor does everyone need it. However, it can be very painful and frustrating to hear of or observe someone who is in desperate need looking for an indication that "my loved one is not gone forever." To illustrate, here is part of a poignant letter I recently received that lays bare the crux of the matter:

I lost my mother in April 1997 to cancer. Because I was nineteen at the time of her death, I never really had the chance to develop an adult relationship with her. Also, her incoherence at the end of her illness made it impossible for me to say all of the things I would have liked to say to her. As a result, I have been waiting patiently for her to make some sort of contact with me.

But I am beginning to grow impatient. It has been about nine months since her death and I haven't heard from her. My sister and sister-in-law have both had vibrant dreams of my mother, but not me. I've waited through so many special occasions such as my own wedding, my birthday, my mother's would-be fiftieth anniversary, and even Christmas, but with no contact from her.

> *I am finding myself very sad lately and I am beginning to think my mother is mad at me, or that maybe I have disappointed her somehow. I really would appreciate any advice you may have on how I can deal with this or even how I can initiate contact with my mother.*

Despite the sadness of this dilemma the fact of the matter is we do not have the answer to what is essentially a philosophical question. Why doesn't this young person or your friend receive their wishes for reassurance at this time? No one can come up with an answer that will assuage their immediate pain. But that does not rule out maintaining hope for the future.

There is one thing you can do to help. Let her know by word and work that you will be there for her whenever she needs you. At this particular time in her mourning (which I am assuming is within weeks of the loved one's death), she is in special need of consistent support she can rely on. Usually, once the funeral is over and everyone goes back to their homes and daily obligations, the mourner is left alone at a time when the real work of mourning is only beginning. However, just because you or anyone else doesn't have the answer to her question, it should not discourage you in your support efforts. You are providing the silent presence of a caring person who is showing love by sharing pain. That is a major factor as she deals with all of the emotions and feelings associated with changes she must confront. Your patient support will help her in the long journey. You may not think you are doing much to help your friend, but let me assure you that your willingness to be around her suffering and distress is something that is most beneficial and will have lasting influence on your relationship.

You have told her the one thing that can be of help, to ask for a sign that her loved one is okay. Encourage her to pray for a sign; prayer is hope in action. Tell her that before she retires each evening to ask for a visitation dream. I believe all prayers are answered—not always with the answer we think we need, not always at the time we want the answer, and often not in the way we expect the answer. But the prayer will be answered. As singer and author Kathy Troccoli advises, in *My Life is in Your Hands,* "When you hear a direct *no* in response to your prayers, remind yourself that there will always be a better yes. God is for you, motivated by a love so strong, so undying, and so wise that we have nothing and no one to fear."

So encourage the mourner to maintain hope, and/or pray daily depending on religious beliefs. Yet be careful not to proselytize. Above all, if your friend feels the deceased is angry at her, make every effort to make it clear that there can be many reasons why there has been no contact (see question 30). Concurrently, you also must remember the mourner has to deal with the practical matters associated with building a new life in the here and now, and she cannot become immobile and preoccupied by looking for a sign. An active interior life, in which the imagery of advance rehearsal, self-talk, and prayer predominate, helps set boundaries that delimit the feelings of isolation that often seem to accompany the journey through change. Still, practical matters and new obligations have to be the central focus. Finally, be sure to remind her that many ADCs occur months and years after the death and in ways totally unexpected. Above all, maintain your hope and your vigil with her; it will strengthen her faith and assist her in the task of adapting to the many changes to be faced.

83. Why do you emphasize in your lectures and discussions that counselors and anyone who provides support for the bereaved should have a thorough understanding of ADC phenomena?

I understand an ADC can often help mourners turn the corner and deal with the loss of a loved one. But it is not clear to me why professional counselors and anyone who helps the bereaved should be well aware of the phenomena. Why should the phenomena be universally known to those who assist mourners?

There are many reasons why the subject of ADC phenomena should be routinely taught in counseling courses and brought to the attention of the general public. Among them are three I must emphasize: understanding the widespread existence of the phenomena would reduce the stress on mourners who have the experience; awareness of the phenomena by counselors and the public would give mourners much needed validation; and education about ADCs would provide a rich resource for use in the coping process.

Specifically, I would recommend the following fundamental concepts be presented, developed, and thoroughly discussed in any ADC education plan offered in conjunction with bereavement support training.

What ADCs Cannot Do

1. ADCs cannot take away the pain of separation nor the pain associated with the sense of loss of part of the self; they do have the potential to reduce the intensity of that pain.

2. ADCs cannot in any way substitute for the mourner's commitment to do his grief work. Dealing with new responsibilities, priorities, and social patterns must be ongoing.

3. ADCs cannot take the place of an understanding, loving support network.

4. ADCs cannot minimize the necessity to identify and mourn secondary losses.

5. ADCs cannot substitute for one special person's healing presence.

6. ADCs cannot substitute for legitimate suffering.

7. ADCs cannot prevent complicated mourning.

What ADCs Can Do

1. ADCs can provide a much needed sense of control and meaning of the death.

2. ADCs can initiate new assumptions, beliefs, and changes in the lives of mourners.

3. ADCs can be a tool for education about loss, grief, and life.

4. ADCs can promote the acceptance of the death of a loved one.

5. ADCs can help mourners articulate their feelings about the death of their loved ones.

6. ADCs can be a resource for mourners to create rituals to assist in adapting to the changes imposed by death.

7. ADCs can help mourners finish unfinished business, heal broken relationships, and establish a new relationship with the deceased.

8. ADCs can reduce anger, guilt, and depression associated with the death of a loved one.

Understanding these concepts can open up a new dialogue about the frequency, meaning, and use of ADC phenomena—all to assist the bereaved. Thorough study of what is presently known about the phenomena, though time consuming, will culminate in understanding an important but neglected facet of the grief process. Furthermore, education about ADCs will also reduce the misinformation and the negative stereotypes that minimize the use of the experience for the benefit of the mourner.

- See also question 88

84. What motivated you to write *After Death Communication: Final Farewells* (Llewellyn, 1997)?

I understand After Death Communication: Final Farewells *was your first work on the subject of ADC phenomena and that it has been translated into other languages. As a grief counselor, you must be the first or one of the first professionals to present an in-depth study of the topic. What was the reason or reasons you decided to undertake such a project in the first place, given the cultural and professional taboos surrounding the subject? By the way, have you taken any heat from your colleagues for taking a stand?*

There are basically two reasons why I decided to put something in print about ADC phenomena. My initial motivation was that at the time of my decision nothing had been written on the topic by a certified grief counselor focusing on the point of view of the bereaved who have the experience. Although, if you looked hard enough, you could certainly find stories about ADCs, there was no book that dealt exclusively with them from the perspective of their impact on the grief process. I thought it was important to get this information out so counselors might consider looking at the topic more closely, as a way of helping their clients. But more importantly, at the time I was convinced that friends and family members of the bereaved who reported an ADC experience needed to understand there was nothing wrong with their grieving loved ones.

The second reason that I wrote on the topic was because the stories I had come across were too convincing with regard to their potential to help the mourner not to be taken seriously. Specifically, I felt these accounts should be brought to the attention of the general public with the hope they could be useful in better understanding the amazing people we are and the uncharted universe in which we live. I should also say I was encouraged by those who would ask me if there was a book on the topic they could read—and I would have to answer I knew of nothing in print.

As for your question about taking heat from colleagues for taking a stand on the importance of ADC phenomena, I'll answer it with one word—yes!

85. Do counselors and caregivers feel there are any therapeutic benefits to ADC experiences?

There are many people who go to counselors for assistance in dealing with many losses in life. Those I have talked to have said their counselors usually believe in certain interventions that they are convinced can provide thera-peutic benefits for the client. Do counselors and caregivers believe ADCs have therapeutic benefits? If they do, what are they?

I regret to say that, generally speaking, the therapeutic benefits of the ADC have not been openly discussed by counselors and professional caregivers, nor have they been systematically studied in the counseling setting. Con-sequently, new members of these two helping professions receive no train-ing in using the ADC as an adjunct to therapeutic intervention with mourners. There are some counselors throughout the country who rou-tinely inquire about the ADC and then go on to use it in some way to help the mourner. I have spoken with some who help mourners validate the ADC experience, often because they themselves have had the experience; they realize its power to assist healing. However, my feeling is that while some counselors and caregivers ask about the experience, few follow up on its meaning to the mourner and use its full potential to create thera-peutic benefits. Consequently, invalidation may be emotionally damaging and stress producing.

Much of this neglect is due to the fact that the nature of the ADC often challenges the worldview of the professional, who therefore refuses to give it careful scrutiny. In fact, it is often dismissed out of hand because of past training in the scientific method. I've had that experience early in my own professional life. Professional counselors are subject to being influenced just like anyone else. The result parallels a universal problem for mourners in our culture: they are highly influenced to hurry up, heal, and get better because of the behavior of others in their support system. In the case with the professional who shuns the ADC experience, he is influenced to quickly dismiss the experience as essentially irrelevant and rely on more conventional approaches to reconcile grief.

However, I see a light at the end of the tunnel. The Association for Death Education and Counseling, a nonprofit educational, professional, and scientific organization, which is on the cutting edge in theory and practice in the areas of death education and counseling, began two years ago accepting a special interest group that will convene annually to discuss ADC and NDE phenomena. This is an important first step for professionals and nonprofessionals alike.

To address your question regarding specific therapeutic benefits, I will list a number of them here. However, this is not the place to deal with each in-depth. (You can learn more about therapeutic benefits in part 6.) To some degree all of the benefits discussed in part 6 can be developed by friends and relatives of the mourner once they become aware of how the ADC can be used. Others, like reducing the intensity of posttraumatic stress disorder, deep depression or guilt, and clarifying emotions belong strictly in the realm of the professional particularly when addressing issues involving complicated mourning. I consider the following as therapeutic benefits that can be utilized by the mourner if needed as a result of experiencing an ADC.

- The expression of feelings and emotions.

- Affirmation and acceptance of the death.

- Reduction of unnecessary suffering.

- Establishment of a new relationship with the deceased.

- A source of rituals for continuity and transition.

- Maintenance of positive memories.

- A means for clarifying emotions and feelings.

- Reduction in the intensity of posttraumatic stress disorder.

- Use as a linking or continuous bonding experience.

- A means of finishing unfinished business and heal relationships.

- A source for reestablishing hope.

- A means of managing STUG (Sudden Temporary Upsurges of Grief) reactions.

- A means for providing a new focus for the mourner.

How these benefits accrue are a function of the nature of the ADC, the creativity of the counselor (particularly in asking the right questions) and mourner, and much time and patience. This is an area those in the counseling and caregiving professions should research, exchange ideas on methodology, and incorporate into in-service training programs.

Finally, the therapeutic potential for nurturing spirituality from the ADC experience has hardly been recognized by the professional community, let alone considered as a means of helping the mourner cope with death. This behavior ignores a large number of studies that show that spiritual and religious beliefs are positively associated with good physical health—and most important—increased mental health. The ADC frequently presents an opportunity for the mourner to rekindle his faith, if it has lagged, or to strengthen it. One's spiritual inclinations can have a profound influence on beliefs about the death of a loved one and the ability to cope with the loss. Actively associating the ADC with one's spirituality (one's belief in something greater than the self), though neglected by medical and health professionals, is a topic worthy of consideration in assisting the bereaved in their work of adapting to the death of a loved one.

86. If the deceased committed suicide, is it less likely one can expect to have an ADC involving that person?

What is your opinion on the frequency of the ADC in relation to the deceased who has taken his own life? Have you found any evidence to suggest the bereaved who are mourning a suicide death are less likely to receive an ADC? This could be important for those providing support for a mourner whose guilt includes the belief that nothing good can come from such a death.

Not infrequently, the person who is mourning a loved one who has committed suicide has to deal with extremely intense emotions. In a clinical setting, counselors often report more intense grief, anger, and depression as well as a host of other emotions that surface as the survivor considers how he could have prevented the death. While all deaths, expected or unexpected, result in a very individual grief response that may be difficult to deal with, the suicide death does carry with it a paralyzing stigma for most. All of this has little to do with whether or not one may experience an ADC. Possible exceptions are those survivors whose intensity of emotion blocks their awareness to receive or accept a contact.

I have not interviewed a sufficient number of people who have had an ADC involving a deceased loved one who had taken his own life in order to make a definitive statement on the subject. I doubt if anyone has. However, I do know many who are mourning deaths by suicide have experienced ADCs. These experiences were every bit as helpful as any other ADC. In my judgment, cause of death has nothing to do with whether or not one experiences an ADC. At the appropriate time, I would counsel those who are mourning the suicide death to hope for, pray for, and look for a sign their loved ones are okay and in a better existence. If a close friend of a mourner came to me for advice on the subject of ADCs, I would suggest, along with some additional support strategies, the same approaches this book has already detailed.

87. How do you deal with critics of ADC phenomena?

I have always been a strong believer in the unseen ever since I was a young-
ster. I think this is because of my mother, who had similar strong beliefs.
Lately, as I have become more open and willing to discuss topics like the
ADC, I have been assailed by some critics—sometimes by those whom I have
considered to be pretty good friends. How can I best deal with the harsh crit-
icism?

Many years ago, I once heard a wise old colleague say there are many times
in life where you have to be thick-skinned and let the taunts of others roll
off your back. That, of course, is much easier said than done, even though
it is good advice. My interpretation of being thick-skinned is that criticism
of various kinds is an inherent part of dealing with controversial issues,
especially those which have been sensationalized and exploited. This is
especially true when you put your side of an issue in print or in a public
forum for all to hear. Then you are fair game for all. So how can you deal
with it?

The first thing to do is check your attitude. What attitude do you normally assume when people are critical of your views? Your attitude can
make a big difference in how you think about criticism coming your way. By
now you should accept the fact that criticism of ADC phenomena (or any
other topics of the unseen variety) is inevitable. As they say, it's the nature of
the beast. Assume you will meet opposition. To be forewarned is to be fore-
armed. It helps if your self-esteem is healthy and you have a sufficient
amount of self-confidence. Then it's easier to take the criticism without taking it personally.

Beware of taking conversational remarks too personally is the second
factor to imprint in your thinking. Don't make the mistake of taking
opposing remarks as a personal attack (even though sometimes it obviously is). Certainly, when you put your ideas out there on the airwaves,
that's a part of you that has become vulnerable. When someone attacks an
idea or puts it down, it's normal to tend to take it as a personal putdown.
Be careful about letting that happen. I have to deal with that as much as
anyone else, whenever someone challenges what I say. Here is where my
colleague's thick-skinned advice comes in handy. Always consider the

source and the disadvantage the person is working from because of their inflexible training and reductionistic thinking.

The third piece of advice I would offer is to avoid direct contradiction of what the person says. As you know, no one wants to hear the words, "You're wrong," as wrong as one may be. It hits a nerve deep inside, and almost as a reflex you want to retaliate. Instead of saying the person is wrong, use remarks such as, "I tend to look at that in just the opposite fashion," or, "I regret I just can't agree with your interpretation." Don't forget, your critic has as much right to his opinion as you do to yours. The point is don't add fuel to the fire with inflammatory rhetoric; it only destroys dialogue. You may even want to close your conversation with some advice a friend of mine received from her mother: "Thank you for being interested enough in my views to offer some interesting comments." Then, in quiet, later, you may want to think about those comments.

Fourth, it is absolutely essential to state your views calmly. Do not raise your voice if you are interrupted, and don't automatically turn up your voice volume because your critic begins to shout out his point of view. The raised voice is the precursor to the shouting match and the loss of any chance at gaining understanding. It's easy to forget we all are slow to accept change, and some people refuse even to consider the possibility of a perspective different from their own. Accept that reality and live with it. The trick is to realize what you are up against. This means assessing and making a decision on the spot at the time of the criticism, defusing the potential flare-up, and gradually finding common ground for agreement.

Fifth, use the following two examples as a way to point out the good that comes from ADC experiences when your opportunity to speak presents itself. More than any other criticism of ADCs, the one I have been confronted with most is that the experiences are orchestrated by the devil himself. Or that, according to the Bible, the dead cannot possibly communicate with the living. Once I listen to the person, I usually respond that if it is the devil, he is completely out of character, because the result of the experience is an overwhelmingly positive one for the mourner. There are too many good things happening for the devil to be the source of the ADC. He would be working against his own cause—as wily as he may be. If the Bible argument is made that the dead cannot communicate with the living, my response is that the Bible also says some people will be given the gift of discerning spirits.

The reason I have given you these two examples is to suggest that you need to decide how to get across to your critics that the good things that accrue from the ADC are too numerous to be a function of things like demons, questionable interpretations, negative impulses, or one's overactive imagination. But you need to have credible answers for these charges whenever they are made. Then expand on that by giving examples of how people have been helped. Concrete examples of positive outcomes are important. Emphasize the large number of people who are helped and how they are helped. Point out that through the ages the positive outcome has an enviable track record. Most scientists, with or without proven experimental evidence about their pet hypothesis, would jump at the chance to boast about their work, if it had the success record ADCs have in easing pain and sorrow.

Sixth, remember that critics have the power of culture (scientifically dominated) on their side, which refuses to recognize the unseen or anything else, unless it can be proven. So sidestep the "no proof" argument. That is, make the statement early in your conversation that there is no way to prove or disprove the ADC experience. This will eliminate a favorite attack argument.

It is because of this argument that occasionally some people who have an ADC experience are denied its fruits. It is easy to let others take your power away and tell you what you experienced, because that's the way our cultural programming works. Group power often dilutes individual power to decide and one begins to second-guess himself. Yet you know what you experienced better than anyone else. That is true reality for you, not manufactured, not in need of scientific proof. It's yours to cherish and use.

Finally, let me comment on the problem of the critic who is not interested in any beneficial discussion, but simply has his mind made up from the start to keep you on the "hot seat." You can usually discern this situation by the first few questions that are asked—ones that aim at your background and look for a flaw to highlight. The assumption is this: By what authority can you speak about ADCs? As soon as you recognize the tactic, bring the discussion to the central issue: What is the ADC? Who has them? How do they help? If the critic refuses to deal with the key issues, answer his authority questions, and as he gets into his viewpoint on the subject, repeatedly say you understand his position. Do not counter with your argument. Graciously end the discussion. Often, by saying you understand his views and not countering, the discussion will naturally come to an end because he is not getting the satisfaction he was looking for. You can't inform someone who refuses to receive information.

88. What topics should I include in an educational program about ADC phenomena?

I would like to put together an educational program for my hospice staff on ADC phenomena and also provide community education on the topic. Where can I obtain materials for such a presentation and what specific topics would you consider essential for my staff to be aware of in order for them to work with the bereaved in our bereavement follow-up program?

Your question addresses what I consider to be a critical need in the training of all hospice personnel. Actually, anyone who has professional responsibilities involving people who are grieving, whether in private practice, working for an agency, or conducting support groups on a volunteer basis, should be knowledgeable about ADCs in order to better serve.

Although I am well aware of the quantity of information that already has to be dealt with in the preparation of staff, since I have been involved in delivering much of this information over the years, ADC awareness has been sorely neglected. At the very least it needs to be normalized and given the green light as an opportunity to help those who are fortunate enough to have the experience. It is my dream that many people in positions to provide educational programs will recognize the potential ADCs have for helping mourners and members of their local communities. These educators can be instrumental in bringing people closer together to discuss issues of life and death including the ADC.

Here is what I believe should be the eleven core topics for your educational ADC program.

1. Definitions and historical background.

2. Fundamental concepts (see question 83).

3. Frequency of the ADC experience.

4. Explanations about when and where ADCs occur.

5. Reports of ADCs: who most often shares the experience.

6. Classification of ADCs.

7. Types of messages received.

8. Changes resulting from the experience.

9. Types of "Negative" ADCs.

10. Explanations for the phenomena.

11. Validation of the ADC and helping the ADCer.

The above are the basics that all professionals, volunteers, and the general public should have access to. I am assuming you will have community education programs on the subject as well. In addition to the above, all who will have direct contact with the bereaved in a support setting should also receive training in the following areas:

12. Inquiring about ADC phenomena with the bereaved.

13. Processing the ADC experience with the bereaved.

14. Applying clinical methods (using specific approaches in utilizing the ADC with those who come to a counselor for therapy).

Discussions on the last three topics should occur in a separate session and be conducted by someone who has used ADC phenomena in a counseling setting.

You can find resources to construct outlines for each of the above (with the exception of clinical applications) by consulting the bibliography at the back of this book. In order to gather information for clinical applications, I would suggest looking for a certified counselor in your area to come in and make a presentation, or set up an interview with the clinician for that purpose.

PART
' 6 '

Helping the Person Who Has an ADC

Questions 89 through 100

Expressing Emotion • Establishing Trust • Gifted Intuitives •
Asking About ADCs • Approaches to Helping •
Finding a Counselor • Related Questions

And someday there shall be such closeness that
when one cries the other shall taste salt.
—Anonymous

89. How can a support person use an ADC to help a mourner express emotion?

Dr. LaGrand, most counselors say that helping a mourner verbalize the emotions and feelings that are teeming within is a fundamental way to provide support. If the person has had an ADC experience, and has shared it with you, how do you go about using it to help the mourner express what is within?

Anyone who provides support for the bereaved on a professional or volunteer basis knows how important it is for the bereaved to be able to express the turmoil that has been building within due to their tragic loss. Why? Because ignoring deep-seated emotions usually results in experiencing them being converted into a host of unwanted physical ailments from digestive disturbances and headaches to insomnia and extreme fatigue. All too frequently, grief becomes extremely complicated because the mourner fails to identify and express hidden emotions and feelings such as guilt and anger that need to be addressed before one can deal with practical matters. But many support persons, especially family and friends of the bereaved, are not aware of the way an ADC can facilitate the expression of emotions. In fact, the therapeutic implications of ADCs have hardly been tapped and provide a wealth of possibilities for changing one's attitudes toward death and toward life.

The opportunities to plumb the depths of the ADC for its emotion expressing possibilities is only limited by your ability to ask questions and to determine how the ADC relates to past events in the mourner's life. The expression of feelings may provide a multitude of positive physiological changes including enhancing immune system function at a time when it is most needed.

Considering all of the above, one of the essential tasks of helping anyone cope with the death of a loved one is to involve him in reviewing the relationship with the person who died. This review, spanning from the beginning of the relationship up to and including the death of the loved one, will necessarily be a time-consuming and emotional journey for most. However, there may be some mourners who, consciously or unconsciously, are likely to avoid the most emotion-arousing memories. The support person should not force the issue of talking about the nature of the relationship that may bring great feeling to the surface for expression. Allow the mourner to set the timetable for his grief work. If there is resistance to reviewing the relationship, let it go for the moment and try at another time.

Consider also the possibility the mourner does not wish to share certain events with you. Your agenda for how she should mourn must not dominate. However, be aware the review of the relationship is important, an arduous affair filled with repetition. Repetition is good: it helps eventually to make what has occurred real. Be prepared to give many hours of your time and to hearing about certain events again and again, especially those surrounding the death. It is healthy and part of the work of mourning. You are helping the mourner by listening with love and respect.

Let me hasten to add that if the mourner trusts you, if she has had an ADC and shares it with you, here is a golden opportunity to help her face the pain of loss and express it. How? By making a thorough inquiry and review of it. This will be the prelude to expressing related incidents and feelings. Just as in reviewing the relationship with the mourner, start at the beginning of the ADC. It is imperative to ask questions such as when, where, and how it occurred. In particular, focus on the message, its meaning, and the use of the experience for the mourner in dealing with the loss of the loved one. In addition, explore whether or not there are parallels between the ADC and its message, and how the deceased lived his life. Often you will find the person saying, "You know, this is just like Brian. He would do something like this." When that happens you have an excellent opening to ask about similar things the deceased used to do when he was alive. In doing so you are helping the mourner bring out feelings she may have been reluctant to express. Through discussion of the ADC she can begin to reexplore the life of the beloved, plumb the moral and value dimensions, and even consider the meaning of her life.

Let us look at an example from an olfactory ADC that occurred to Marion after the death of her father:

"This Helped Me Tremendously"

I was in bed thinking about my father and speaking aloud to him. I asked him to give me a sign if he could hear me. I started to smell cigarette smoke, a smell closely related to my father. My husband, son, and daughter entered the bedroom and all verified the smell of smoke. (Nobody in my home is a smoker.) Since there was no logical explanation, I believe my father was giving me the sign I asked for. The message was "I'm here, I hear you." This helped me tremendously; it was extremely comforting and pulled me out of a sad mood.

This brief experience is rich with opportunity to explore Marion's relationship with her father. You could begin by asking her about his smoking habits, when she first remembered him smoking as a child, and what it was like growing up in a home where your father smoked. You could pursue the idea of whether his smoking influenced her not to smoke. All through this, Marion will have to recall her relationship with her father and it will call forth feelings and emotions. You could also bring up the subject of how Marion's father had been there for her as she was growing up, as he is now, and ask her about what circumstances prevailed when she remembers him stepping in to help.

Whether you are a friend, volunteer, or professional counselor, suggest the mourner write down specific phrases or interpretations about the ADC that can be used later in discussing the event and how it can be utilized to cope with the loss. Be sure to use the dream ADC to talk about qualities and experiences with the person when he was alive. Ask the mourner why she thinks the ADC took place. Help her see the importance of this connection as a sign of ongoing love. Ask if the event has brought peace and comfort.

Encourage the mourner to immediately begin using the ADC as a coping tool. It's an unexpected gift to deal with the loss. Emphasize thinking about it when she wishes to banish the sadness and think about all the good things that have been a part of the relationship. Suggest using the ADC to remind herself of the love and care which are eternal. Through the conversation generated by your questions, the similarities in the ADC to previous life events, and the focus on the deceased, you will be giving the mourner ample opportunity to bring feelings to the surface that she will want to share.

Last, but not least, you will have the opportunity at some point in the conversation to ask two seed-planting questions: "What would your loved one want you to do in dealing with his death?" and "Does the ADC say anything about how your loved one would expect you to respond?

90. Should you ask someone who is mourning if she has had an ADC?

Because of the nature of the ADC and the demeaning way some people look on the experience, it may be a touchy subject to bring up with someone who is mourning. Should you, at some point in your support work, bring up the subject, and what is the best way to go about the task?

In answering your question, I am assuming you are a close friend of the bereaved and the person trusts you and is seeking, or has accepted, your support in dealing with his loss. Obviously, asking about such an intimate experience should not be taken lightly. It is not something everyone involved with the bereaved should attempt. But it is something that should be routinely asked at the right time, in the right place, and by the right person. Furthermore, asking about the experience is something that should take place only after it is clear the relationship between you and the mourner is strong. That means only after speaking with him about his loss on a number of occasions. It goes without saying, therefore, that an inquiry should not be made early in your support work.

As an aside, I disagree with counselors who ask the question about ADC phenomena during their intake (first) interview. It is my contention that some mourners, not yet sure about their relationship with the counselor, are reluctant to give out that type of information. They are not sure how the counselor might respond to the information or are fearful they might be labeled negatively (and this is an unneeded stressor for the mourner at this time). At best, they may not give a clear picture of the ADC in order to protect their true feelings.

Ask we must, or risk losing a wealth of information that is fertile ground for furthering the progress of one's grief work. But ask later, when you sense the relationship between you and the mourner is strong. I am also aware that on occasion it is abundantly clear that the mourner and the counselor (sometimes the support person) may, in their initial contact, hit it off so well that anything can be said or asked. There are exceptions to the rule that only you can sense and then proceed accordingly.

Asking the question about experiencing ADC phenomena can be accomplished directly or indirectly. Here are some of examples.

- "Jim, many people have a strong sense or feeling of connection with their loved ones. Have you ever felt as though Sara was especially near?"

- "Alice, have you ever sensed Don's presence or had an experience where you felt he was close by?"

- "Fred, at times you must feel Joanne is far away. Have you ever had occasion to feel that she is particularly close?"

- "Martha, have you ever had an experience that you thought was a 'sign' or a message from your husband?"

Sometimes you may introduce the topic by saying that mourners often talk out loud to the deceased. Then ask if the mourner has had any experiences where he thought the deceased was communicating with him. You may also bring up the subject through first talking about dreams of the deceased. Dreams are marvelous vehicles for interacting with the beloved and obtaining useful information for the coping process. Again, let me emphasize the importance of sensing when to ask the question, particularly when a trusting relationship has been established. Also, be sure the question is posed where there is privacy so the response will not be unduly influenced.

91. How do you establish trust so you can ask the mourner whether she has had an ADC?

It is obvious, unless you have good rapport with a mourner, especially a trusting relationship, you cannot expect the person to share the experience. Yet in order for the ADC to be fully utilized, it would seem that talking about it is essential. So how do you establish the trust that can lead to openness and the freedom to talk about deep feelings?

Keep in mind that those who are mourning the death of a loved one need safe places and safe people. That is, they need privacy so they can express their feelings openly without feeling embarrassed, and they need the companionship of a trusted friend, relative, or confidant who will allow them to feel what they are feeling. All of this should occur in a nonjudgmental environment in which the survivor feels free to accept or reject the support offered. Mourners especially need to be allowed to stay in charge of their mourning and not be manipulated by support persons to respond in a particular way. Society already is inherently manipulating in this regard and wants the mourner to quickly get back to normal and not display emotion.

In establishing a trusting relationship, few things are more important than reliability. For example, in 1980, I was on a team providing support for our first hospice patient who was dying of lung cancer. Gerald had been told he had two months to live by one doctor and less than three months by another. I first met him, lying in bed at his home in a rural area of northern New York state one month after he had outlived both of their prognoses. To say the least, he was angry at being told by two doctors that he was going to die in a short period of time—with all of the anxiety that entails—but he was still able to function quite well. In fact, four months later he surprised me one day when I walked into his home and he was sitting up in a living room chair. At a later date, he even did some repairs on his home.

As do all who are dying, Gerald was grieving the loss of all his relationships to the world. Our hospice team was diligent with its care and was led by a brilliant young physician's assistant who was highly skilled in pain management. Every day someone from the team came to visit this fifty-four-year-old man, and every day he surprised us with his strength and vigor. Six months after he was supposed to have died he was out driving his truck. During all this time (he lived for eighteen months) I went to see him every Tuesday and Thursday afternoon. Whether it rained or snowed (and we had some heavy snowstorms in the north country) I was there. He knew he could rely on me to show up at his door when I said I would be there, something every professional caregiver is taught early in training.

The moral of this brief story is that consistent respectful presence resulted in a deep trusting relationship. Consistency (which creates the expectation of support), reliability (which creates belief in the caregiver as a person), and respect (which creates feelings of self-esteem in the person you are helping) are the hallmarks of any trusting relationship regardless of the nature of the loss or illness.

After his death, I had to go back and review for myself why, a couple of months earlier, he had said to me, "If it wasn't for you, I don't think I would be here now." At the time, that statement floored me. Later, I came to realize our trust developed because he could count on me; I listened intently—with my eyes as well as my ears—and never talked to him differently than I would any other friend. Through all of this he was always in charge of his dying. This respectful service to another is something anyone can give if he decides to provide support for someone who is grieving. The main task is to learn to be around someone in pain. You need no special words or phrases, simply your humble presence.

Trust, therefore, flows from consistent presence, being a good nonjudgmental listener, never talking down to a mourner as though he is a victim, and from the gentle honesty that always exists between two friends.

92. What should someone do if a friend or family member who is in mourning comes to you and says he has had an ADC?

If, without warning, a mourner decides to share his ADC experience with you, is there any particular initial response that can help facilitate the exchange? What approach have you used in putting the mourner at ease so that he realizes you are open to his experience?

The best preparation for the experience is obviously to have basic knowledge about ADC phenomena so you do not immediately suspect something is not right with the mourner. That is easier said than done. All too often a support person is startled by the revelation. For example, suppose you were presented with the following ADC that Chris Tozzo (you met her daughter in question 56) of Sarasota, Florida experienced shortly after the death of her husband.

The ring my husband ordered for me arrived after his death. Within one week, one of the stones in the ring was missing, which was very upsetting to me. I tried to locate it for three days with no luck. On the fourth day, I came

home from taking my children to school and walked into the kitchen. I
dropped on my knees to the floor and started to cry. I reached for the dust-
pan and brush and was making sweeping motions, as I had done about four
times since the loss of the stone, and I said out loud, "Please God, help me
find it." In the silence there was a tinkling of bells like wind chimes—and
the stone fell through the air and landed in front of me.

I believe my husband knew how much the ring meant to me and found
a way to return the lost stone. A message I received from the experience was
that souls do not automatically go on if the persons left behind are not
ready. On his deathbed I had told him I could not do it without him and I
think he stayed to be sure I was okay. It was a beautiful experience, but it
made me miss him more than ever. It did give me peace thinking he was
watching over us.

This experience certainly belongs in the most intriguing category. I
interviewed Chris at her home and asked her many questions regarding
her ADC. I am confident it occurred to her as she stated. So where can you
begin? By all means, begin by making every effort to respond with sincere
interest, encouraging the mourner to tell you about the experience including when and where it happened. Hold in check your culturally ingrained
reflex to suspect something is not right with the mourner as her story
unfolds. Your demeanor is crucial here.

In particular, be advised that your nonverbal communication is much
more important in this situation than anything you may say. As the communication experts tell us, if someone sends a mixed message, that is, if
you say one thing but your body language says something else (disinterest,
disbelief, alarm, etc.), the listener will usually accept what is conveyed in
nonverbal terms. Also keep in mind that the mourner will be studying you
carefully for signs of disbelief.

Current communication theory suggests that the vast majority of our
messages are read nonverbally. That is why it is so important to be aware of
how you communicate with your body posture, gestures, eyes, voice tone,
and facial expression in your interaction with anyone you are trying to
help. Therefore, when you are told by the mourner she has had an extraordinary experience, make every effort to give your undivided attention, seek
details with great sincerity, and give open support. Later, if the event proves

to be a misperception or misunderstanding, you will still have maintained your trusting relationship with the mourner. You have lost nothing, but you have allowed the mourner to realize she can come to you with her most intimate thoughts.

If you are around others when the mourner breaks the news, ask if she would like to go where there is more privacy. Find a place to sit down so you can have a long talk, as usually appears warranted in these situations. Be sure to stay in close conversational range and lean slightly forward toward the mourner. All of this will show your interest and sincerity that is critical at this time. I try to show joy and belief in my facial expression when I hear the story and, at various points in the telling, I may nod my head to show acceptance of what I am hearing. If appropriate, I may show agreement by saying others have had similar experiences. Or I may say, "you seem to have received a wonderful gift," when I realize the mourner is convinced of the authenticity of her experience. Let the mourner direct and dominate the conversation. Good listening means conscious intent, conveying the language of acceptance with timely nonverbal communication, listening with your heart, and listening for the feelings that accompany the words.

93. Do you ever recommend that a mourner who has not had an ADC visit a spiritual medium to help her realize the loved one lives on?

I have heard that some people who are mourning feel they must have some assurance their loved one lives on in another life. Consequently, they search out the most popular spiritual medium or psychic in their area, spend a considerable amount of money, and hope for the best. What is your feeling about doing this sort of thing? Do you recommend it to your clients?

Visiting a person who purports to have ability to make contact with a deceased loved one is a big step to take, for many have questionable credentials. I say that because there is no guarantee that the experience will be a positive one (as the mourner expects) or that the person being consulted actually possesses extraordinary intuitive ability. In fact, it could be a disaster. Consequently, I would always let the mourner decide and would not initiate or directly recommend the consultation.

However, if the choice is made to go, I feel obligated to inform the mourner what to expect and ask her what she knows about the person she wants to visit. If possible, I would try to arrange to interview the medium (or gifted intuitive as I prefer to call them). Furthermore, the mourner should find out as much as possible about fees and about whether the meeting will be conducted as part of a group sitting or if she will be alone. In a group sitting, though less expensive, there may be less chance of meeting one's specific needs. In any event, I would continue to support the mourner and not only prepare her for the visit, but also process the visit with her after it takes place.

Again, it is important to support the mourner in her search for meaning. It is also important to inform the mourner that if there is no contact it is not the fault of the deceased. Some mourners have interpreted lack of contact as implying the deceased did not wish to send a message to the survivor, and they have become angry at the deceased or more depressed. We have to remember that intuitives have good days and bad days just like everyone else. They may not be able to make the connection for any number of reasons, if at all possible. (The standard explanation given by many parapsychologists for the supposed contact with the deceased is the psi ability of the intuitive who is picking up information from the mind of the mourner, so-called mind reading.)

Are there individuals mourning the death of a loved one who go to an intuitive and have positive results? There certainly are! In a recent conversation with a woman who went to a sitting involving three hundred people, she shared the following results.

> I decided to go to a sitting with an intuitive that involved three hundred people and only ten were going to be able to have him read for them. I heard him go through several people in the audience and he was so accurate I was sure they must have been planted there. He couldn't be that good. Then he started talking about someone he had an image of who had been killed in an aircraft accident and two others raised their hands and began to speak. But then he clarified it further and it wasn't for them. All of a sudden I realized he was talking about my husband and he came over to me. Everything he told me was correct and he could not have known the information beforehand. I have always been skeptical, but not anymore.

Let me emphasize it is important to consider in depth one's expectations of having a sitting with a gifted intuitive. What do you hope will be the result of the relationship? To feel the deceased is in a better place? To know the deceased is happy and lives on? To understand the deceased is concerned about the survivor? To complete unfinished business? Perhaps the most important question to ponder before a visit is how such a visit will help one better cope with the absence of the loved one. As one woman stated in closing a letter to me about her fifteen-year-old son, who died in a bicycle accident, and about her ADCs after his death: "I have been to psychics, spent lots of money, but finally realized that I will not ever have him on this earth. That was a very difficult thing for me to accept." This comment carries much wisdom for all who are mourning: no one, including a gifted intuitive, is going to take away the pain of having to cope with the absence of the loved one. Coping with the death of a loved one inevitably means learning to live again without the physical presence of that person and dealing with all the adjustments in lifestyle that are necessitated. That is the work of grief—to learn new ways to deal with a different world—no one can do that for the mourner.

Another important rule of thumb: avoid the tendency to become reliant on intuitives and fixated on receiving proof positive that the loved one has been contacted and is in another existence. Often, mystery must prevail. Poet John Keats (who died in his twenties) said in a letter to his brother "One must be at ease amid uncertainties." I have seen mourners who appear to be conducting their grief work in large part on what intuitives tell them. Beware! Mourners who rely solely on others (after the early days of grief) are further complicating their grief by failing to assume responsibility for adapting to the changes imposed by the death, while limiting the development of skills and abilities essential for integrating the loss into life. Mourning the death of a loved one demands that we learn new ways to deal with a world that has changed, to appreciate and cherish the gifts the life of the deceased has presented, and to integrate the relationship into a new world.

94. How can you decide on the content of the message if nothing is said by the deceased?

In many ADCs there is no verbal communication. How do you decide what the contact means for a mourner? I am thinking of situations where a person is seen by the mourner but there is no audible sound.

To begin with, you do not decide what the contact experience means for the mourner. That person alone decides. This does not mean you have to refrain from making suggestions in addition to whatever the mourner deduces from the experience. In practice, you will be able to ask questions that can help the mourner find additional meaning and comfort. That aside, much can be learned from the experience by examining the visual characteristics, that is, the nonverbal features.

Nonverbal communication is a part of our everyday life and we all become accustomed to communicating not only with our voices, but with many personal gestures including eye contact, nodding the head, smiling, and hand gestures. Many of our nonverbal signs are uniquely personal. The experts tell us that in some instances we do not even realize what nonverbal signs we are using. Nevertheless, showing up, just being there, sends a profound fundamental message. Presence makes a very personal statement: *I care.* The fact that a deceased loved one, an angel, or a Supreme Being appears is saying much about the relationship between the mourner and the messenger. The specific message received depends on the perception of the mourner. Here are ten questions the mourner may ask himself, or a support person or counselor may want to ask the mourner, in discussions about meaning and messages. At the appropriate time, developing the full meaning of the encounter can provide insight to help the mourner decide how to use the ADC as a coping tool.

- Where did the encounter occur? Perhaps it was in an intimate place often shared with the deceased and has special meaning.

- What was the person wearing? Did his clothing make a statement?

- How did he look? Healthy? Whole? Strong? Vibrant?

- What did his eyes say? Happy? Caring? Loving? Hopeful?

- What was his facial expression? Radiant? Alert? Enthused?

- Was he smiling? What does his smile mean to you? Was there a frown?

- Was he standing, sitting, or walking, and what does that imply?

- Did he make any gestures with hands or arms?

- Did he reach out to touch you?

- What was the distance between you and the loved one when he appeared?

Distance alone is a powerful message. Did he sit on the edge of the bed? Was he standing next to your chair or bed?

Here is a visual ADC that Sara Costello experienced. She had just given birth to her daughter when she was informed her grandmother had died as the result of falling down the steps at her home. After reading her story, consider how some of the ten questions might be applied to illuminate the messages and the meaning she received through the experience.

"It Was Her Way to Let Me Know that She Had Seen My Baby"

My grandmother had eleven children. Her first child was a boy who died at birth. Then she had ten girls, all of whom had two to eight children each, plus she had many great grandchildren. At the time of her death, I was in the hospital, having just given birth to my daughter on July 4. We were all very close to my grandmother, so when my sister told me she had died on July 7, the first thing I thought and said to my sister was, "You know, my baby was the only one she hasn't seen."

Of course, after that, I asked my doctor to send me home early, which he did. Back when this happened, they kept you in the hospital a lot longer than they do now. I left the hospital that day and my neighbor watched my baby while I went to the funeral home. I never made it to the funeral, but I loved my grandmother very much. I thought of all the things she would do for me when she visited. I thought, "Well, life goes on and she's with God." She was a very religious woman. Every chance she had, she was always saying the rosary.

On July 10, at about 2:00 A.M., I got up for the baby's feeding, heated the bottle, fed and changed her, and put her back in the bassinette sound asleep. As I sat back down on the bed and was slipping off my slippers, I heard her whimpering and looked over at the bassinette. There was my grandmother, standing bent over the bassinette, smiling. The baby's hand was extended up and it looked like she was shaking her hand, and also smiling at me. I looked and couldn't believe my eyes. I rubbed them and looked again; she kept shaking the baby's hand and smiling at me. I looked and rubbed my eyes three times before I screamed. Then she just vanished.

I really don't know why I screamed; I guess just out of shock. To this day, I am so mad at myself for screaming. This is a memory I'll have for the rest of my life. I often think of my grandmother now and I always tell her I am sorry. I know she would never have harmed either of us; I feel so bad about my actions. It was her way to let me know she had seen my baby. And the experience helped me to understand more about death; it showed me there is a life after death and that death should not be feared.

Sara was able to read many of the nonverbal signs (shaking hands, smiling, etc.) that were presented by the appearance of her grandmother and readily used them to deduce message and meaning. Much more discussion could now take place based on her description of the ADC and the use of the discussion questions. She regretted having screamed and has made it an issue that overshadows the comforting meaning of her grandmother's visit. On the other hand, she has received much that has changed her perceptions of death.

In using any ADC to cope with the death of a loved one, it is helpful to carefully examine the account from beginning to end. Look at all nonverbal features, even when there is an auditory ADC (tone, pitch, volume, setting in which it occurred) and explore their meaning. This procedure may provide new images and details that the mourner can use to strengthen his belief in the experience and hope in the future. Good support work, like good counseling, depends more on asking the right questions than on having the right answers.

95. How do you use the ADC experience to help mourners retain positive memories of their loved ones?

If an ADC is a specific event in which a mourner senses a closeness or a sign from the deceased loved one, it is obviously something he won't forget right away. In order to use the ADC to assist the mourner in holding on to positive memories and cope with his loss, what can be said or done to facilitate the process? How do I approach the mourner with this idea?

When a loved one dies, a physical presence and relationship ends, but there will always be a deep intimate relationship with the deceased based on memories. Usually such memories are especially strong and surface at special family gatherings, holidays, and often when the mourner is in a place where he has been with his beloved in the past. In fact, memories are critical grieving tools that one can use to look back on all the good times and recall what was received and learned from the deceased. These are opportunities, if you are a support person, to facilitate this important recollection process by being open to the sharing of these memories and encourage the mourner to talk about feelings. For example, look for opportunities to help the mourner recall when he felt loved. When you feel loved, you feel connected, you feel you belong. Help the mourner recall those loving memories of belonging and harvest the wisdom of the experience. Include the ADC as a belonging/restoring event in the process. It is part of the new loving relationship that has to be established after the death of the beloved. Suggest to the mourner that he has received a gift through the ADC that bestows love and is part of the memories to include in establishing the new relationship with the deceased.

The first step you as support person can take in introducing the idea of using the ADC to build positive memories is to start pattern building. That is, willingly accept and build on memories of the past—or of the dying process and the funeral—which the mourner chooses to share with you. At the first sharing of any memory take the opportunity to recognize its importance by pointing out its merits. ("That's an important memory to hold on to." Or "That memory has much meaning for you.") By example, you are saying it's okay to share memories, even the sad ones, and you will always be there to listen. And of course, you are providing great support to your friend or family member.

It is often best to introduce the importance of the ADC as a positive memory source at a time when the topic normally comes up in conversation—occasionally even on the first exchange about the experience—if, without question, it has been obviously a welcomed event. ("What another beautiful memory you now have of Jane.") Generally, suggesting this idea comes later when the mourner or you introduce the topic into the conversation. I usually say something like, "You know, Bev, you have a wonderful experience to use in dealing with your loss," and then go on to explain how it can be used, especially when one is feeling low. Place emphasis on the reality of the loved one's happiness, his wanting the mourner to adjust and reengage life, and that he will always be caring.

The ADC can be used as a resource for building or linking positive memories of the deceased from the past to the present. Because memory is a powerful motivator of behavior, sharing memories with others that are accepting of the practice will help the mourner normalize his feelings. Often, emotion accompanies the sharing process and it is to be accepted without fanfare (although with warmth and support) as a common response to such thoughts. Equally important is encouraging the incorporation of the ADC into memory sharing with those who hold similar beliefs about the experience, because reinforcing the ADC provides an additional resource to turn to and to strengthen the acceptance of the loss. Memory helps create new patterns of behavior; it profiles and directs us. Thus, people who have a contact experience are not just helped through their grief, they are often motivated to adopt a new perspective on life, appreciate what they still have, and/or reinforce long held spiritual beliefs—all of which result in critical behavioral changes.

Like the stories we heard as children, ADC stories do not grow old; they renew and refresh. One fond remembrance turns into the recollection of another. These memories can encourage the bereaved to undertake new goals and assume new roles; bring goodness into the lives of others. One can be motivated by what the deceased had accomplished, how she cared for others, what changes she inspired. These precious memories are part of personal histories and those of our children.

Sometimes an ADC can help a family member who did not have the experience as much or more than it does the person who is the direct recipient of the experience. Louise Schnur of Auburn, California shares just such an account, one in which memories can be fashioned for all concerned.

"Milt's Dream Has Helped Me Too"

My brother Jack died from emphysema. He was also severely crippled with arthritis and had been in a wheel chair for several years prior to his death. It was May 24, 1990, and it was Jack's fifty-eighth birthday. My husband Milt and I had gone to the hospital to celebrate his birthday. He was in a coma and also in a fetal position from crippling arthritis when we arrived. When I looked at him I thought to myself, "He looks so uncomfortable."

Suddenly, Jack opened his eyes and smiled at the balloon that I had tied to the foot of his bed. Quickly, I placed each birthday card in front of his face and read it out loud. Afterwards, Milt and I sang "Happy Birthday" to him. A few seconds later, he slipped back into a coma again and we left for home.

We visited with Jack again the following day, arriving at the hospital at 10 A.M. Although he was still in a coma, I began talking to him about God and how everyone—grandmother, grandfather, and father who had all died several years ago—were all waiting to welcome him back home. I also told him he had done the best he could, and if he was ready to go, all he had to do was to follow the light and go home to God. I just kept talking over and over again about God and family members who had died. Suddenly, the strangest thing happened. His body began to move slowly. Within a few minutes, he was completely straight in the bed. With tears in my eyes, I knew he was in spirit.

Because we didn't want him to die alone, we stayed until 7:30 that evening. I hated to leave him then, but we had a long drive back home. The next morning, I got a call from the hospital. Jack had died at 3:47 A.M. He obviously chose that time of day to leave to spare us the pain of his death.

Five days later, Jack came to Milt in a dream. Jack, who was healthy and strong, was walking along side of Milt. Suddenly, Jack turned to Milt and said, "I'm happy and I'm well." And that's when Milt woke up. At first I was hurt and confused because Jack didn't come to me. But after thinking about it that whole day, I finally understood why he had chosen Milt and not me. It was because Milt didn't believe in an afterlife and I did. Jack, of course, didn't know that about Milt before he died. It was after he died that he knew that, and obviously wanted Milt to know that there is life after death and that he was now whole and well.

Although Milt is still somewhat skeptical about a life after death, the dream did help him with Jack's death. And Milt's dream has helped me too, because I know Jack is with God and free of pain and suffering.

The specific use of the ADC depends on the message(s) the mourner has drawn from the experience and his needs. In this instance, the message was twofold: he's whole again and he's happy. Thus, in talking about the ADC, the subject of no longer being in pain can be talked about and expanded upon as well as the happiness found in his new existence. When the message is also one of happiness, as indicated, or if one hears "I'm fine, I'm all right" then, likewise, expand on the various implications of the statement and how the deceased looked and spoke. You will be helping to construct new memories.

Another reason for reinforcing the message of the ADC is because through repetition the mourner can ingrain the most needed memory (freedom from pain, happiness, caring, love, etc.) deeply in his or her memory banks. Encourage the person to repeat it, or parts of the experience, and on appropriate occasions to tell others. For example, on an anniversary or at Christmas or Hanukkah, the recollection of the ADC is especially appropriate. Explore with the mourner when might be the most appropriate times. Let the person assume control of when to utilize the experience in the coping process.

As for introducing the idea of using the ADC to retain positive memories, the basic approach is to be straight forward at a time when you intuitively feel it is appropriate. Simply suggest and explain. Emphasize focusing on positive memories is helpful to anyone who has suffered through the death of a loved one. Memories associated with the ADC can take their rightful place among many of those memories generated from past experiences. Help the mourner identify times in the past that bring happy memories of the deceased (i.e., "When was the most recent joyous time that you and Bill shared?").

Using the ADC as part of "remember when" sessions can assist in posing questions such as how the deceased inspires us, what would she recommend in this situation or that, or how would she change a negative into something positive. The ADC is made to order for retaining positive memories of the deceased because, as psychology tells us, emotion and memory are inextricably linked. We need to take advantage of this fact and assist the bereaved in establishing memories of love and commitment. And what better way can we pay respect to our deceased loved ones than by using what we have learned from them.

96. What can you do when one family member receives an ADC and other family members feel slighted?

What can be done in a situation where one family member reports having an ADC, tells the rest of the family, and discovers one or several others feel hurt because they would like a similar experience? Is there something I can say to ease the feeling other family members have who have not been honored by the deceased? Why does such a dilemma occur?

I can appreciate the thinking of those who believe a family member has had a sign from a deceased loved one and wonder why they have been left out of the loop. In reality, those who have not received the gift of the ADC are asking the same question all mourners—and each of us—ask many times throughout life, "Am I loved?" The question isn't posed in exactly those terms; it is masked in numerous hopes and the little things that occur daily that make us feel wanted and needed. The death of the loved one, who is often the primary reinforcement that the mourner was loved, now frames for the mourner in a dramatic way the same question, "Am I still loved?" Therefore, it should come as no surprise other family members are questioning why they have not had some sign because they too want tangible evidence that love is ongoing. I would like to have it; you would like to have it.

Does this mean other family members will automatically feel left out? Not at all. In some instances there will be some family members who do not believe in ADC phenomena. There are still others who will be so overjoyed the ADC occurred to someone in the family they do not feel overlooked.

Why does one family member receive a contact and other family members do not? No one has the answer to that one, although we can speculate. It is possible one family member is much more open to spiritual phenomena than others. Or, perhaps that one family member was in special need of a particular sign because of the nature of the emotional investment in the deceased and the person's distraught frame of mind.

I once had a letter from a young woman whose mother died and her husband sensed the presence of her mother on several occasions, including at the moment of death when he was not present at the hospital (a crisis ADC). These were enough for her, because as she said, "I had to know if she was completely free from pain, that at last she was happy. I had to know. I couldn't have gone on if I didn't know she was okay." Her husband's responses were most significant for her because they helped answer her critical question. She believed the husband's ADCs were meant for her and they probably were. However, they also had a major impact on his beliefs. His ADCs were unusual because his wife would ask her mother a question and he would receive her response. This is another example of the great diversity of the ADC.

One might also suggest that perhaps the family member who received the contact would be most believable and best able to relay the essence of the contact to others. Then too, the person who received the sign may have been the only person who was looking for one or who had prayed for one. In any event, the dilemma of those who feel left out can be addressed by looking at the event as a family happening.

I don't mean to underestimate the difficulty of the task one faces in helping those who wish they could receive a sign. Whether you can present a plausible explanation or suggest an avenue of hope or meaning regarding the felt omission, it will not magically erase that left out feeling for some. But try you must. Here is an approach I recommend. First, delight in the fact the family has truly been touched by the extraordinary; they have been singled out, honored. That an ADC has happened at all is deeply meaningful with many implications. The deceased (or an angel, the Divine) knows the message will be heard by all. It may be stated it was to be shared by all who will listen and believe. Focus on the concept the event was a family affair ("Your family has indeed been blessed."), relayed through one family member for the benefit of all who loved the deceased.

Secondly, highlight the specifics of the message. What was the intent of the message? To show caring? Concern? Love? To inform about peace? Happiness? Freedom from pain? These are messages for all primary mourners that need to be shared and discussed as appropriate and applicable to all in the family. They are usually not exclusive one-person communications. You can find help in developing these approaches by talking to the person who received the contact. He or she will be delighted to know when other family members believe in the experience and will want to share the rich rewards and insights that assist in accepting the death and coping with the loss.

97. Can you use an ADC to create a ritual so the mourner can say goodbye to the deceased and let him go?

I know rituals can have powerful healing effects on people who are going through major life transitions and that we all continue to use rituals to reinforce beliefs and meaning in our lives. Do you see the ADC being used by some mourners as part of a ritual to finish unfinished business, to let go, to say goodbye, or to strengthen the bond between mourner and deceased, if necessary?

The ADC can be used in all the ways you have mentioned and then some. Rituals for those who are mourning the death of a loved one are an excellent means of regaining a sense of control at a time when disorganization seems to be everywhere. The use of the ADC can provide a large assortment of choices to meet specific needs of the mourner. Rituals may be formal or informal, short or long, take place indoors or outside, and provide for participation to whatever degree the mourner desires. In addition to those already mentioned, therapeutic ritual involving the ADC can be fashioned to signal forgiveness, expiate guilt, act out and release feelings, memorialize, affirm the reality of the death, provide a sense of continuity, confront unresolved grief, and act as a linking object to the deceased. The biggest obstacle in meeting these ritual needs is a lack of support for the mourner to proceed in this endeavor and a lack of ideas for utilizing the ADC.

Constructing appropriate ritual begins with the mourner; it has to conform to his desires and belief system. Next, the question of what the ritual is to address has to be considered. The mourner should be asked if there is a behavior he wants to initiate though the ADC ritual—reconciliation, a demonstration of continuity, to use it to symbolically accommodate the deceased's presence, or to say farewell. Is there a message to be conveyed such as, "we'll always love you, thank you for everything, you will live on in our hearts?" Friends or counselors can then assist in making suggestions for creating a ritual with the ADC.

Here is a time when even the wounded inner child (the child in each of us regardless of age) can begin to heal through ritual use of the ADC. The mourner can forgive himself for the pain, real or imagined, he may have caused in the life of the loved one or that the loved one caused the mourner. The ADC becomes the staging ground for reinterpreting what was once a painful failure by looking at the good that has since occurred. Depending on the nature of the ADC, here are some possibilities for rituals that can be employed in a variety of settings. Remember, a ritual can be as simple as sitting down with a cup of tea to ruminate about the ADC or using it in a more dramatic show of love and caring with loved ones present; it can also be a one-time event or repeated on special occasions.

- Draw, paint, or sketch the ADC or a significant part of it. Frame it and have family or friends sign it. Display the creative result permanently or on special occasions when honoring the deceased as part of a celebration of a life that has been lived. An ADC dream image is especially applicable to the above.

- If there are objects involved in the ADC experience—such as a stone, ornament, flower, beach shell—they can be preserved or mounted as a reminder. The object or a part of it may also be used to bid the deceased farewell in a ritual of transition. The object can be taken to a familiar place and placed in tribute, or taken to a body of water and released in the waves.

- Make a collage that represents various aspects of the deceased's life and include some part of the ADC experience in it.

- Take a picture or drawing of the ADC and use it as part of a wreath to put on the gravestone.

- Make use of any parts of the ADC that included birds, animals, or other wildlife that symbolize certain meaning to the mourner and/or in the life of the deceased. Have a likeness of the particular wildlife painted or purchase a picture of it to place in an appropriate setting in the home.

- Draw memories of the deceased, including memories associated with the ADC, and hang them on a mobile to be used as part of the ritual. You may also want to include words like *hope, thanks,* and *love* inscribed so they can be read as the mobile turns. This can initiate memories and expression of emotions. Use the drawing or other memorabilia as part of a book of remembrances.

- In a quiet setting, reconstruct the ADC experience as a way to initiate dialogue with the loved one and to express unexpressed wishes, regrets, and love.

- Decide to use the ADC experience in a way to remember the deceased on an anniversary or other significant occasion. One may repeat the ritual on each anniversary of the death either at home, at the cemetery, or in a natural setting. This may involve other family or friends or be used alone by the mourner.

- Incorporate the ADC as part of the inner work of spiritual development and in thanksgiving for favors received. Focus on the goodness that comes through the recollection of the experience and how that goodness fits into personal beliefs about the afterlife and a Supreme Being. Using the ADC to develop spiritual insight can turn the past and the future into the now; one can mend the past and endorse the future and whatever it may bring.

- On holidays, cook the loved one's favorite dish (or make a dessert). Serve it as part of a "remember when" session and include the ADC experience as part of the celebration of remembrances.

To illustrate the use of the ADC as a ritual for bringing closure, here is a dream state experience that happened to Jane Foster of Danville, Illinois.

"My Belief is That He Was Truly with Me"

We were living in Huntington, New York, at the time of my husband's death from a cardiac infarction. He died in Manhattan where he was working. On the day of his death, I was having parent-teacher conferences in the Brentwood School District, where I was working. I remember wondering how something so important could have happened without me being aware of it. Our children were in high school, being sixteen and seventeen years old. After his death, I went to work and church, otherwise I stayed home. He had been such a family-involved person that I felt it would be unforgivable if something happened to one of the children while I was out having a good time. I wouldn't have been able to explain it to him or to myself. At the time of his death, I did not believe in an afterlife. It didn't seem logical that one might be rewarded through eternity, or punished, because of these few years on earth. My husband was even more adamant about that than I.

Hube died November 19, 1970. In August 1973, I was in bed in one of those half-asleep, half-awake periods, when I dreamed I was in the front room of our home and that an unfamiliar blue car had pulled into our drive. My husband got out of the car with his clothes hanger-satchel over his shoulder and came around the car on his way into the house. I knew he had been away and I went out the front door onto the stoop to greet him. He greeted me, saying that he was really rested. I responded that was good, as he had been so very tired. As he came closer, I sank down onto the steps and said, "This isn't real; you're dead." He sat down beside me and said, "I'm sorry," and held my hand firmly. I felt his hand and saw some little white spots on his hand that I had forgotten. I was crying. However, when I awoke I was not crying; I was feeling happy. Explicit was the message that he was rested. Implicit was that he was off about his business. I don't know why, but it seemed to me that his "business" was another life. One of my reactions to his presence was, "I'll bet he was surprised," that is, surprised to find there was more to his existence than the one he had on earth.

I've taken classes and been in workshops that try to teach dream remembrance. I seldom remember dreams, but this one I can't forget. At any rate, I know the dream appearance could have been my subconscious telling me that it was time to move on. My belief is he was truly with me and telling me in effect to let go and get on with my life.

Because Jane believes her husband did visit her, she could use this ADC in a ritual of transition by engaging him in conversation to say goodbye, though he will never be forgotten. This is done by finding a quiet setting, relaxing, replaying the dream, and saying her goodbyes at her choosing. She could also use it as a linking object, to recall fond memories, to grow spiritually, and to remember him on his birthday or their anniversary. As time goes by, she may choose to reassess her ADC experience and decide to use it in a different way. She may even interpret it differently, so as to open up new avenues of ritual (and control) through the years.

The above are only a few of many possible uses of the ADC. One thing is certain: whatever the need of the mourner, together you can find a way to utilize the ADC in the creation of a ritual. A therapist who has used the ADC in working with mourners will also be able to integrate its use into other ritual behaviors by closely analyzing its contents and helping assess current needs.

98. How can an ADC be used as a linking object to maintain a bond with the deceased?

In the literature on grief, some writers talk about the use of linking objects that form a symbolic bond with the deceased. This can be helpful when griev-ing, or it may impede progress, depending on how the linking object is per-ceived. Can the ADC be used as a linking object, and if it can, how would you suggest it be used?

First, let's define what is meant by a linking object. Linking objects are vir-tually anything that the mourner perceives as symbolically linking him with the deceased. The object could be a favorite medal, cup, trinket, pic-ture, book, letter—the list is endless. It may also include a special memory associated with the deceased that gives special meaning. This is where the ADC could be utilized as the mourner chooses.

I would like to emphasize that not everyone needs a linking object to feel especially close to the deceased loved one. Clearly, linking objects are not used by all mourners. I make that statement because it is all too easy to think everyone mourning the death of a loved one must have an object that makes the relationship strong and ongoing. That is not necessarily so. There are many mourners who have no need for this symbolic emotional reminder because they have been able to integrate their loss into their lives. They believe all is well with the deceased, want to let go, and say goodbye. Others wish to have an active continuing bond.

The former have no intention of forgetting the loved one. Instead they see the death with different eyes and want to begin the reorganization process of their lives. The latter choose a different road to adaptation. The lack of need for a linking object in no way means the mourner does not want to retain some of the deceased's possessions. Keep in mind a linking object is extraordinarily invested with emotion and keeps the deceased close in a symbolic bond. Therefore, a linking object may, as time goes by, become an obstacle to going on with life as the mourner tries to keep the deceased alive and relies too much on interacting with the object.

Can the ADC be used as a linking object or memory? Yes. The ADC can serve as a way to nurture or maintain the relationship through simple recollection and playback as desired. Of course, like any linking object, one has to be careful about using it in such a way as to refuse to acknowledge the deceased is gone and will not be physically present again. The mourner can invest too much of the self in any linking object to his or her detriment. When this occurs the mourner is constantly living in the past and has not begun the task of building a new life without the deceased. Healthy use of the ADC as a linking object is directly dependent on the emotional needs and disposition of the mourner. As in so many aspects of life, from nutrition to stress management, balancing the use of a linking object with the duties and responsibilities of life in the present tense is essential.

99. What have you learned from mourners who have had an ADC that can help other mourners who have not had the benefit of this experience?

In speaking to mourners who have had an ADC, are there any insights you have gained that other mourners might be able to use in dealing with their losses? I wonder if there are some techniques or approaches that could help in the long struggle to adapt to the changes and loneliness that so often are a part of transition.

Invariably, one of the first things that comes to mind when I think of what could help other mourners who have not had the experience is the conviction there is another existence. One theme that is constant through the ADC experience is the recognition by the mourner that his loved one lives on. How this concept is conveyed to the mourner who has not had an ADC is a matter that needs careful thought and review. Initially, you need to be well aware of the beliefs about an afterlife held by the mourner and intuitively sense when to plant the seed of suggestion that his loved one lives on. Do not push the point, however. Say what you need to say in your own intimate style and then wait for a response. If there is none, let it go for the time being. On a future occasion, you may wish to suggest the same idea again, using slightly different words and phrases.

Do not minimize the impact of your suggestion merely because there is little or no response. There may well be good reason (embarrassment, guilt, shame, shyness) why the mourner chooses not to respond at the time. What is most important is your willingness to be present and not be deterred in any way in providing comfort simply because you have received a negative or lukewarm response or no response at all. Mourners are dealing with all kinds of issues and thoughts. At a future time they may recall your suggestion, for better or for worse. Remember too, you can make inroads on the loneliness that often accompanies grief by maintaining consistent contact with the mourner. Your presence is of inestimable value, even though you may not see outward signs of it in the behavior of the mourner.

Your visits, telephone calls, and invitations to the mourner will be of great help, but they will not eliminate the loneliness that only the deceased could fill. He must deal with the feelings of powerlessness to change the past, the need to be temporarily dependent on others (it's a healthy dependency to be encouraged), and the inability to explain the why of the tragedy. Eventually, all of this has to give way to reconstruction. That is where the mourner must begin the long journey of change, decide "I am going to make it through this," and reinvest in life. You cannot do it for the mourner, but you can encourage him in those directions. It is especially important to tactfully reinforce the powerful and critical concept that he can adapt, he can get through this dark night of his life.

You can only do so much. The mourner then must decide to slowly return to self-reliance, and reorganize his life. As important as human contact is in adapting to the death of a loved one, there is no ADC or living person who can do the inner work every mourner must accomplish in order to reengage life. The task of finding peace of mind after the death of a loved one is, at root, a process the mourner must gradually work on and be responsible for, although much support in the long journey comes from counselors, friends, and family. Be aware how social isolation adds to the problems of readjustment and often leads to unneeded health problems. To avoid this you can encourage activities the mourner enjoys and assist in facilitating social interaction.

Those who have had an ADC can use it to help themselves in their readjustment, but they still have to do much work. Specifically, I have learned from mourners who have had an ADC, as well as from those who have not had the experience, that grief work is highly individual. You can emphasize to the mourner not to fall into the trap of comparing how he is mourning with how another friend or family member is mourning. No one owns the book on grief. We all have specific individual relationships and investments in those who have died and grieve them in our own personal ways. The depth of grief is only known to the mourner. Generally, the grief process takes much longer than we have been conditioned to believe; it hurts for a lot longer time than expected, sometimes for years and years. Reassure your friend his grief is one of a kind, that he will never be abandoned (even though that feeling may persist), that he is free to take extra time to move at his own pace, and that he need not be dictated to by others. It is okay for the mourner to be assertive.

Mourners also tell us successful maneuvering through the minefield of grief is accomplished by avoiding these obstacles:

- Refusing to be comforted or to take a break from grief, thinking that it is demeaning to the memory of the deceased (accept invitations to go out for dinner or interact with old friends).

- Living in the past and "the way it used to be," forgetting that major loss changes us and demands that we deal with secondary losses that always accompany major loss (be aware the loss of a spouse or a child also means the loss of certain dreams, routines, and expectations and the need to create new ones).

- Refusing to seek out others who have dealt with similar losses and can be symbols of hope (at the appropriate time join a support group or talk to others who have worked through similar losses).

- Avoiding friends and memories of the deceased (memories are there for a purpose: to be shared and treasured and become tools for reinvestment).

- Refusing to resist friends who want you to "be your old self" in a hurry (mourning is not time bound).

- Failing to recognize the importance of expressing emotion (mourning is an individual process and crying is a coping, liquid emotion that is an action of the heart).

- Refusing to face grief head-on and work through the pain of loss (openly acknowledge and move toward the pain and talk about it).

- Failing to establish new routines, to begin new traditions, and to stop anticipating the old routines involving the deceased. (Accept the sudden upsurges of grief, the "grief attacks," as normal. Continue to gradually build new skills, adapt to the new world, and slowly let go of the old)

- Not understanding that taking action eventually changes emotion (commit yourself to action even when you awake and wish you did not have to face the day). As they say in Alcoholics Anonymous, the largest self-help group in the world, "Fake it till you make it." Act as you wish to be is just good mental health.

- Not realizing that ultimately everything needed to cope with the death of a loved one lies within (Seek your own wisdom, your faith, your spiritual self, as you keep reaching for your goal of peace of mind).

At the opportune moment, you may wish to rephrase one of the above into a positive idea to help the bereaved deal with loneliness and the task of coping with change. But don't push; honor boundaries. Be careful about insisting on a particular course of action—which you are convinced is needed—because only the mourner can choose when he is ready to act.

100. How can you find a counselor who is open to discussing an ADC with you?

Given the fact that the ADC is just emerging as a tool that professional counselors can use to help the bereaved, there must be many counselors who still dismiss it as little more than an annoyance in the process of coping with the death of a loved one. Is it possible to find out, before you go for counseling, if the counselor is open to the phenomena?

I regret to say there is no directory or organization that lists counselors who deal with ADC phenomena. However, there are some ways to hurdle this obstacle and find a professional suitable to your needs. You can begin by asking the bereavement coordinator at your local hospice to recommend a counselor in your area. There are also counselors who deal with spiritual matters that you can inquire about through your local church or county mental health center. The latter often maintain a list of counselors, in addition to its own staff, with a description of the type of counseling offered. You may also want to contact the Association for Death Education and Counseling (ADEC), an international nonprofit organization with offices in Hartford, Connecticut. ADEC is the oldest interdisciplinary organization in the field of dying, death, and bereavement. They will be able to put you in touch with counselors who can assist you in your search. Obviously, you can also ask for referrals from others you know who have been in therapy. Sometimes this is the best way to find the professional you feel you would want to work with.

In any event, whether or not you are able to quickly find a counselor specifically knowledgeable about ADC phenomena, it is important to remember to check out those you are considering and inquire about their certification, where they were trained, how long they have been practicing, and their fee schedule. I often feel most people put much more time in selecting an automobile or boat than in choosing a person to help them cope with traumatic change. It is easy to see why. When hurting we want relief as soon as possible and we are often willing to sacrifice time to find help. If that is the case, let me recommend a few considerations for your first visit to help insure you have made the right choice.

Do you feel good rapport being in this counselor's presence? It should not take you several sessions to decide if this is a person you can connect with and build trust. What is the feeling? Do you feel safe, comfortable, and believe you can form a good relationship with the person?

You have to decide whether this person is right or wrong for you and, most importantly, whether you can be completely honest and open with him/her. Does the counselor interact with you in a way that you feel understood and you feel you can share your deepest sentiments?

Can you sense whether the person is dominating and overpowering, or gentle and caring, or perhaps somewhere in between? Do you feel you can work with someone possessing any of these characteristics?

Ask about ADC phenomena if the counselor does not bring up the subject in the intake interview. Carefully listen to how the topic is handled, particularly what is not said. Was the topic quickly dealt with? Was sincere interest shown? What did the counselor say nonverbally?

Pay attention to your intuitive feelings about your visit—the office setting, the counselor as a good person, his organization, and the sense of empowerment or lack of it that surfaces. Even though you may have reservations, go with your intuition.

I know we can all make mistakes with our first impressions. Still, give yourself credit to sense what is right for you, even though you are hurting. If you don't feel a sense of connection, if you don't feel you're in the place you should be, that the chemistry isn't right, then it is probably best for you to keep looking, as difficult as it may be. Don't let discouragement seep into your thinking. Help can be found. There are professionals out there you can connect with and who will help you in utilizing your ADC.

‿

Epilogue: A Friendly Place

Albert Einstein once said: "The most important question all of us must answer is whether the universe is a friendly place or not." For many bereaved people of all ages, especially children and the grieving elderly population, the world often suddenly turns unfriendly, even fearful. Despite the daily menu of conflict and confrontations which continually highlight the front pages of newspapers, we can be proactive and reinforce the conviction that the world is still a friendly place. It begins with a single friendly gesture.

We all should be aware of the implications of a friendly environment in which to live and mourn losses. That atmosphere helps mourners regain lost self-esteem, allows them to reinvest in life, reduces the stress of adaptation, and enhances emotional and physical health. Throughout recorded history, people who have lived through an ADC experience have found the world to be a friendly place once again. Let's make every effort to help the bereaved use the ADC in a way in which they can integrate their losses into life. The result will feed the eternal thirst to find meaning. Along the way we will all benefit from better understanding the world of nonphysical reality and realize too that it is another friendly place.

Life is eternal
Love is immortal
Death is only a horizon
A horizon is nothing save the limit of our sight
—Author Unknown

Author's Request

I am continually searching for additional accounts of ADC's from anyo*
who has had the experience when mourning the death of a loved one.
you have had the experience, or have a child who has reported the expe*
ence, and would be willing to share it with me for possible inclusion in
future publication, please write to me at the following address:

Lou LaGrand
Loss Education Associates
450 Fairway Isles Drive
Venice, Florida 34292-3659

Your ADC experience may help someone else who is coping with t*
loss of a loved one and has had a similar experience—but needs validati*
from someone like you. It would be especially helpful to hear from reade*
in other parts of the world in order to compare similarities and differenc
in experiences.

Thank you for your help.

Glossary

Active listening: the skill of listening to what another person is saying and feeling through awareness of body language and demeanor as well as words. Then the listener creatively reflects those feelings and thoughts back so the person knows he or she is truly understood.

Advance rehearsal: a coping technique in which the mourner anticipates specific events when the absence or memory of the deceased loved one will cause much anxiety, creates a plan and practices it, in order to deal with the situation if and when it occurs.

Anomaly: something that deviates from the normal or common order, is irregular, or is very difficult to classify.

Apparition: a ghostly figure, a specter.

Auricular locution: hearing a voice that seems to becoming from outside of the body.

Bereavement: the condition of having experienced a meaningful loss; an objective fact.

Biopsychosocial-spiritual model: a model depicting the effects of biological, social, psychological, and spiritual factors on behavior.

Bodymind: all those functions connected with the central nervous system that control mental, physical, and emotional behavior. The bodymind continues to function whether we are conscious or not and includes the intuitive mind or faculty.

Broken heart syndrome: a phrase used by medical and counseling professionals referring to the lethal effects of social isolation associated with the grief response, particularly the effects on the cardiovascular and immune systems, leading to the death of the mourner.

Channeler: one who purports to be able to communicate between this world and the spirit world. Sometimes referred to as a medium or psychic.

Clairvoyance: The ability to acquire information about objects or events at great distances by means not involving the known senses.

Collective apparition: an apparition seen by more than one person simultaneously.

Collective unconscious: in Jungian psychology, a part of the unconscious mind shared by everyone.

Corporeal vision: a vision in which a physical body is seen.

Crisis apparition: the appearance of the now-deceased loved one at the moment of death or shortly before or after.

Disenfranchised grief: grief that ensues when a loss occurs that the mourner cannot openly acknowledge, publicly mourn, or obtain social support. Losses through death of pets or ex-spouses or from stillbirths, miscarriages, and abortions are examples of potential sources of disenfranchised grief.

Endocrine system: a system of the body in which glands (often referred to as ductless glands) secrete hormones directly into the blood stream. According to body-mind medicine, this system is intricately linked to other systems in the body and can be influenced by thought processes.

ESP: the acronym for extrasensory perception.

Ghost: the spirit of one who has died, especially one that appears in bodily likeness to living persons.

Grief: the normal emotional and physical response to any meaningful loss.

Grief work: the often difficult task of establishing new routines, priorities, and traditions in adjusting to the absence of a deceased loved one, including the withdrawal of emotional investment (but not the memories) in the deceased and the reinvestment of that emotion in other worthwhile pursuits.

Hallucination: a false or distorted perception of objects or events usually resulting from emotional disorganization or as a response to a drug.

Hypnagogia: the point between being half-asleep and half-awake. It is considered to be a highly creative state.

Imaginative locution: hearing a voice that comes from within the self.

Inner child: the child in everyone, regardless of age, often wounded early in life when dependency needs are not met.

Institute of Noetic Sciences: a research foundation, educational institution, and membership organization dedicated to the study of the mind and its diverse ways of knowing.

Intake interview: the initial meeting between a mourner and a counselor in which the counselor does a loss history and obtains other information to better understand influences that may be affecting the way a person is grieving.

Internal communication: a method of communication using the imagination to access and explore the inner relationship we have with a deceased loved one. See *Your Loved One Lives On Within You* (Berkley/Putnam, 1997) by Alexandra Kennedy.

Intellectual vision: a term used by some to describe having felt the presence of someone who has died. Nothing is actually seen.

Intellectual locution: receiving an interior message without hearing a voice. Mind-to-mind or telepathic communication.

Intuition: the power or faculty of attaining to direct knowledge or cognition without rational thought or inference; immediate cognizance or conviction without rational thought.

Intuitive (gifted): one who purports to be able to communicate with those who have died. Also referred to as a spiritual medium or a psychic and sometimes as a channeler.

Linking objects: physical objects, as well as dreams and memories, which are used by a mourner to form a symbolic link to the deceased loved one.

Metaphysics: the philosophical study of the nature of reality.

Mind-body medicine: a medical approach that considers thoughts and emotions as playing a major role in promoting the health of the body.

Mourning: the active process of sharing one's grief with another in adapting to the absence of the deceased loved one and establishing a new identity.

Mystical experience: an experience having a spiritual quality involving direct contact or communication with ultimate reality or God.

Naturalism: a system of belief holding that all phenomena can be explained in terms of natural causes and laws without attributing moral, spiritual, or supernatural significance to them.

Near-death experience (NDE): an experience reported by people believed to be on the brink of death, that may include out-of-body experiences, seeing deceased loved ones, going through a tunnel-like phenomena, seeing a being of light, and the passage of one's consciousness into another dimension.

Neuropeptide: any of a variety of short-chain peptides or informational substances which link the brain, body, and behavior. Originally thought to be only in the brain, they have been found throughout the body and form a complex network of communication.

Nonlocal mind: a part of consciousness that is not subject to or confined by space or time. Many believe that the mind operates nonlocally, transcending both space and time, and is the reason for many normally unexplainable communications and healings.

Paradigm: an example that serves as a pattern or model. Also used to indicate a particular worldview or way of looking at life.

Parapsychology: the science focused on the study of paranormal or psi phenomena. The term was first used by philosopher-psychologist Max Dessoir in Germany in the nineteenth century.

Precognition: the ability to randomly predict the future in a way other than through logical inference; foreknowledge of events.

Precognitive dream: a dream providing information about a future waking event before the event occurs and about which the dreamer would not previously have had received any information though usual sense perception.

Primary mourner: one who is directly related to the deceased or who possesses a deep emotional investment in the deceased.

Psi: the twenty-third letter in the Greek alphabet commonly used to indicate the unknown. It is also used to refer to intuitive or psychic knowing and collectively referring to telepathy, clairvoyance, precognition, and psychokinesis as psi phenomena.

Probability theory: the theory of analyzing and making statements regarding the probability of uncertain events occurring.

Psychoneuroimmunology: the study of the network of relationships between the nervous system, the endocrine system, the gastrointestinal system, and the immune system.

Recurrent localized apparition: an apparition seen in more or less the same form by several different people in approximately the same location at different times. Commonly referred to as a ghost.

Reductionism: the theory that all complex phenomena, including ADCs, can be explained by examining the basic physical mechanisms involved. In practice, reductionistic thinking often simplifies complex phenomena to the point of minimizing or distorting it.

Remote viewing: a nonlocal (not subject to space/time constraints) phenomena that involves the ability to describe and experience activities that are taking place at great distances from the person. It has been suggested by some researchers that remote viewing and psychic healing are connected. The U.S. government has funded studies on this phenomena.

Scientism: the belief that the scientific method used in investigating the natural sciences should be applied in all fields of inquiry.

Secondary losses: additional losses which are associated with the death of a loved one and usually accompany all major losses. Secondary losses may include, but not be limited to, changes in income, loss of transportation, changes in living arrangements, education plans, and geographical location. Loss of one's dreams which involved the deceased is often a special concern. These losses need to be talked about and mourned.

Scientific method: the principles and empirical processes of discovery and demonstration considered necessary for scientific investigation. It includes formulation of a hypothesis, the observation of phenomena, and experimentation to demonstrate or invalidate the truth of the hypothesis.

Self-talk: the conversation we continually have with ourselves throughout the day and which can be helpful or hurtful to our self-esteem depending on what is said.

Society for Psychical Research: formed in London in 1882, this was the first organization of scholars, scientists, and other professionals to band together for systematic study of unexplainable or paranormal phenomena. The SPR has accumulated thousands of documented cases of the extraordinary over the years.

Subconscious mind: the part of the mind below the level or awareness of conscious perception.

Synchronicity: a theory proposed by Carl Jung suggesting that the coincidence of events seem to be meaningfully although not causally related.

Telepathy: the transmission of information between two people by some means other than normal sensory perception. Also referred to as mind-to-mind communication. The term was coined by F. W. H. Myers in 1882.

Unconscious mind: a part of the mind containing elements such as memories and repressed desires that are not subject to conscious perception or control but that often affect conscious thought and behavior.

Vision: a sight seen in a dream, ecstasy, or trance-like state. Also, the mystical experience of seeing as if with the eyes of a supernatural being.

Year of the firsts: a term used by grief counselors to refer to all of the significant events, dates, and social gatherings that the survivor faces for the first time without the deceased loved one. These occasions are usually times in which great emotional pain is experienced and the bereaved may need comfort and support.

Suggested Readings on ADC Phenomena

The following readings have been offered to give the reader a variety of choices in examining ADC experiences. Inclusion of a specific title does not necessarily imply that I endorse the book in whole or in part. This reading list will hopefully provide you with the opportunity to appreciate the great diversity of situations in which the experience unfolds, insight into the people who have been gifted with the experience, and an awareness of differences of opinion on the subject among authors and researchers.

Anderson, J. W. *Where Miracles Happen*. Brooklyn, NY: Brett Books, Inc., 1994.

Bosco, A. "White Bird." *Guideposts*. (September, 1966).

Bramblett, J. *When Goodbye is Forever: Learning to Live Again After the Loss of a Child*. New York: Ballantine Books, 1991. (See pages 147–157.)

Canfield, J. and M. Hansen. *Chicken Soup for the Soul*. Deerfield Beach, FL: Health Communications, Inc., 1993. (See pages 5–7.)

Chance, S. *Stronger than Death: When Suicide Touches Your Life*. New York: W. W. Norton, 1992. (See pages 114–116.)

Cosgrove, J. "Our Consoling Visitor." *Venture Inward*. (January/ February, 1994).

Cox–Chapman, M. *The Case for Heaven*. New York: G.P. Putnam, 1995. (See pages 33–34, 39.)

Currie, I. *You Cannot Die*. Rockport, MA: Element Books, 1995. (See pages 19–20.)

Devers, E. "Experiencing the Deceased." *Florida Nursing Review* 2 (January 1988): 7–13.

Devers, E. *Goodbye Again: Experiences with Departed Loved Ones*. Kansas City: Andrews and McMeel, 1997.

Durkee, C. and J. Cooper. "The Bee Gees Search for Life After Disco." *People*. (August 7, 1989).

Finley, M. *Whispers of Love.* New York: Crossroads, 1995.

Freeman, E. *Touched by Angels.* New York: Warner Books, 1993. (See pages 1–9.)

Garfield, P. *The Dream Messenger.* New York: Simon and Schuster, 1997.

Gean, C. "Awakened by an Angel." *Bereavement Magazine* (July/August, 1994).

Gottlieb, A. "How Your Dreams Can Heal You." *McCall's* (July 1994): 84, 86–89, 138.

Greeley, A. "The Paranormal is Normal: A Sociologist Looks at Parapsychology." *The Journal of the American Society for Psychical Research* 85 (1991): 367–374.

Greeley, A. *Religion as Poetry.* Transaction Publications, 1995. (See chapter 12.)

Greeley, A. *The Sociology of the Paranormal.* Beverly Hills, CA: Sage Publications, 1975.

Green, M. and Mathison, D. "The Drama Behind Mask." *People.* (March 18, 1985).

Guggenheim, W. and J. Guggenheim. *Hello from Heaven.* New York: Bantam, 1996.

Halberstam, Y. and J. Leventhal. *Small Miracles.* Holbrook, MA: Adams Media Corporation, 1997. (See pages 143–144.)

Haraldsson, E. "Survey of Claimed Encounters with the Dead." *Omega* 19 (1988–89): 103–113.

————. "The Lyenger-Kirti Case: An Apparitional Case of the Bystander Type." *Journal of the Society for Psychical Research* 54 (1987): 64–67.

Harlow, S. R. *A Life After Death.* New York: Doubleday, 1961. (See Chapters 3 and 4.)

Hart, H. "Six Theories About Apparitions." *Proceedings of the Society for Psychical Research* 50 (1956):153–239.

Hull, J. and M. *Heaven—Why Doubt?* 21 Wynstay Rd., Wirral, Merseyside, England, L47 5AR: The Wynstay Press, 1997.

Hurley, T. "Dwelling with the Mystery of Death." *Noetic Sciences Review* (Spring 1994): 6–7.

Jung, C. *Memories, Dreams, Reflections.* New York: Vintage Books, 1965. (See pages 312–314.)

Kastenbaum, R. *Is There Life After Death?* London: Multimedia Books Limited, 1995. (See pages 90–96.)

Kelsey, M. *Dreams: A Way to Listen to God.* New York: Paulist Press, 1978.

Klass, D., P. Silverman., and S. Nickman. (eds.), *Continuing Bonds.* Philadelphia: Taylor and Francis, 1996.

Kübler–Ross, E. *Death is of Vital Importance.* Barrytown, NY: Station Hill Press, 1995. (See pages 95–98.)

LaGrand, L. *After Death Communication: Final Farewells.* St. Paul, MN: Llewellyn Publications, 1997.

———. "Are We Missing Opportunities to Help the Bereaved?" *The Forum Newsletter*, Vol. 23 (September/October 1997): 5.

———. "Extraordinary Experiences of the Bereaved." *The PSI Researcher* (November 1996) No. 23:8–11.

Lewis, C. S. *A Grief Observed.* New York: Bantam, 1980. (See pages 85–87.)

———. *Life Beyond Death.* Pleasantville, NY: The Reader's Digest Association, Inc. 1992. (See pages 90–92, 98–99.)

Lightner, C. *Giving Sorrow Words.* New York:Warner Books, 1990. (See pages 212–214.)

Linn, E. *Premonitions, Visitations and Dreams.* P.O. Box 6939, Incline Village, Nevada, 89450: The Publisher's Mark, 1991.

Lord, J. "This May Sound Crazy . . ." *MADDvocate.* (Spring, 1991. Published by Mothers Against Drunk Driving).

Maitland, R. *The Snettisham Ghost.* London: Psychic Press, n.d., 1956.

Martin, J. and P. Romanowski. *Love Beyond Life.* New York: HarperCollins, 1997.

Matott, J. *My Garden Visits.* New York: Ballantine Books, 1996.

McCarthy, D. "One Gold Angel." *Catholic Digest* (August 1992).

Morrell, D. *Fireflies.* New York: E.P. Dutton, 1988. (See pages 33–47.)

Morse, M. *Parting Visions.* New York: Villard Books, 1994.

Morsilli, R. "I Still See Him Everywhere." *Reader's Digest* (July 1984).

Olsen, P., J. Suddeth, P. Peterson, and C. Egelhoff. "Hallucinations of Widowhood." *Journal of the American Geriatrics Society* 33 (1985): 543–547.

Owens, N. "My Gift From God." *Sharing and Healing*. (April/ June, 1994).

Rees, W. "The Hallucinations of Widowhood." *British Medical Journal* 4 (1971): 37–41.

Rogo, D. "Spontaneous Contact with the Dead: Perspectives from Grief Counseling, Sociology, and Parapsychology." In Doore, G. *What Survives?* Los Angeles: Jeremy P. Tarcher, 1990. (See pages 76–91.)

Seymour, S. and H. Neligan. *True Irish Ghost Stories*. New York: Causeway Books, 1974. (See pages 146–174.)

Sparrow, S. *I Am With You Always*. New York: Bantam, 1995.

von Franz, Marie–Louise. *On Dreams and Death*. Boston: Shambala, 1986. (See pages xv, 111–114, 133.)

Wakefield, D. *Expect a Miracle: The Miraculous Things That Happen To Ordinary People*. San Francisco: HarperSanFrancisco, 1995. (See chapter 8.)

Walker, P. R. *Every Day's A Miracle*. New York: Avon Books, 1995. (See pages 85–87.)

Williams, O. *Temptations*. New York: G.P. Putnam, 1988. (See page 163.)

Winter, W. *The Life of David Belasco*. New York: Benjamin Bloom, Inc., 1972 (See pages 466–468.)

Wiitala, G. *Heather's Return*. Virginia Beach, VA: A.R.E. Press, 1996.

Zinsser, W. (ed.) *Spiritual Requests: The Art and Craft of Religious Writing*. Boston: Houghton Mifflin, 1988. (See pages 105–106.)

Bibliography

Anderson, J. W. *Where Angels Walk.* Sea Cliff, New York: Barton and Brett, 1992.

Bohm, D. *Quantum Theory.* New York: Dover, 1989.

———. *Wholeness and the Implicate Order.* London: Routledge, 1996.

Burnham, S. *A Book of Angels.* New York: Ballantine Books, 1990.

Burton, R. *The Anatomy of Melancholy.* London: G. Bell and Sons, Ltd., 1924.

Chopra, D. *Quantum Healing.* New York: Ballantine, 1990.

———. *The Seven Spiritual Laws of Success.* San Rafael, CA: Amber–Allan Publications, 1994.

Cicero, Marcus Tullius. *On Divination.* Translated by Hubert M. Poteat. Chicago: University of Chicago Press, 1950.

Department of Health and Human Services, U. S. Public Health Services, Centers for Disease Control and Prevention, Atlanta, Georgia.

Dickens, C. *My Early Life.* United Kingdom: Aurum Press, 1997.

Dossey, L. *Healing Words.* San Francisco: HarperCollings, 1993.

Evans–Wentz, W. (ed.) *The Tibetan Book of the Dead.* New York: Oxford University Press, 1957.

Flammarion, C. *The Unknown.* New York: Harper and Brothers Publsihers, 1900.

Fontana, D. *The Secret Language of Symbols: A Visual Key to Symbols and their Meaning.* San Francisco: Chronicle Books, 1994.

Frankl, V. *Man's Search for Meaning.* New York: Washington Square Press, 1968.

Freeman, E. *Touched by Angels.* New York: Washington Square Press, 1968.

Gallup, G. and F. Newport. "Belief in Paranormal Phenomena among Adult Americans," *Skeptical Inquirer,* 1991, vol. 15, 136–146.

Greeley, A. and R. McReady. "Are We a Nation of Mystics?", *New York Times Magazine,* January 26, 1975.

Gurney, E., F. Myers and F. Podmore. *Phantasms of the Living,* vol. 2, London: Kegan, Paul, 1886.

Herbert, N. *Quantum Reality.* New York: Anchor Books, 1987.

———. *Elemental Mind.* New York: Dutton, 1993.

Jung, C. *Memories, Dreams, Reflections.* New York: Random House, 1961.

Kalish, R. and D. Reynolds. *Death and Ethnicity: A Psychocultural Study.* Los Angeles: Andrus Gerontology center, 1976.

Keller, T. and D. Taylor. *Angels: The Lifting of the Veil.* Charlottesville, VA: Hampton Roads Publishing Company, 1994.

Kennedy, A. *Your Loved One Lives on Within You.* New York: Berkeley Books, 1997.

Kübler–Ross, E. *On Death and Dying.* New York: Macmillan, 1969.

———. *Death is of Vital Importance.* Barrytown, NY, Station Hill Press, 1995.

Lewis, C. S. *A Grief Observed.* New York: Bantam, 1980.

Mackenzie, A. *Hauntings and Apparitions.* London: Grenada Publishing Ltd., 1983.

Margenau, H. and R. Varghese, (eds.), *Cosmos, Bios, Theos: Scientists Reflect on Science, Religion, and the Origins of the Universe, Life and Homo Sapiens.* Chicago: Open Court Publishing, 1992.

Moody, R. *Life After Life.* New York: Bantam, 1976.

Morsilli, R. "I Still See Him Everywhere," *Reader's Digest.* July 1984.

Myers, F. W. H. *Human Personality and Its Survival of Bodily Death.* New Hyde Park, New York: University Books, 1961.

Osis, K. and E. Haraldsson. *At the Hour of Death.* New York: Avon, 1977.

Pert, C. *Molecules of Emotion.* New York: Scribner, 1997.

Reittinger, D. Department of Psychology, College of St. Rose, Albany, NY, 12203.

Selye, H. *The Stress of Life* (Rev. ed.). New York: McGraw–Hill, 1976.

Sidgwick, E. *Phantasms of the Living.* New Hyde Park, NY: Univeristy Books, 1962.

Sorokin, P. *The Crisis of Our Age.* London: One World Publications, 1992.

Troccoli, K. *My Life is in Your Hands: Devotions to Help You Fall More Deeply in Love with Jesus.* Grand Rapids, MI: Zonderan, 1997.

Ullman, M. and S. Krippner. *Dream Studies and Telepathy.* New York: Parapsychology Foundation, 1970.

Index

A

Accepting death, 215, 238
Active listening, 216
Advance rehearsal, 228, 245
After-death communication
    and emotional blocks, 94
    and establishing trust, 263
    and expression of emotion,
        214, 224, 287
    and fear of the unknown, 93
    and linking objects, 283
    and retaining positive memo-
        ries, 273, 276–277
    and ritual, 218, 279–281, 283
    and suicide, 15, 30, 90, 128,
        180, 251
    and visits to a spiritual
        medium, 47, 267
    and the unconscious mind, 38,
        52, 85–86, 88, 104, 226–229
    asking abou, 262, 263
    definition of, 4
    finding a counselor, 288
    positive influences, 201–256
Afterlife, 3, 12, 30, 83, 89–91, 112,
    133, 184, 198, 217, 220, 227,
    276, 281–282, 285
Agnostics, 83, 114, 183–185
Alcoholism, 43, 139
Allen, Steve, 101
All Saints Day, 106
Anderson, Joan Wester, 49

Angel Collectors Club, 47
Angels, 47–49, 58–59, 75, 102, 177
Anger, 29, 81, 94, 132, 144, 202,
    227, 247, 251, 259
Anglican, 105
Apparitions, 26–27, 42, 46, 52, 62,
    64–65, 67, 105, 136–138, 156
Approaches to helping, 259, 279,
    284
Asking about ADCs, 262–263
Association for Death Education
    and Counseling, 249, 288
Atheists, 183–185
Attitude, 171–173, 185, 196,
    222–223, 252
Auditory ADC, 90, 111, 116, 122,
    133, 272
Autoscopic NDE, 9

B

Beliefs, 19, 43, 49, 64, 69, 71–73,
    83, 85, 89, 92–93, 106, 171,
    190, 209–210, 225–228, 240,
    245, 250
Believing, 68–71, 91, 196
Believing is seeing, 68–71, 104
Bible, 7, 48, 103, 236, 253–254
Bird & Animal ADC, 37, 129
Blessed Mother, 47
Bodymind, 17
Bohm, David, 62, 130
Bowlby, John, 104

☽ REACH FOR THE MOON

Llewellyn publishes hundreds of books on your favorite subjects! To get these exciting books, including the ones on the following pages, check your local bookstore or order them directly from Llewellyn.

ORDER BY PHONE

- Call toll-free within the U.S. and Canada, 1-800-THE MOON
- In Minnesota, call (651) 291-1970
- We accept VISA, MasterCard, and American Express

ORDER BY MAIL

- Send the full price of your order (MN residents add 7% sales tax) in U.S. funds, plus postage & handling to:

  Llewellyn Worldwide
  P.O. Box 64383, Dept. K406-5
  St. Paul, MN 55164–0383, U.S.A.

POSTAGE & HANDLING

(For the U.S., Canada, and Mexico)

- $4.00 for orders $15.00 and under
- $5.00 for orders over $15.00
- No charge for orders over $100.00

We ship UPS in the continental United States. We ship standard mail to P.O. boxes. Orders shipped to Alaska, Hawaii, The Virgin Islands, and Puerto Rico are sent first-class mail. Orders shipped to Canada and Mexico are sent surface mail.

International orders: Airmail—add freight equal to price of each book to the total price of order, plus $5.00 for each non-book item (audio tapes, etc.).

Surface mail—Add $1.00 per item.

Allow 2 weeks for delivery on all orders.
Postage and handling rates subject to change.

DISCOUNTS

We offer a 20% discount to group leaders or agents. You must order a minimum of 5 copies of the same book to get our special quantity price.

FREE CATALOG

Get a free copy of our color catalog, *New Worlds of Mind and Spirit*. Subscribe for just $10.00 in the United States and Canada ($30.00 overseas, airmail). Many bookstores carry *New Worlds*— ask for it!

Visit our web site at www.llewellyn.com for more information.

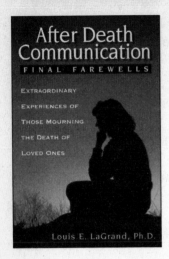

After Death Communication

Final Farewells

Louis E. LaGrand, Ph.D.

"I saw my dead son standing in the hall-way near the stairs to his bedroom. He was wearing a favorite hat. I wanted to believe he was happy."

In this moving and compassionate work, a pioneer in after-death communication research guides you through one of the most empowering of human experiences.

Forty-two percent of people surveyed claim to have had some type of after-death contact with a loved one. This book examines a wide variety of those experiences—seeing, hearing, or sensing the presence of the deceased; feeling a touch; smelling a fragrance; meeting the loved one in a vision or dream; unusual appearances of birds and animals; and a host of other unexplainable happenings—all of which have provided millions of grieving people with relief that their loved ones still live on. Dr. LaGrand takes the experience out of the realm of illusion, and also shows how support persons can assist the bereaved to use these experience to go on with their lives.

1-56718-405-7
6 x 9, 256 pp.
$12.95